Salvaging Damaged dBASE®Files

The **DATA BASED ADVISOR**® Series
Lance A. Leventhal, Ph.D., Series Director

SECOND EDITION

Salvaging Damaged dBASE®Files

Step-by-step procedures for recovering data and restoring damaged files.

Paul W. Heiser

Microtrend™ Books

TRADEMARKS

Clipper	Nantucket Corporation
dBASE, dBASE II, dBASE III,	
dBASE III PLUS, dBASE IV	Ashton-Tate, Inc.
dBFix, UnFrag	Paul Mace Software
dBXL	WordTech Systems
Disk Repair	International Business Machines, Inc.
DiskMinder	Westlake Data Corporation
dSALVAGE, dSALVAGE Professional	Comtech Publishing Ltd.
FoxBASE, FoxBASE+	Fox Software
IBM, IBM PC, PC-DOS	International Business Machines, Inc.
MS-DOS	Microsoft Corporation
Norton Utilities	Peter Norton Computing
SBT	SBT Corporation
Sidekick	Borland International

ISBN 0-915391-33-3

Library of Congress Card Catalog Number: 89-43072

Microtrend™ Books
Slawson Communications, Inc.
165 Vallecitos de Oro
San Marcos, CA 92069

Edited by Lance A. Leventhal, Ph.D., San Diego, CA
Front Cover design by Lorri Maida
Interior design by Dave Morgan, Slawson Communications, Inc.

Printed in the United States
10 9 8 7 6 5 4 3 2 1

Contents

Tables

Figures

About the Author

Paul Heiser's involvement with software and file recovery is the story of a hobby that got out of hand. While living in Tokyo in 1975, he stumbled into the world of microcomputers. One thing led to another and he eventually left a Fortune 500 management position to start his own consulting business. A client's severely damaged dBASE datafile steered him into the arena of file recovery, a specialty that was practically nonexistent. He is now regarded as the foremost authority on this subject by the dBASE community, including the good folks at Ashton-Tate, Fox Software, Nantucket, SBT, and Data Based Solutions.

Paul writes custom dBASE applications, teaches dBASE courses at the University of Rochester, and is the author of *Mastering dBASE II The Easy Way* (Prentice Hall), *The dBASE II Cash Manager* (Prentice Hall), and the first edition of *Salvaging Damaged dBASE Files* (Comtech Publishing). He is also the developer of the award-winning dSALVAGE file recovery software.

His formal background is physics in which he holds a Master's degree from UCLA. If you look carefully at a map of the Queen Elizabeth Range in Antarctica, you will see Mt. Heiser, a mountain named in recognition of Paul's participation in an expedition there in the late 1950's.

About the Series Editor

Lance A. Leventhal is the author of 25 books, including *80386 Programming Guide, 68000 Assembly Language Programming, Programmer's Guide to QuickC 2, and Microcomputer Experimentation with the IBM PC*. His books have sold over 1,000,000 copies and have been translated into many foreign languages. He has also helped develop microprocessor-based systems and has served as a consultant for Disney, Intel, NASA, NCR, and Rockwell.

Dr. Leventhal served as Series Editor on Personal Computing for Prentice-Hall and as Technical Editor for the Society for Computer Simulation. He has lectured throughout the United States on microprocessors for IEEE, IEEE Computer Society, and other groups.

Dr. Leventhal's background includes affiliations with Linkabit Corporation, Intelcom Rad Tech, Naval Electronics Laboratory Center, and Harry Diamond Laboratories. He received a B.A. degree from Washington University (St. Louis, Missouri) and M.S. and Ph.D. degrees from the University of California, San Diego. He is a member of the AAAI, ACM, ASEE, IEEE, IEEE Computer Society, and SCS.

Foreword

by
David Kalman
Editor-in-Chief, *Data Based Advisor*

It's 3 a.m. and an important project is due tomorrow. But you have somehow damaged a major dBASE datafile. Where can you turn for quick relief if there's nothing in your medicine cabinet? The answer is to call on Paul Heiser, the leading healer of sick databases. He knows what to do, and he shares his knowledge with you in the second edition of *Salvaging Damaged dBASE Files*.

What tools do you need? Where do you start? What procedure should you follow? How do you know when recovery is complete? Pundits have joked that, "You can't be too rich or too thin." Paul Heiser would say, "You can't be too knowledgable about dBASE file damage and recovery."

Heiser provides an inside look at file structures, disk directories, and file allocation tables. He explores diagnosis and repair techniques using a variety of tools, including Debug, Norton Utilities, IBM's Disk Repair, Disk Minder, dBFix, and his own dSALVAGE. He gives you the information required to combat even the most insidious forms of dBASE file damage.

In my experience, Paul Heiser is the undisputed dBASE file master. He has already helped thousands of dBASE II, dBASE III, and dBASE III PLUS users with the first edition of *Salvaging Damaged dBASE Files*. In the second edition, he now covers dBASE IV and the advanced tools of the trade, while still providing valuable new insight to dBASE III and dBASE III PLUS users.

In the business world, data is a precious asset. Its collection, organization, and maintenance represent a major investment. Paul Heiser's *Salvaging Damaged dBASE Files,* 2nd edition protects your dBASE data investment like a comprehensive insurance policy. Unlike insurance, Heiser's book has no loopholes and no expiration date.

Acknowledgments

Grateful acknowledgment is made to:

Taeko, my wife and business partner, for keeping my nose to the grindstone.

Adam Green for his continuing support and for persuading me to develop dSALVAGE.

David Irwin, David Kalman, and Tom Rettig for their unceasing encouragement.

Steve Hoffman, whose trashed dBASE file stimulated my interest in file recovery.

David Morgan, the production editor, and the staff of Slawson Communications.

Special thanks goes to Lance Leventhal, my editor, whose wonderful wordsmithing helped make a highly technical subject easy to read.

Preface

Few things are more frustrating than trying to use your only copy of a large, valuable datafile only to be told that it is "not a dBASE database" ... or you can access only fourteen records from a twenty-thousand record file ... or you see a large section of a document in the middle of your datafile or....??! I use the word "few" advisedly. Death, taxes, children, and sauerkraut-flavored ice cream can be more frustrating.

Many users have never experienced datafile damage. They are careful. They are cautious. They leave the tags on their mattresses and accept full responsibility for all copyright violations before opening their software packages. They make backups religiously. They feel safe. They say, "That will never happen to me." Then—to quote the inimitable Jackie Gleason—BANG ZOOM their file goes up in smoke. Two years of irreplaceable data vanishes in a flash.

Users who make frequent backups of their datafiles sometimes get a false sense of security. They may not be aware of the existence of damage, particularly in a large datafile, when creating a backup. Restoring from it, instead of providing the complete recovery they expect, can destroy their data permanently. So backup by itself, no matter how complete and consistent, does not solve the damage problem.

Sooner or later you will need this book and the valuable insight it provides into ways to preserve, diagnose, and recover datafiles. If you had the foresight to buy it before disaster struck, you will be prepared. If disaster has already struck, this book will help you survive it and live happily ever after (well, at least you will survive!). Its purpose is to give you an intimate understanding of: (1) the structure of dBASE datafiles; (2) the nature, symptoms, and causes of datafile damage; and (3) the tools and methods for diagnosing and salvaging damaged datafiles.

The subject is not an exciting one. Most people do not find a description of datafile damage and what to do about it to be a "sit-on-the-edge-of-your-chair- and-gnaw-at-your-fingernails" thriller. The topic is highly technical, requires a lot of detailed analysis, and is dear to the heart of practically nobody. Yet it is an important subject. It can help you avoid file damage and repair damage you cannot avoid.

Despite the importance of file damage to dBASE users and the frequency with which it occurs, very little has been written on the subject.

This book is for anyone who uses dBASE (any version), FoxBASE, Clipper, dBXL, or any database management software that uses dBASE's DBF datafile format. We will refer to any such software as dBASE. While we fully recognize and respect Ashton-Tate's ownership of the dBASE name, it is simply too clumsy to say "dBASE, FoxBASE, Clipper, dBXL, or any database management software that uses the DBF datafile format of dBASE and the command syntax of dBASE" every time we want to refer to the relevant software. Hence, we will simply say "dBASE"; this use should not be construed as implying any generic quality to the name.

Through no fault of the software manufacturer, you will inevitably face a damaged dBASE datafile sooner or later. The damage can be caused by human error, computer malfunction, software conflicts (particularly involving terminate-and-stay-resident (TSR), disk-caching, or driver software), an electrical power interruption while you are working with a file, faulty applications software, or other events beyond your control. Whatever the cause, you may be left with a corrupted file. The damage may make dBASE unable to recognize the file or even open it when asked to do so.

People sometimes ask me why dBASE files appear to be particularly vulnerable to damage. The question implies a premise that I do not accept. Certainly, large files are more easily damaged than small ones since they occupy more disk space and thus offer a larger target for disturbances. Database files (unlike document files, spreadsheet files, applications, programs, utilities, and the like) tend to grow as you add data to them. They resemble the paper files that eventually overflow whatever cabinet or floor space they occupy. Not only, therefore, do the files grow, but so do their chains in the File Allocation Table, the infamous FAT (discussed later). Besides, dBASE has a very large user base and has been around for a long time. All these factors may easily lead one to believe incorrectly that dBASE files are especially vulnerable or unstable.

As we said, nearly every dBASE user can expect to experience datafile damage. Those who have not yet faced the problem can expect to eventually. The issue is not "IF" you will have file damage, but "WHEN". I receive many calls from panicky users who have just encountered damage in a valuable datafile. I often hear them say, "I never thought this would happen to me." It WILL HAPPEN to you, and you should be prepared for it.

To give you a solid preparation, we will start with datafile fundamentals, explain the forms of file damage, and guide you through many recovery procedures.

Chapters 1 through 3 discuss computer files in general and datafiles in particular. You will also find useful information about memo fields and files.

Chapters 4 through 7 deal with disk directories, File Allocation Tables, data storage on disks, and anomalies that produce damage symptoms.

Chapter 8 introduces today's most advanced software tools for diagnosing and recovering damaged datafiles.

Chapters 9 through 11 discuss ZAP'd, PACK'd, and erased datafiles and the pitfalls of file unerasing.

Chapters 12 through 21 show you how to use software tools to diagnose and recover damaged datafiles.

Chapter 22 discusses specialized editors designed for use with datafiles.

The procedures we discuss will enable you to diagnose and salvage most damaged dBASE datafiles, regardless of their size and whether the damage is internal or at the DOS level. In most cases, you can recover all the data. In some cases, some good data may have actually been replaced or overwritten, but most of it will still be intact (even though dBASE may refuse to access it). Occasionally, the damage may be so diffuse and scattered that recovery is impractical. Our procedures and tools will allow you to salvage most datafiles that have not been physically overwritten and to restore them to a dBASE-compatible state.

Once you have read this book, you will be a certified healer of sick or damaged databases, worthy of receiving commendations, the eternal gratitude of your patients, and (best of all) exorbitant fees. The author will even be pleased, for a small charge, to send you an official-looking certificate to hang on your office wall. Please indicate your choice of color, language (Latin, Greek, Sanskrit, or dBASE), and emblem. But remember that Plato wrote, "...the true physician...is not a mere moneymaker."

Anatomy of a File
or
All about Bits, Bytes, and ASCII

This book spends a lot of time describing files and referring to such things as bytes, memory addresses, and ASCII characters. If you are not sure what some or all of them are, this chapter is for you. You may compare it to the course that teaches aspiring doctors how to speak incomprehensible jargon and write indecipherable prescriptions.

Visible and Invisible Characters

Let's begin with a simple example. Little Jimmy is at summer camp and wants to write his parents to let them know what is happening. He has an old portable typewriter they gave him because nobody can read his handwriting. One evening, Jimmy composes the letter shown in Figure 1-1.

```
Dear Mom & Dad,

Almost a week has gone by since I came to
summer camp. I thought that camp would be
boring like last year, but it's been fun so
far.

I have a new friend. His name is Billy. He
is 7 years old and has a little yellow dog.
I never saw a dog like that before.
Yesterday Billy's dog ate one of the
counsellors. I asked Billy what kind of dog
it was and he said, "Before I cut off his
tail and painted him yellow, he was an
alligator."

Well, bye now. I'll write another letter
next week.
```

Figure 1-1. *Jimmy's Letter on a Typewriter*

Let's look at the letter in detail. It consists of things you can see and things you cannot. We are not even considering the groans caused by the old alligator joke.

The things you can see are the symbols the typewriter prints on the paper. All of them are familiar to you. Some are letters, some are digits, some are punctuation marks, and some are other symbols (such as "&").

The things you cannot see include carriage returns and line feeds. When Jimmy reached the end of a line, he pushed the typewriter's "carriage return" lever. This did two things: (1) it moved the carriage back to its the left margin (a carriage return); and (2) it advanced the paper one line (a line feed). In the typed letter, you can see the results of his action, namely, lines beginning at the left margin.

However, you cannot actually see the carriage returns and line feeds themselves. If Jimmy had typed his letter with a computer word processor rather than on a manual typewriter, the screen would look the same as the paper version. However, the computer would actually put special characters in the text to represent carriage returns and line feeds.

 ## Bits, Bytes, and ASCII

If Jimmy had recorded his letter on a computer disk, he would have to give it a name. It would be a *file*, and its name would appear in a list of files or *directory*. The directory listing would also show the size of the file in bytes (a *byte* holds one character) and the date and time when it was last saved.

Each character in Jimmy's letter (even the non-printing ones) is stored on disk as a byte. A byte, in turn, consists of 8 smaller units of information called *bits*. The bit is the basic unit of information storage on disk or in the computer's memory. Like a light switch, it has only two possible conditions (or values): ON or OFF. If we call the OFF condition 0 and the ON condition 1, every character consists of eight ones or zeros. Since a byte contains 8 bits, each of which must be 0 or 1, it can have only 256 possible values. If we list them in numerical order, they are as follows:

```
00000000
00000001
00000010
00000011
00000100
00000101
00000110
00000111
00001000
00001001
    .
    .
    .
11111101
11111110
11111111
```

A moment's thought will show you that half of these bytes (that is, 128 of them) have 0 as the leading (leftmost) bit and half have 1 as the leading bit. The 128 bytes that start with 0 are special. They represent the 128 characters that you can produce by pressing keys on your computer's keyboard. We refer to them as ASCII characters. *ASCII* stands for American Standard Code for Information Interchange.

A capital 'A', for example, has the ASCII representation 01000001. Lowercase 'z' has the ASCII representation 01111010. The digit '3' has the ASCII representation 00110011. Appendix C contains a complete listing of ASCII characters.

Although the computer handles bytes as collections of 1's and 0's, it is not convenient for us to handle them that way. They are simply too long and difficult to understand. Instead, we handle them as numeric values and express them in decimal or in any other number system we choose.

 # Hexadecimal Numbers—A First Look

Although the decimal number system is in common use, it is not the most convenient when dealing with computers.

The best number system to use when dealing with computers is base 16 or *hexadecimal*. Appendix D discusses hexadecimal numbers in detail.

The decimal number system is based on 10, because people have 10 fingers. It uses 10 symbols (0,1,2,3,4,5,6,7,8, and 9) to represent numeric values. The hexadecimal number system, however, is based on 16 and therefore requires 16 symbols to represent numeric values. It is popular on planets where inhabitants have 16 fingers or where computers rule. The first six letters of the alphabet serve as the extra six symbols needed to complete the set of digits. Hence, in hexadecimal (or simply hex) notation, the sixteen symbols are 0, 1, 2, 3, 4, 5, 6, 7, 8, 9, A, B, C, D, E, and F. A through F can be either uppercase or lowercase. In this book, we will generally use uppercase.

We can represent each bit combination described earlier as a decimal or hexadecimal number.

Let's look at the list again and add the decimal and hex representations, as shown in Table 1-1.

Table 1-1. Hexadecimal Conversion Table		
HEXADECIMAL NUMBER	**DECIMAL EQUIVALENT**	**BINARY EQUIVALENT**
00	0	00000000
01	1	00000001
02	2	00000010
03	3	00000011
04	4	00000100

(continued on next page)

Table 1-1. Hexadecimal Conversion Table *(continued)*

HEXADECIMAL NUMBER	DECIMAL EQUIVALENT	BINARY EQUIVALENT
05	5	00000101
06	6	00000110
07	7	00000111
08	8	00001000
09	9	00001001
0A	10	00001010
0B	11	00001011
0C	12	00001100
0D	13	00001101
0E	14	00001110
0F	15	00001111
10	16	00010000
11	17	00010001
12	18	00010010
13	19	00010011
14	20	00010100
15	21	00010101
.	.	.
.	.	.
.	.	.
FD	253	11111101
FE	254	11111110
FF	255	11111111

As noted, the ASCII characters are the first 128 combinations. Specifically, they are the bit combinations from 00000000 through 01111111 (the decimal numbers from 0 through 127 or the hex numbers from 00 through 7F).

 **Text Files**

Let's return to Jimmy's letter. Figure 1-2 shows it both as hex values and as ASCII characters. We have used "cr" for carriage return and "lf" for line feed.

```
44 65 61 72 20 4D 6F 6D-20 26 20 44 61 64 2C 0D
 D  e  a  r     M  o  m      &     D  a  d  ,  cr

0A 0D 0A 41 6C 6D 6F 73-74 20 61 20 77 65 65 6B
 lf cr lf A  l  m  o  s  t     a     w  e  e  k

20 68 61 73 20 67 6F 6E-65 20 62 79 20 73 69 6E
    h  a  s     g  o  n  e     b  y     s  i  n
```

```
63 65 20 49 20 63 61 6D-65 20 74 6F 0D 0A 73 75
 c  e     I     c  a  m  e     t  o cr lf  s  u

6D 6D 65 72 20 63 61 6D-70 2E 20 20 49 20 74 68
 m  m  e  r     c  a  m  p  .        I     t  h

6F 75 67 68 74 20 74 68-61 74 20 63 61 6D 70 20
 o  u  g  h  t     t  h  a  t     c  a  m  p

77 6F 75 6C 64 20 62 65-0D 0A 62 6F 72 69 6E 67
 w  o  u  l  d     b  e cr lf  b  o  r  i  n  g

20 6C 69 6B 65 20 6C 61-73 74 20 79 65 61 72 2C
    l  i  k  e     l  a  s  t     y  e  a  r  ,

20 62 75 74 20 69 74 27-73 20 62 65 65 6E 20 66
    b  u  t     i  t  '  s     b  e  e  n     f

75 6E 0D 0A 73 6F 20 66-61 72 2E 0D 0A 0D 0A 49
 u  n cr lf  s  o     f  a  r  . cr lf cr lf  I

20 68 61 76 65 20 61 20-6E 65 77 20 66 72 69 65
    h  a  v  e     a     n  e  w     f  r  i  e

6E 64 2E 20 20 48 69 73-20 6E 61 6D 65 20 69 73
 n  d  .        H  i  s     n  a  m  e     i  s

20 42 69 6C 6C 79 2E 0D-0A 48 65 20 69 73 20 37
    B  i  l  l  y  . cr lf  H  e     i  s     7

20 79 65 61 72 73 20 6F-6C 64 20 61 6E 64 20 68
    y  e  a  r  s     o  l  d     a  n  d     h

61 73 20 61 20 6C 69 74-74 6C 65 20 79 65 6C 6C
 a  s     a     l  i  t  t  l  e     y  e  l  l

6F 77 0D 0A 64 6F 67 2E-20 20 49 20 6E 65 76 65
 o  w cr lf  d  o  g  .        I     n  e  v  e

72 20 73 61 77 20 61 20-64 6F 67 20 6C 69 6B 65
 r     s  a  w     a     d  o  g     l  i  k  e

20 74 68 61 74 20 62 65-66 6F 72 65 2E 0D 0A 59
    t  h  a  t     b  e  f  o  r  e  . cr lf  Y

65 73 74 65 72 64 61 79-20 42 69 6C 6C 79 27 73
 e  s  t  e  r  d  a  y     B  i  l  l  y  '  s

20 64 6F 67 20 61 74 65-20 6F 6E 65 20 6F 66 20
    d  o  g     a  t  e     o  n  e     o  f

74 68 65 0D 0A 63 6F 75-6E 73 65 6C 6C 6F 72 73
 t  h  e cr lf  c  o  u  n  s  e  l  l  o  r  s

2E 20 20 49 20 61 73 6B-65 64 20 42 69 6C 6C 79
 .        I     a  s  k  e  d     B  i  l  l  y

20 77 68 61 74 20 6B 69-6E 64 20 6F 66 0D 0A 64
    w  h  a  t     k  i  n  d     o  f cr lf  d
```

```
6F 67 20 69 74 20 77 61-73 20 61 6E 64 20 68 65
 o  g     i  t     w  a  s     a  n  d     h  e

20 73 61 69 64 2C 20 22-42 65 66 6F 72 65 20 49
    s  a  i  d  ,     "  B  e  f  o  r  e     I

20 63 75 74 20 6F 66 66-0D 0A 68 69 73 20 74 61
    c  u  t     o  f  f crlf h  i  s     t  a

69 6C 20 61 6E 64 20 70-61 69 6E 74 65 64 20 68
 i  l     a  n  d     p  a  i  n  t  e  d     h

69 6D 20 79 65 6C 6C 6F-77 2C 20 68 65 20 77 61
 i  m     y  e  l  l  o  w  ,     h  e     w  a

73 0D 0A 61 6E 20 61 6C-6C 69 67 61 74 6F 72 2E
 s crlf a  n     a  l  l  i  g  a  t  o  r  .

22 0D 0A 0D 0A 57 65 6C-6C 2C 20 62 79 65 20 6E
 " crlfcrlf W  e  l  l  ,     b  y  e     n

6F 77 2E 20 20 49 27 6C-6C 20 77 72 69 74 65 20
 o  w  .        I  '  l  l     w  r  i  t  e

61 6E 6F 74 68 65 72 20-6C 65 74 74 65 72 0D 0A
 a  n  o  t  h  e  r     l  e  t  t  e  r crlf

6E 65 78 74 20 77 65 65-6B 2E 0D 0A 1A
 n  e  x  t     w  e  e  k  . crlf eof
```

Figure 1-2. *Jimmy's Letter in ASCII Form*

Figure 1-2 illustrates how a computer stores text in a file — not as a sequence of characters, but as a sequence of numbers, shown here in hex format. Pay particular attention to the hex values 0D and 0A. They are the ASCII *carriage return* and *line feed*, respectively. Also note the last character in the file. It is 1A hex, a value often used to mark the end of a file. Most personal computer software, including dBASE, uses 1A hex to designate the so-called end-of-file or EOF character.

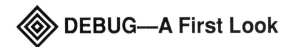 DEBUG—A First Look

As we said, Jimmy may record (save) his file on disk. He may also load it back into his computer's memory, producing a copy (or *memory image*). There are many ways to load a file into memory. A word processor can load it; so can many other types of software.

Some programs let you see all the characters in the file (including ones that are normally invisible). They may also let you change or move characters, search for particular characters or combinations, etc. Such programs are generally called *debuggers* or *debugging tools*. In IBM PC and PC-compatible computers, the most common debugger is DEBUG. It is usually on the DOS Supplemental Programs disk.

Let us next look at Jimmy's letter as DEBUG would display it. We will cover DEBUG more thoroughly later in Chapter 8. Its D (Dump) command (see Appendix B) displays the letter as shown in Figure 1-3.

```
26D4:0100  44 65 61 72 20 4D 6F 6D-20 26 20 44 61 64 2C 0D   Dear Mom & Dad,.
26D4:0110  0A 0D 0A 41 6C 6D 6F 73-74 20 61 20 77 65 65 6B   ...Almost a week
26D4:0120  20 68 61 73 20 67 6F 6E-65 20 62 79 20 73 69 6E    has gone by sin
26D4:0130  63 65 20 49 20 63 61 6D-65 20 74 6F 0D 0A 73 75   ce I came to..su
26D4:0140  6D 6D 65 72 20 63 61 6D-70 2E 20 20 49 20 74 68   mmer camp.  I th
26D4:0150  6F 75 67 68 74 20 74 68-61 74 20 63 61 6D 70 20   ought that camp
26D4:0160  77 6F 75 6C 64 20 62 65-0D 0A 62 6F 72 69 6E 67   would be..boring
26D4:0170  20 6C 69 6B 65 20 6C 61-73 74 20 79 65 61 72 2C    like last year,
26D4:0180  20 62 75 74 20 69 74 27-73 20 62 65 65 6E 20 66    but it's been f
26D4:0190  75 6E 0D 0A 73 6F 20 66-61 72 2E 0D 0A 0D 0A 49   un..so far.....I
26D4:01A0  20 68 61 76 65 20 61 20-6E 65 77 20 66 72 69 65    have a new frie
26D4:01B0  6E 64 2E 20 20 48 69 73-20 6E 61 6D 65 20 69 73   nd.  His name is
26D4:01C0  20 42 69 6C 6C 79 2E 0D-0A 48 65 20 69 73 20 37    Billy...He is 7
26D4:01D0  20 79 65 61 72 73 20 6F-6C 64 20 61 6E 64 20 68    years old and h
26D4:01E0  61 73 20 61 20 6C 69 74-74 6C 65 20 79 65 6C 6C   as a little yell
26D4:01F0  6F 77 0D 0A 64 6F 67 2E-20 20 49 20 6E 65 76 65   ow..dog.  I neve
26D4:0200  72 20 73 61 77 20 61 20-64 6F 67 20 6C 69 6B 65   r saw a dog like
26D4:0210  20 74 68 61 74 20 62 65-66 6F 72 65 2E 0D 0A 59    that before...Y
26D4:0220  65 73 74 65 72 64 61 79-20 42 69 6C 6C 79 27 73   esterday Billy's
26D4:0230  20 64 6F 67 20 61 74 65-20 6F 6E 65 20 6F 66 20    dog ate one of
26D4:0240  74 68 65 0D 0A 63 6F 75-6E 73 65 6C 6C 6F 72 73   the..counsellors
26D4:0250  2E 20 20 49 20 61 73 6B-65 64 20 42 69 6C 6C 79   .  I asked Billy
26D4:0260  20 77 68 61 74 20 6B 69-6E 65 20 6F 66 0D 0A 64    what kind of..d
26D4:0270  6F 67 20 69 74 20 77 61-73 20 61 6E 64 20 68 65   og it was and he
26D4:0280  20 73 61 69 64 2C 20 22-42 65 66 6F 72 65 20 49    said, "Before I
26D4:0290  20 63 75 74 20 6F 66 66-0D 0A 68 69 73 20 74 61    cut off..his ta
26D4:02A0  69 6C 20 61 6E 64 20 70-61 69 6E 74 65 64 20 68   il and painted h
26D4:02B0  69 6D 20 79 65 6C 6C 6F-77 2C 20 68 65 20 77 61   im yellow, he wa
26D4:02C0  73 0D 0A 61 6E 20 61 6C-6C 69 67 61 74 6F 72 22   s..an alligator"
26D4:02D0  2E 0D 0A 0D 0A 57 65 6C-6C 2C 20 62 79 65 20 6E   .....Well, bye n
26D4:02E0  6F 77 2E 20 20 49 27 6C-6C 20 77 72 69 74 65 20   ow.  I'll write
26D4:02F0  61 6E 6F 74 68 65 72 20-6C 65 74 74 65 72 0D 0A   another letter..
26D4:0300  6E 65 78 74 20 77 65 65-6B 2E 0D 0A 1A 1A 1A 1A   next week.......
```

Figure 1-3. *Jimmy's Letter as Displayed by DEBUG*

DEBUG's display has three parts. The numbers in the leftmost column are the "addresses" or locations in computer memory where the characters are stored temporarily. The sixteen 2-digit numbers in the center are the hex values of the stored characters. The rightmost column shows the ASCII characters themselves. Each row displays the contents of sixteen consecutive addresses in computer memory. The address in the leftmost column is the first of them.

The addresses appear as two 4-digit hex numbers separated by a colon. The ones to the left of the colon are called *segment numbers,* and those to the right are called *relative addresses* or *offsets.* **Whenever we refer to addresses in this book, we will mean the relative addresses.** For more information on memory addressing, see Appendix E. You can think of the complete addresses as resembling references to an encyclopedia using volume numbers and page numbers.

Note that the first address shown is 0100. When DEBUG loads a file into memory, it puts the first byte at address 0100.

In the rightmost section of the display, you see the ASCII characters corresponding to the hex values in the center. However, some ASCII characters are non-printing. They are the 32 characters with hex values 00 through 1F and the one with hex value 7F. When a memory location contains one of these values, DEBUG puts a period (.) in the corresponding location in the ASCII display.

There is one subtle point about the ASCII display. If a memory location contains a byte with a hex value greater than 7F, DEBUG will show the character obtained by changing the leftmost bit from 1 to 0. For example, the hex value C2 appears as "B" in the ASCII display since the binary representation of C2 is 11000010 and the value 01000010 is the letter "B".

 ## Summary

Computers treat characters as numbers. The most convenient form for expressing the numbers is hexadecimal, a number system based on 16. Files consist of collections of characters (or numbers) and can be stored on disk or in your computer's memory. When stored in memory, each character is at a location that has a unique address. DEBUG is a utility program that can load a file into memory for you to examine and modify.

Understanding
dBASE Datafiles

◈ Datafile Components

This chapter examines the components of DBF datafiles. Before now, you may
have viewed the data in them only as dBASE presents it in LISTings, the EDIT
or BROWSE mode, or other conventional displays. You may have learned, by
listing a datafile's structure, that it has components besides the data itself. In fact,

a DBF datafile consists of three distinct parts: header, record area, and end-of-file marker, as shown in Figure 2-1.

Figure 2-1. *Architecture of a DBF Datafile*

The file header contains information about the structure of the data records and the file as a whole. The information includes the field names, types, widths, number of decimal places (numeric or floating point fields only), and (dBASE IV only) a flag that indicates whether the field is a key in a multiple index (MDX) file. The header also contains the date of the last file update, number of records in the file, size of the header itself, and the size of each record. Appendix A has descriptions of dBASE headers for easy reference.

The header's size varies in dBASE (except in dBASE II where it is always exactly 521 bytes). It depends on how many fields the records have.

dBASE III/III PLUS allows five types of fields: character, numeric, date, logical, and memo. dBASE IV allows one additional type: floating point. As you will see, the contents of a memo field are not stored in the DBF file, but instead reside in a separate DBT file. The memo field itself contains only a pointer to the associated text.

The entire file is stored on disk as a series of characters (or bytes). It starts with the first byte of the file header and ends with the end-of-file marker (ASCII character 1A hex). The tools and utilities that we will use to examine files in detail work with hexadecimal numbers. The hex number 1A is equivalent to the decimal number 26. It is the character produced when you press Ctrl-Z on the keyboard.

◈ dBASE III PLUS Files

To illustrate the form of a dBASE III PLUS datafile, we use a sample that contains every type of field. We will call it TEST3.DBF. Figure 2-2 shows its structure.

```
Structure for database: test3.dbf
Number of data records:      3
Date of last update   : 11/26/88
Field  Name          Type       Width    Dec
    1  NAME          Character     10
    2  AMOUNT        Numeric        8      2
    3  START         Date           8
    4  CONFIRMED     Logical        1
    5  NOTES         Memo          10
** Total **                       38
```

Figure 2-2. *Sample dBASE III PLUS Datafile Structure*

Note that the numeric field (AMOUNT) has a width of 8 with two decimal places.

Our sample file contains the following data:

```
Record#  NAME        AMOUNT START   . CONFIRMED NOTES
      1  Harry     12345.25 06/15/88 .T.        Memo
      2  Roger        12.34 10/12/88 .F.        Memo
      3  Phil          0.25 12/15/88 .T.        Memo
```

We put the following text in the NOTES field of two records of TEST3.DBF. The NOTES field of the third record is blank.

```
Record#  notes
      1  Historically a slow payer.  Do not let balance exceed
         limit.

      2  Very small orders and many returns as well.
```

dBASE III PLUS Header

The first 32 bytes of a dBASE III PLUS datafile hold specific information about the file as a whole. The remaining header bytes hold the field definitions. We refer to the first byte as #1 (although programmers often refer to it as #0, mainly to differentiate themselves from normal human beings). Table 2-1 describes the header contents.

Table 2-1. dBASE III PLUS File Header

Byte Number(s) Contents

Byte Number(s)	Contents
1	Version number byte. 83 hex if the file contains a memo field; 03 if it does not.
2 - 4	Date of the last update. Byte 2 is the year, byte 3 the month, and byte 4 the day. As the values are all hex numbers, the sequence 58 0B 1A represents 88 (for 1988), 11 (for November), and 26 (for the 26th day of the month). 58 hex equals 88 decimal, 0B hex equals 11 decimal, and 1A hex equals 26 decimal.
	Note that the 1A hex in the date example is the dBASE end-of-file marker (Ctrl-Z). It can appear in the file as well as at the end. Its meaning is position-dependent, not universal.
5 - 8	Number of records in the file (least significant byte first). This is the record count that you see in dBASE when you LIST STRUCTURE (or display the RECCOUNT() function). For a healthy file, it is also the number displayed by the COUNT command. COUNT actually counts the records, whereas RECCOUNT() and the value displayed in the STRUCTURE listing come directly from bytes 5 through 8 of the file header. Thus LIST STRUCTURE and COUNT may give different values for a damaged file.
9 and 10	Number of bytes in the file header (least significant byte first). For example, if these bytes are C2 00, the file header consists of the first 194 bytes of the file, since 00C2 hex is 194 decimal.
11 and 12	Length of the records in the file (least significant byte first). For example, if the bytes are 26 00, the record length is 38 characters since 0026 hex is 38 decimal.
13 - 32	Reserved for dBASE
bytes 33 - end of header minus 1	Groups of 32 bytes defining the names, types, and widths (and decimal places if applicable) of the fields. Each group consists of:
1 - 10	Field name (an ASCII string), padded with nulls (zeros) at the right
11	Always zero
12	Field type (see Table 2-2)
13 - 16	Reserved for dBASE
17	Field width. For example, a value of 1B hex indicates that the field is 27 characters wide, since 1B hex equals 27 decimal.
18	Number of decimal places in a numeric field, 0 if the field is not numeric
19 - 32	Reserved for dBASE
last header byte	0D hex, indicating the end of the field definitions. The next byte is either the first byte of the first record or 1A hex (the end-of-file marker) if the file contains no records.

Table 2-2. dBASE III PLUS Field Types		
Designation		
ASCII **Hex**		**Type**
C	43	Character
D	44	Date
L	4C	Logical
M	4D	Memo
N	4E	Numeric

If you know how many fields a dBASE III PLUS file structure has, you can easily calculate the length of its header from the equation

$$\text{Header Length} = 33 + F \times 32 \tag{2-1}$$

where F is the number of fields. For example, if a dBASE III PLUS file has 12 fields per record, the header is $33 + 12 \times 32$ or 417 bytes long.

Thus, the size of the dBASE III PLUS file header depends on the number of fields. If the records have only one field, the file header is a mere 65 bytes. If they have the maximum number of fields (128), the header is 4129 bytes (over 60 times larger!). This is unlike dBASE II where the file header is always 521 bytes, no matter how many fields there are.

◈ Detailed Analysis of a dBASE III PLUS File

To delve into the internals of a datafile, you must examine it from outside dBASE since dBASE hides some information. We entered dBASE III PLUS to create the sample file TEST3.DBF and add data to it. But now that we want to examine the file, we will exit from dBASE and invoke the DOS utility DEBUG. Using DEBUG is not as difficult as you may think. Nor can it cause any havoc if you use it only to read or examine files.

To use DEBUG, you must, of course, have a copy of it on your disk. It is called DEBUG.COM or DEBUG.EXE in the directory. You may invoke it by simply typing its name at the DOS prompt and pressing the Enter (Return) key. You may also include a file specification on the command line as we do here.

Important Warning: If the specified file is too large to fit into the available memory space, your computer may hang up and require re-booting. Not a pleasant prospect. You must handle large files in a different way. For example, you can examine them with a sector editor such as DiskMinder (discussed in Chapter 8). To learn if your file is small enough, run CHKDSK (discussed in Chapter 6) to determine how many free bytes of memory your computer has. Subtract the size of DEBUG (obtained from a directory listing) from this. If the result is smaller than your file, the file is too large.

If DEBUG and TEST3.DBF are on the same disk and in the same directory, you can give the command

```
DEBUG TEST3.DBF
```

at the DOS prompt. If DEBUG and TEST3.DBF are on different disks or in different subdirectories, your file specification must include drive and path information.

When you press the Enter key, DEBUG loads itself into memory, moves itself to the top of low memory, and then loads TEST3.DBF into memory, beginning at address 0100.

Once DEBUG has loaded itself and the datafile, it displays its prompt, a hyphen. It provides no other information, so it is not user-friendly. Appendix B contains a DEBUG command list with examples. At this point, if you press **D** (for Dump), then Enter, you will see a display that resembles the first 8 lines of Figure 2-3. The first four hex digits of the addresses will probably be different for your computer. To get the entire display as shown, give the more elaborate command

```
D 100 23F
```

and press the Enter key. It instructs DEBUG to display the contents of memory addresses 0100 through 023F.

```
17B9:0100  83 58 0B 1A 03 00 00 00-C1 00 26 00 00 00 00 00   .X........&.....
17B9:0110  00 00 00 00 00 00 00 00-00 00 00 00 00 00 00 00   ................
17B9:0120  4E 41 4D 45 00 00 00 00-00 00 00 43 03 00 28 4C   NAME.......C..(L
17B9:0130  0A 00 00 00 01 00 00 00-00 00 00 00 00 00 00 00   ................
17B9:0140  41 4D 4F 55 4E 54 00 00-00 00 00 4E 0D 00 28 4C   AMOUNT.....N..(L
17B9:0150  08 02 00 00 01 00 00 00-00 00 00 00 00 00 00 00   ................
17B9:0160  53 54 41 52 54 00 00 00-00 00 00 44 15 00 28 4C   START......D..(L
17B9:0170  08 00 00 00 01 00 00 00-00 00 00 00 00 00 00 00   ................
17B9:0180  43 4F 4E 46 49 52 4D 45-44 00 00 4C 1D 00 28 4C   CONFIRMED..L..(L
17B9:0190  01 00 00 00 01 00 00 00-00 00 00 00 00 00 00 00   ................
17B9:01A0  4E 4F 54 45 53 00 00 00-00 00 00 4D 1E 00 28 4C   NOTES......M..(L
17B9:01B0  0A 00 00 00 01 00 00 00-00 00 00 00 00 00 00 00   ................
17B9:01C0  0D 20 48 61 72 72 79 20-20 20 20 20 31 32 33 34   . Harry     1234
17B9:01D0  35 2E 32 35 31 39 38 38-30 36 31 35 54 20 20 20   5.2519880615T
17B9:01E0  20 20 20 20 20 20 31 20-52 6F 67 65 72 20 20 20       1 Roger
17B9:01F0  20 20 20 20 20 31 32 2E-33 34 31 39 38 38 31 30       12.34198810
```

```
17B9:0200   31 32 46 20 20 20 20 20-20 20 20 20 32 20 50 68   12F          2 Ph
17B9:0210   69 6C 20 20 20 20 20 20-20 20 20 20 30 2E 32 35   il            0.25
17B9:0220   31 39 38 38 31 32 31 35-54 20 20 20 20 20 20 20   19881215T
17B9:0230   20 20 20 1A 89 46 FC 83-3E EC 86 00 74 0B C7 46      ..F.....t..F
```

Figure 2-3.   dBASE III PLUS Datafile as Displayed by DEBUG

We are now ready to examine the details of the TEST3.DBF datafile.

Note that the first byte (at address 0100) is 83. It indicates that the file is a dBASE III PLUS (or dBASE III or compatible) datafile with at least one memo field. If the file had no memo fields, this byte would be 03.

The next three bytes are 58 0B 1A, indicating a last update on November 26, 1988 as explained in Table 2-1.

The next four bytes are 03 00 00 00, indicating three records in the file.

The next two bytes are C1 00, indicating that the file header occupies 193 bytes (00C1 hex = 193 decimal).

The next two bytes are 26 00, indicating a record width of 38 characters (0026 hex = 38 decimal).

Since the next 20 bytes are reserved, let's skip to the one at address 0120. It is 4E hex (78 decimal), an ASCII N. It is the first character in the first field name. The rest of the name is 41 4D 45 (the ASCII characters 'AME'), followed by six zeros (nulls) to fill the 10-byte space. Hence we see the word 'NAME', the name of the first field in the file.

The next byte is always zero.

The next byte contains 43 (ASCII 'C'), indicating a character field.

The next four bytes (03 00 28 4C) need not concern us. dBASE uses them.

The next byte (at address 0130) is 0A hex (10 decimal), indicating a field width of 10.

The next byte is 0, indicating no decimal places.

The next 14 bytes need not concern us.

We have now arrived at the next field definition. The 10 bytes starting at address 0140 begin with the word 'AMOUNT' (that is, hex 41 4D 4F 55 4E 54), the name of the second field.

The byte at address 014B is 4E hex (ASCII N), indicating a numeric field.

Skipping the next four bytes, we come to the 08 at address 0150, followed by 02 at address 0151. They indicate that the AMOUNT field is 8 characters wide, including two decimal places.

After proceeding similarly through the next three fields, we finally come to the byte at address 01C0. Its value (0D) indicates the end of the file header. The next byte (at address 01C1) is the start of the actual data.

Beginning at address 01C1, the data records are laid out end to end. Within each record, the fields are laid out end to end. Looking at the first record, we see 20 hex (the 'space' character) at address 01C1. It is the delete status flag. 20 hex (an ASCII space) means that the record has not been marked for deletion. 2A hex (an ASCII asterisk) would mean that it has been.

The next ten addresses contain the name 'Harry' (48 61 72 72 79 hex), followed by five spaces (20 hex) to fill the 10-character field width.

Next we see the values 31 32 33 34 35 2E 32 35 (representing the ASCII characters '1' '2' '3' '4' '5' '.' '2' and '5') that form the number 12345.25. 2E is an ASCII decimal point.

Immediately thereafter, we see a date field (START) containing 31 39 38 38 30 36 31 35. They are the hex values of the ASCII characters '1' '9' '8' '8' '0' '6' '1' and '5' forming, of course, the date 19880615 (or June 15, 1988).

The next byte (at 01DC) is 54 hex, an ASCII T, indicating a logical 'true' in the CONFIRMED field.

The next 10 bytes (starting at address 01DD and extending through 01E6) contain the pointer used by dBASE to find the contents of the memo field (NOTES) for this record. (We will discuss such pointers in Chapter 3). This completes the first record. The second one starts with the next byte.

If you proceed similarly through the remaining two records of the file, you will eventually come to address 0233. It contains the end-of-file marker 1A, the last byte of the file. Data beyond it is not part of the file.

◆ dBASE III Files

A dBASE III file header is identical to a dBASE III PLUS header with one exception. A dBASE III header has an extra byte between the 0D hex marking the end of the last field definition and the first byte of the first record. Although Ashton-Tate designers must have had a future use in mind for the extra byte, they did not follow through in dBASE III PLUS or dBASE IV. Instead, it simply disappeared.

Because of the extra byte, the formula for computing the length of a dBASE III header is

$$\text{Header Length} = 34 + F \times 32 \qquad\qquad \textbf{(2-2)}$$

where F is the number of fields per record.

◆ dBASE IV Files

dBASE IV has some new datafile features. Specifically, it has a new field type and a provision for indicating whether a field is an index key in a multiple index (MDX) file. The result is that a dBASE IV file header differs slightly from its dBASE III PLUS cousin.

To illustrate the form of a dBASE IV datafile, we use a sample containing every valid field type. We call it T4M.DBF. Figure 2-4 shows its structure.

```
Structure for database: T4M.DBF
Number of data records:        3
Date of last update   : 12/01/88
Field  Field Name  Type        Width   Dec    Index
    1  NAME        Character    10             Y
    2  AMOUNT      Numeric       8      2      N
    3  STARTDATE   Date          8             Y
    4  VAR1        Float        20      3      N
    5  VAR2        Float        10             N
    6  PAID        Logical       1             N
    7  NOTE        Memo         10             N
**  Total  **                   68
```

Figure 2-4. *Sample dBASE IV Datafile Structure*

As you can see, the file structure differs from a dBASE III or III PLUS file by having an extra column that indicates (with Y or N) whether a field is an index key in an MDX file.

Also note fields 4 and 5. They are floating point fields, a new type provided in dBASE IV. Both numeric and floating point fields have a maximum width of 20.

The header bytes are allocated as listed in Table 2-3. Once again, we will call the first byte #1.

Table 2-3. dBASE IV File Header

Byte Number(s)	Contents
1	Version number byte. 8B hex if the file contains a memo field; 03 if it does not. An exception is the SQL system file (discussed later in this chapter) which has 63 hex as its first byte. dBASE IV recognizes it as a read only file.
2 - 4	Date of the last update. Byte 2 is the year, byte 3 the month, and byte 4 the day.
5 - 8	Number of records in the file (least significant byte first)
9 and 10	Number of bytes in the file header (least significant byte first)
11 and 12	Length of the records in bytes (least significant byte first)
13 and 14	Reserved for dBASE
15	Incomplete transaction flag, value of 0 or 1.
16	Encryption flag: 1 if the file is encrypted, 0 if not.
17 - 28	Reserved for local area network usage.
29	Indicates whether the file has an associated production MDX file: 1 if it does and 0 if it does not.
30 - 32	Reserved for dBASE
33 - end of header minus 1	Groups of 32 bytes defining the names, types, widths, decimal places (if applicable), and index key indicator of the fields. Each group consists of:
1 - 10	Field name (an ASCII string), padded with nulls (00 hex) if necessary at the right.
11	Always zero
12	Field type (see Table 2-4)
13 - 16	Reserved for dBASE
17	Field width. For example, 1B hex indicates that the field is 27 characters wide (1B hex = 27 decimal).

(continued on next page)

Table 2-3. dBASE IV File Header *(continued)*

Byte Number(s)	Contents
18	Number of decimal places in a numeric or floating point field, 0 if the field is neither numeric nor floating point.
19 and 20	Reserved for dBASE
21	Work area identifier
22 - 31	Reserved for dBASE
32	Indicates whether the field is a key in a multiple index (MDX) file: 1 if it is, 0 if not.
last header byte	0D hex, indicating the end of the field definitions part of the header. It is followed by the first byte of the first record or by 1A hex (the end-of-file marker) if the file contains no records.

Table 2-4. dBASE IV Field Types

Designation		Type
ASCII	Hex	
C	43	Character
D	44	Date
F	46	Floating Point
L	4C	Logical
M	4D	Memo
N	4E	Numeric

As viewed with DEBUG, our sample dBASE IV file appears as shown in Figure 2-5.

```
33D2:0100  8B 58 0C 01 03 00 00 00-01 01 44 00 00 00 00 00   .X........D.....
33D2:0110  00 00 00 00 00 00 00 00-00 00 00 00 01 00 E0 01   ................
33D2:0120  4E 41 4D 45 00 00 00 00-00 00 00 43 05 00 05 8A   NAME.......C....
33D2:0130  0A 00 00 00 01 00 00 00-00 00 00 00 00 00 00 01   ................
33D2:0140  41 4D 4F 55 4E 54 00 00-00 00 00 4E 0F 00 05 8A   AMOUNT.....N....
33D2:0150  08 02 00 00 01 00 00 00-00 00 00 00 00 00 00 00   ................
33D2:0160  53 54 41 52 54 44 41 54-45 00 00 44 17 00 05 8A   STARTDATE..D....
33D2:0170  08 00 00 00 01 00 00 00-00 00 00 00 00 00 00 01   ................
33D2:0180  56 41 52 31 00 00 00 00-00 00 00 46 1F 00 05 8A   VAR1.......F....
33D2:0190  14 03 00 00 01 00 00 00-00 00 00 00 00 00 00 00   ................
33D2:01A0  56 41 52 32 00 00 00 00-00 00 00 46 33 00 05 8A   VAR2.......F3...
33D2:01B0  0A 00 00 00 01 00 00 00-00 00 00 00 00 00 00 00   ................
33D2:01C0  50 41 49 44 00 00 00 00-00 00 00 4C 3D 00 05 8A   PAID.......L=...
33D2:01D0  01 00 00 00 01 00 00 00-00 00 00 00 00 00 00 00   ................
33D2:01E0  4E 4F 54 45 00 00 00 00-00 00 00 4D 3E 00 05 8A   NOTE.......M...
33D2:01F0  0A 00 00 00 01 00 00 00-00 00 00 00 00 00 00 00   ................
33D2:0200  0D 20 48 61 72 72 79 20-20 20 20 20 31 32 33 34   . Harry     1234
33D2:0210  35 2E 32 35 31 39 38 38-31 30 31 34 20 20 20 20   5.2519881014
33D2:0220  20 20 20 20 20 20 20 20-20 31 36 37 2E 32 39 34         167.294
33D2:0230  20 20 20 20 20 20 35 33-32 31 54 30 30 30 30 30        5321T00000
33D2:0240  30 30 30 30 32 20 53 68-65 6C 64 6F 6E 20 20 20   00002 Sheldon
```

```
33D2:0250  20 20 20 33 37 2E 39 33-31 39 38 38 31 32 30 31    37.9319881201
33D2:0260  20 20 20 20 20 20 20 20-20 20 20 20 20 20 37 33               73
33D2:0270  2E 30 32 31 20 20 20 20-20 20 20 34 33 32 20 30    .021      432 0
33D2:0280  30 30 30 30 30 30 30 30-31 20 53 61 6C 6C 79 20    000000001 Sally
33D2:0290  20 20 20 20 20 34 39 36-37 2E 30 31 31 39 38 38         4967.011988
33D2:02A0  31 31 32 31 20 20 20 20-20 20 20 20 20 20 20 20    1121
33D2:02B0  20 20 20 34 2E 30 39 37-20 20 20 20 20 37 32 33       4.097      723
33D2:02C0  35 34 54 20 20 20 20 20-20 20 20 20 1A 00 00    54T          ...
33D2:02D0  00 00 00 00 00 00 00 00-00 00 00 00 00 00 00 00    ...............
```

Figure 2-5.   dBASE IV Sample Datafile as Displayed by DEBUG

The first byte of the file is 8B hex, indicating that it contains memo fields.

Please also note the bytes at addresses 013F and 017F. They are 01 hex, indicating that the NAME and STARTDATE fields are keys in an MDX multiple index file.

The 0D hex at address 0200 is the final byte of the header. The 1A hex at address 02CD is the dBASE end-of-file marker.

Note that data is stored in the same format in numeric fields and floating point fields. See, for example, the eight boldface bytes starting at address 020C (a numeric field containing the value 12345.25) and the twenty boldface bytes starting at address 021C (a floating point field containing the value 167.294).

Note also that the memo field pointers are left-filled with zeros (ASCII value 30 hex), rather than with spaces as in dBASE III PLUS. See, for example, the ten bytes starting at address 023B.

Ashton-Tate's decision to use 03 or 8B as the first header byte of a dBASE IV file is surprising. On the one hand, dBASE III PLUS can open a dBASE IV file that does not contain a memo field. But, if the file contains a floating point field, dBASE III PLUS cannot deal with it. On the other hand, the decision to use 8B for a dBASE IV file that contains memo fields was evidently made to prevent dBASE III/III PLUS from opening the file. This protects the dBASE IV DBT file from being edited in dBASE III/III PLUS. Since the DBT files have different formats, such editing would corrupt the DBT file. Following Ashton-Tate's historical trend, one would have expected to see 04 or 84 as the first header byte of a dBASE IV datafile, depending on whether it contained memo fields.

The incorporation of SQL capability into dBASE IV has produced another minor variant of the DBF datafile. It appears in the SQL system files (SYS*.DBF) that are copied into the SQLHOME subdirectory at installation. They have the same format as a conventional dBASE IV datafile except that their first byte is 63 hex. SQL operations maintain them automatically. Although they can be opened with the USE <filename> command of dBASE IV, they cannot be edited since dBASE treats them as read only. dBASE III or III PLUS cannot open them.

◈ Converted dBASE II Files

There is one case in which a dBASE III/III PLUS file header deviates from the description in this chapter. It involves a datafile converted to dBASE III PLUS format from dBASE II using the Ashton-Tate dCONVERT utility.

Let us start with a dBASE II file that appears as shown in Figure 2-6 when viewed with DEBUG.

```
2F90:0100   02 05 00 08 1E 58 95 00-53 55 52 4E 41 4D 45 00   .....X..SURNAME.
2F90:0110   00 00 30 43 0F 30 30 00-46 4E 41 4D 45 00 00 00   ..0C.00.FNAME...
2F90:0120   00 00 30 43 0F 30 30 00-53 54 52 45 45 54 00 00   ..0C.00.STREET..
2F90:0130   00 00 30 43 23 30 30 00-43 49 54 59 00 00 00 00   ..0C#00.CITY....
2F90:0140   00 00 30 43 12 30 30 00-53 54 41 54 45 00 00 00   ..0C.00.STATE...
2F90:0150   00 00 30 43 02 30 30 00-5A 49 50 00 00 00 00 00   ..0C.00.ZIP.....
2F90:0160   00 00 30 43 05 30 30 00-41 43 43 54 4E 4F 00 00   ..0C.00.ACCTNO..
2F90:0170   00 00 30 4E 05 30 30 00-50 41 49 44 55 50 00 00   ..0N.00.PAIDUP..
2F90:0180   00 00 30 4C 01 30 30 00-4C 41 53 54 54 52 41 4E   ..0L.00.LASTTRAN
2F90:0190   00 00 30 43 06 30 30 00-43 41 54 45 47 4F 52 59   ..0C.00.CATEGORY
2F90:01A0   00 00 30 4E 02 30 30 00-41 52 45 41 43 4F 44 45   ..0N.00.AREACODE
2F90:01B0   00 00 30 43 03 30 30 00-54 45 4C 00 00 00 00 00   ..0C.00.TEL.....
2F90:01C0   00 00 30 43 08 30 30 00-53 4C 4E 41 4D 45 00 00   ..0C.00.SLNAME..
2F90:01D0   00 00 30 43 0F 30 30 00-53 46 4E 41 4D 45 00 00   ..0C.00.SFNAME..
2F90:01E0   00 00 30 43 0F 30 30 00-4F 52 44 45 52 00 00 00   ..0C.00.ORDER...
2F90:01F0   00 00 30 4E 03 30 30 00-0D 00 00 00 00 00 00 00   ..0N.00.........
2F90:0200   00 00 00 00 00 00 00 00-00 00 00 00 00 00 00 00   ................
2F90:0210   00 00 00 00 00 00 00 00-00 00 00 00 00 00 00 00   ................
2F90:0220   00 00 00 00 00 00 00 00-00 00 00 00 00 00 00 00   ................
2F90:0230   00 00 00 00 00 00 00 00-00 00 00 00 00 00 00 00   ................
2F90:0240   00 00 00 00 00 00 00 00-00 00 00 00 00 00 00 00   ................
2F90:0250   00 00 00 00 00 00 00 00-00 00 00 00 00 00 00 00   ................
2F90:0260   00 00 00 00 00 00 00 00-00 00 00 00 00 00 00 00   ................
2F90:0270   00 00 00 00 00 00 00 00-00 00 00 00 00 00 00 00   ................
2F90:0280   00 00 00 00 00 00 00 00-00 00 00 00 00 00 00 00   ................
2F90:0290   00 00 00 00 00 00 00 00-00 00 00 00 00 00 00 00   ................
2F90:02A0   00 00 00 00 00 00 00 00-00 00 00 00 00 00 00 00   ................
2F90:02B0   00 00 00 00 00 00 00 00-00 00 00 00 00 00 00 00   ................
2F90:02C0   00 00 00 00 00 00 00 00-00 00 00 00 00 00 00 00   ................
2F90:02D0   00 00 00 00 00 00 00 00-00 00 00 00 00 00 00 00   ................
2F90:02E0   00 00 00 00 00 00 00 00-00 00 00 00 00 00 00 00   ................
2F90:02F0   00 00 00 00 00 00 00 00-00 00 00 00 00 00 00 00   ................
2F90:0300   00 00 00 00 00 00 00 00-00 20 5A 75 63 6B 65 72   ......... Zucker
2F90:0310   6D 61 6E 20 20 20 20 20-20 20 41 64 64 69 73 6F 6E  man       Addison
2F90:0320   20 42 2E 20 20 20 20 20-34 31 36 20 47 61 72 66   B.      416 Garf
2F90:0330   69 65 6C 64 20 41 76 65-6E 75 65 20 20 20 20 20   ield Avenue
2F90:0340   20 20 20 20 20 20 20 20-20 20 20 42 6F 73 74 6F          Bosto
2F90:0350   6E 20 20 20 20 20 20 20-20 20 20 20 20 4D 41 30   n            MA0
```

Figure 2-6. *dBASE II Datafile as Displayed by DEBUG*

As long as we are looking at a dBASE II file, we might as well say a few words about it. The dBASE II header differs from the dBASE III PLUS header in the following ways:

1. It is always 521 bytes long, regardless of the number of fields per record.

2. It has file information (version indicator, number of records, date of last update, and record length) in its first eight bytes. The first byte is always 02.

3. Each field is specified in a block of 16 bytes.

4. There is a 0D hex immediately after the last field definition.

5. If there are fewer than 32 fields per record, the space between the last field definition and the end of the header is filled with nulls (zeros).

After converting this file to dBASE III PLUS format, the header appears as shown in Figure 2-7.

```
2F90:0100  03 56 01 1E 55 03 00 00-21 04 95 00 00 00 00 00   .V..U...!.......
2F90:0110  00 00 00 00 00 00 00 00-00 00 00 00 00 00 00 00   ................
2F90:0120  53 55 52 4E 41 4D 45 00-00 00 00 43 00 00 00 00   SURNAME....C....
2F90:0130  0F 00 00 00 00 00 00 00-00 00 00 00 00 00 00 00   ................
2F90:0140  46 4E 41 4D 45 00 00 00-00 00 00 43 00 00 00 00   FNAME......C....
2F90:0150  0F 00 00 00 00 00 00 00-00 00 00 00 00 00 00 00   ................
2F90:0160  53 54 52 45 45 54 00 00-00 00 00 43 00 00 00 00   STREET.....C....
2F90:0170  23 00 00 00 00 00 00 00-00 00 00 00 00 00 00 00   #...............
2F90:0180  43 49 54 59 00 00 00 00-00 00 00 43 00 00 00 00   CITY.......C....
2F90:0190  12 00 00 00 00 00 00 00-00 00 00 00 00 00 00 00   ................
2F90:01A0  53 54 41 54 45 00 00 00-00 00 00 43 00 00 00 00   STATE......C....
2F90:01B0  02 00 00 00 00 00 00 00-00 00 00 00 00 00 00 00   ................
2F90:01C0  5A 49 50 00 00 00 00 00-00 00 00 43 00 00 00 00   ZIP........C....
2F90:01D0  05 00 00 00 00 00 00 00-00 00 00 00 00 00 00 00   ................
2F90:01E0  41 43 43 54 4E 4F 00 00-00 00 00 4E 00 00 00 00   ACCTNO.....N....
2F90:01F0  05 00 00 00 00 00 00 00-00 00 00 00 00 00 00 00   ................
2F90:0200  50 41 49 44 55 50 00 00-00 00 00 4C 00 00 00 00   PAIDUP.....L....
2F90:0210  01 00 00 00 00 00 00 00-00 00 00 00 00 00 00 00   ................
2F90:0220  4C 41 53 54 54 52 41 4E-00 00 00 43 00 00 00 00   LASTTRAN...C....
2F90:0230  06 00 00 00 00 00 00 00-00 00 00 00 00 00 00 00   ................
2F90:0240  43 41 54 45 47 4F 52 59-00 00 00 4E 00 00 00 00   CATEGORY...N....
2F90:0250  02 00 00 00 00 00 00 00-00 00 00 00 00 00 00 00   ................
2F90:0260  41 52 45 41 43 4F 44 45-00 00 00 43 00 00 00 00   AREACODE...C....
2F90:0270  03 00 00 00 00 00 00 00-00 00 00 00 00 00 00 00   ................
2F90:0280  54 45 4C 00 00 00 00 00-00 00 00 43 00 00 00 00   TEL........C....
2F90:0290  08 00 00 00 00 00 00 00-00 00 00 00 00 00 00 00   ................
2F90:02A0  53 4C 4E 41 4D 45 00 00-00 00 00 43 00 00 00 00   SLNAME.....C....
2F90:02B0  0F 00 00 00 00 00 00 00-00 00 00 00 00 00 00 00   ................
2F90:02C0  53 46 4E 41 4D 45 00 00-00 00 00 43 00 00 00 00   SFNAME.....C....
2F90:02D0  0F 00 00 00 00 00 00 00-00 00 00 00 00 00 00 00   ................
2F90:02E0  4F 52 44 45 52 00 00 00-00 00 00 4E 00 00 00 00   ORDER......N....
2F90:02F0  03 00 00 00 00 00 00 00-00 00 00 00 00 00 00 00   ................
```

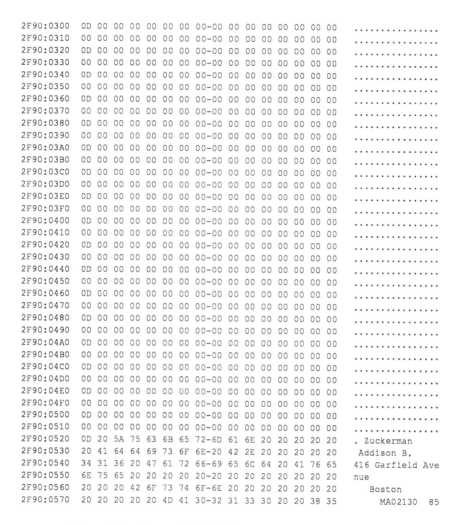

```
2F90:0300  0D 00 00 00 00 00 00 00-00 00 00 00 00 00 00 00   ................
2F90:0310  00 00 00 00 00 00 00 00-00 00 00 00 00 00 00 00   ................
2F90:0320  0D 00 00 00 00 00 00 00-00 00 00 00 00 00 00 00   ................
2F90:0330  00 00 00 00 00 00 00 00-00 00 00 00 00 00 00 00   ................
2F90:0340  0D 00 00 00 00 00 00 00-00 00 00 00 00 00 00 00   ................
2F90:0350  00 00 00 00 00 0D 00 00-00-6D 00 00 00 00 00 00 00   ................
2F90:0360  0D 00 00 00 00 00 00 00-00 00 00 00 00 00 00 00   ................
2F90:0370  00 00 00 00 00 00 00 00-00 00 00 00 00 00 00 00   ................
2F90:0380  0D 00 00 00 00 00 00 00-00 00 00 00 00 00 00 00   ................
2F90:0390  00 00 00 00 00 00 00 00-00 00 00 00 00 00 00 00   ................
2F90:03A0  0D 00 00 00 00 00 00 00-00 00 00 00 00 00 00 00   ................
2F90:03B0  00 00 00 00 00 00 00 00-00 00 00 00 00 00 00 00   ................
2F90:03C0  0D 00 00 00 00 00 00 00-00 00 00 00 00 00 00 00   ................
2F90:03D0  00 00 00 00 00 00 00 00-00 00 00 00 00 00 00 00   ................
2F90:03E0  0D 00 00 00 00 00 00 00-00 00 00 00 00 00 00 00   ................
2F90:03F0  00 00 00 00 00 00 00 00-00 00 00 00 00 00 00 00   ................
2F90:0400  0D 00 00 00 00 00 00 00-00 00 00 00 00 00 00 00   ................
2F90:0410  00 00 00 00 00 00 00 00-00 00 00 00 00 00 00 00   ................
2F90:0420  0D 00 00 00 00 00 00 00-00 00 00 00 00 00 00 00   ................
2F90:0430  00 00 00 00 00 00 00 00-00 00 00 00 00 00 00 00   ................
2F90:0440  0D 00 00 00 00 00 00 00-00 00 00 00 00 00 00 00   ................
2F90:0450  00 00 00 00 00 00 00 00-00 00 00 00 00 00 00 00   ................
2F90:0460  0D 00 00 00 00 00 00 00-00 00 00 00 00 00 00 00   ................
2F90:0470  00 00 00 00 00 00 00 00-00 00 00 00 00 00 00 00   ................
2F90:0480  0D 00 00 00 00 00 00 00-00 00 00 00 00 00 00 00   ................
2F90:0490  00 00 00 00 00 00 00 00-00 00 00 00 00 00 00 00   ................
2F90:04A0  0D 00 00 00 00 00 00 00-00 00 00 00 00 00 00 00   ................
2F90:04B0  00 00 00 00 00 00 00 00-00 00 00 00 00 00 00 00   ................
2F90:04C0  0D 00 00 00 00 00 00 00-00 00 00 00 00 00 00 00   ................
2F90:04D0  00 00 00 00 00 00 00 00-00 00 00 00 00 00 00 00   ................
2F90:04E0  0D 00 00 00 00 00 00 00-00 00 00 00 00 00 00 00   ................
2F90:04F0  00 00 00 00 00 00 00 00-00 00 00 00 00 00 00 00   ................
2F90:0500  0D 00 00 00 00 00 00 00-00 00 00 00 00 00 00 00   ................
2F90:0510  00 00 00 00 00 00 00 00-00 00 00 00 00 00 00 00   ................
2F90:0520  0D 20 5A 75 63 6B 65 72-6D 61 6E 20 20 20 20 20   . Zuckerman
2F90:0530  20 41 64 64 69 73 6F 6E-20 42 2E 20 20 20 20 20   Addison B.
2F90:0540  34 31 36 20 47 61 72 66-69 65 6C 64 20 41 76 65   416 Garfield Ave
2F90:0550  6E 75 65 20 20 20 20 20-20 20 20 20 20 20 20 20   nue
2F90:0560  20 20 20 42 6F 73 74 6F-6E 20 20 20 20 20 20 20      Boston
2F90:0570  20 20 20 20 20 4D 41 30-32 31 33 30 20 20 38 35        MA02130   85
```

Figure 2-7. *Converted dBASE II Datafile as Displayed by DEBUG*

Note the anomaly in the converted file header. It looks like a conventional dBASE III PLUS header through address 02FF, but then it has a succession of 32-byte groups, each starting with 0D hex and containing 31 nulls. If you count groups and add the number of actual fields, you find that the sum is 32, the maximum number of fields in a dBASE II file. Hence we see that the resulting header is of fixed length, the length of a conventional header for a dBASE III PLUS file having 32 fields per record. If we removed all bytes from addresses 0300 through 051F, we would have a conventional dBASE III PLUS header.

The unusual header poses no problem for dBASE, but it can cause havoc for other software designed to read dBASE files. There is a simple way, however, to transform this header into the conventional dBASE III PLUS format. The only thing you need to do is invoke dBASE, open the file, and copy it to another file with the dBASE COPY command. The new file will have a proper header.

 **Record Format**

So far we have dealt exclusively with file headers. But there is one thing you should know about the records in the file, aside from the fact that they consist of a long, continuous stream of characters. You may have noted, when listing the structure of a datafile, that the length of each field appears and that the bottom line of the display shows a TOTAL. If you sum the individual field widths, you will find that the result is one less than the TOTAL.

The reason for the discrepancy is that dBASE allocates an extra byte in each record for a "delete status flag." It is the first byte of every record. It has only two permissible values in a healthy datafile. They are 27 hex (the asterisk character), indicating a record marked for deletion, and 20 hex (the space character), indicating an unmarked record. When you DELETE or RECALL a record, dBASE changes the delete status flag.

dBASE also uses this position to hold the end-of-file marker (1A hex) immediately after the last character of the last record. You may think of the marker as an extra "record" containing only a delete status flag. If, somehow, a 1A crept into the flag position in a valid record, dBASE would regard it as the actual end-of-file for a LISTing or a COPY, regardless of what the header says about the number of records in the file.

 **Summary**

A dBASE datafile consists of three parts: header, record area, and end-of-file marker. dBASE II file headers have a fixed length (always 521 bytes), but header length in all other versions depends on the number of fields. The header contains field definitions and information about the file as a whole (dBASE version, date of last update, record count, record length, etc.). To examine headers in detail, you must use a debugger or sector editor.

3

dBASE Memo
Fields and Files

If you use dBASE III/III PLUS/IV, you probably know how convenient memo fields are for storing free-form text such as biographical sketches, sales representatives' notes, technical abstracts, and product descriptions. dBASE II lacked this feature. Unlike other types of fields, the contents of memo fields are not stored directly in the DBF datafiles. Instead, the memo field contains a ten-digit number (or *pointer*), but the text itself is elsewhere. It is in a file with the same name as the datafile, but with an extension of DBT rather than DBF. dBASE creates the DBT file automatically when you include a memo field in a datafile, either by creating a new file structure or by modifying an existing one.

The ten-digit pointer tells dBASE where to find the actual text in the DBT file. The pointer consists of ten ASCII digits, most significant digit first. In the event of file damage, you may need to find memo text without dBASE's help. We will therefore discuss how dBASE constructs the pointer and what it really means.

If you consult the ASCII table in Appendix C, you will see that 'space' has a hex value of 20 and that the ASCII digits 0 through 9 have the values shown in Table 3-1.

Table 3-1. ASCII Values of the Decimal Digits		
ASCII Digit	Decimal Value	Hex Value
0	48	30
1	49	31
2	50	32
3	51	33
4	52	34
5	53	35
6	54	36
7	55	37
8	56	38
9	57	39

It is easier to relate an ASCII digit to its hex value than to its decimal value. Just strip off the first hex digit and you have it. We will use hex notation when discussing memo field pointers because debugging tools and sector editors generally display digits in hex.

Now let's look at how dBASE stores a ten-digit pointer in the memo field of a DBF datafile. The digits are stored as ASCII characters rather than as numbers; the least significant digit comes last (that is, in the rightmost character position). dBASE III PLUS uses spaces for leading zeros, but dBASE IV uses zeros. For example, dBASE III PLUS stores 127 as:

```
20 20 20 20 20 20 20 31 32 37
```

dBASE IV stores it as:

```
30 30 30 30 30 30 30 31 32 37
```

The pointers tell dBASE where to look in the DBT file for the text associated with a particular memo field. As soon as you enter a single character into the field (and, of course, save it using Ctrl-End), dBASE immediately reserves a block of 512 bytes in the DBT file to hold it. As you add text, dBASE will continue to store it in the 512-byte block until it overflows. dBASE will then reserve another 512-byte block. (This is not strictly true when you edit a memo field, but we will treat that complication later). A collection of blocks for a particular memo form a *memo group*.

Each block is at a particular location in the DBT file. The first one starts at the 513th character position. 513 may seem to be an odd starting number, but think of the file locations in hex. If the first byte (or position) in the file is hex 0, the first block of memo text starts at byte 200 hex. As the block is 512 bytes long, its last position is byte 3FF hex, and the first position of the next block is byte 400 hex. Hence, dBASE assigns starting locations for blocks at multiples of 200 hex, starting at byte 200 hex. Byte 200 hex is the 513th character position if you start counting at 1.

Do not confuse the byte locations just mentioned with the memory addresses displayed by the debugger. When DEBUG loads a file into your computer's memory, it does not load it at address 0000. Instead, it loads the file at address 0100.

Hence, when loaded into memory, the address of a particular character is its hex byte location in the file plus 100 hex. Figure 3-1 shows this.

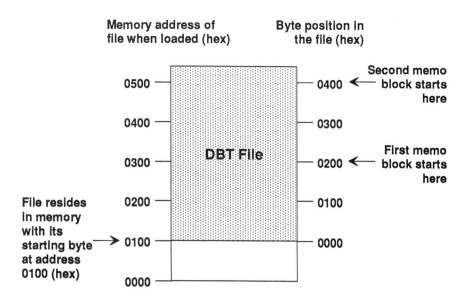

Figure 3-1. *DBT File Loaded into Memory by DEBUG*

There is one major difference between dBASE III PLUS memo groups and dBASE IV memo groups. In dBASE III PLUS, the first byte of a group contains the first character of the memo text. In dBASE IV, however, each group starts with an 8-byte group header, followed immediately by the memo text. Table 3-2 describes the group header.

Table 3-2. dBASE IV DBT File Group Header	
Bytes	Meaning
1-2	Indicate whether the text is the contents of a dBASE III PLUS memo field. FFFF indicates that it is not. In the initial release, the bytes are always FFFF, but future releases might use other values.
3-4	Number of bytes in the group header (least significant byte first). In the initial release, the value is always 8, but it could change in future releases.
5-8	Total number of bytes in the memo text, including the group header (least significant byte first).

For example, if the first eight bytes of a group header are

```
FF FF 08 00 2B 01 00 00
```

then you would know the following:

- The text is the contents of a dBASE IV memo field, not dBASE III PLUS.

- The group header is eight bytes long.

- The memo is 299 bytes long (including the eight header bytes), since 12B hex = 299 decimal.

Now that you understand the format of a DBT file, the task of finding a particular body of text in a memory-resident copy of one, based on the pointer in the related DBF file, is not difficult. In fact, you can use the following simple formula:

$$\text{DBT file address in memory} = 300 + (N\text{-}1) \times 200 \qquad \textbf{(3-1)}$$

where N is the pointer's hex value. All numbers in the formula are hex.

For example, suppose that a memo field contains

```
20 20 20 20 20 20 20 20 31 32
```

This is equivalent to decimal 12 or hex 0C. N, therefore, is 0C hex and N-1 is 0B hex. Multiplying 0B hex by 200 hex gives 1600 hex. Adding 300 hex gives 1900 hex. Hence the address of the beginning of the related block of text in the memory-resident DBT file is 1900. A calculator with hex capabilities is the only reasonable way to do the arithmetic, short of having six extra fingers attached surgically or painting A through F on your toes. Or perhaps I could sell you a pair of "Heiser's Hex Gloves" (trademark applied for), which have eight fingers on each hand.

With this knowledge, you can often reconstruct a corrupted DBT file (assuming that you can read most or all of its text). You can use DEBUG for small files or a sector editor like DiskMinder for large ones. DiskMinder (discussed in Chapter 8) can handle files of any size.

A more important consideration, however, is that this knowledge will allow you to modify memo-field pointers altered by datafile damage. You can even move memo-field text from one record to another within a file or duplicate it without re-entering it. All you must do is change a pointer. You can use dSALVAGE Professional's Record Editor for this purpose since it allows you to access and alter any field, including memo fields. We will discuss dSALVAGE fully later.

Before we leave the subject of memo fields, we should mention an interesting sidelight to dBASE III PLUS DBT files. As we noted, dBASE reserves file space in blocks of 512 bytes. If you put a small amount of text in a memo field (less than 512 characters), dBASE reserves a single 512-byte block in the DBT file. If later you add text so that the total exceeds 512 characters, dBASE will reserve a new group (consisting of as many blocks as are required) in the DBT file, but will not remove the original block.

The new group will contain all the text now in the memo field. The old block will contain only the original text. The strange thing is that dBASE never reuses the old block. It just stays in the DBT file and occupies disk space. Clearly, reassigning the space would increase disk utilization. We suspect, however, that Ashton-Tate made a conscious tradeoff between disk utilization and processing time. You can always compact the DBT file by copying the DBF datafile with the dBASE COPY command.

There is one other tidbit of information about dBASE III PLUS memo files that you might find useful some day. If your dBASE III PLUS DBF datafile contains a memo field and you erase its associated DBT file, dBASE will refuse to open it. You can solve this problem in a surprising way. Just create a dummy DBT file with the correct name. It does not matter what it contains. You can create it with the DOS COPY command. For example, if your DBF file is SAMPLE.DBF, just give the following command at the DOS prompt:

```
COPY CON SAMPLE.DBT
```

Now type a character or two, press the F6 function key (or Ctrl-Z), then press Enter. dBASE will open the datafile, but you will see nothing, of course, if you try to access the memo field text. This trick is unnecessary in dBASE IV; it will alert you to the missing DBT file and create an empty one automatically if you wish.

 **Summary**

Memo text is stored in a DBT file rather than in the memo field of a DBF datafile. The DBF file contains only a pointer to the text. If you know the pointer's value, you can find the related text in the DBT file with a debugger or sector editor. More important, by changing a pointer in a given record, you can reassign text to the record's memo field without having to reenter it with dBASE's text editor.

If you repair a damaged datafile and lose memo field pointers in the process, you can replace them using a debugger or sector editor. You cannot use dBASE to view or change the pointers.

4

Disk Directories and File Allocation Tables

Both hard and floppy DOS disks contain regions assigned to specific purposes. They include the directory, a "map" of the file storage area, and the file storage data area itself. The "map" is called the File Allocation Table, or FAT for short.

When you format a disk, DOS organizes it into concentric tracks and pie-shaped sectors. A typical 5 1/4-inch 360K double-sided double-density floppy disk formatted in this way contains 40 tracks and 9 sectors on each side of its surface. Each sector can hold 512 bytes (or characters) of data.

As files are stored on disk, DOS allocates space in increments of clusters. A cluster is not the same size for all disks. On a 360K floppy disk, it consists of two sectors that can hold 1024 bytes (1K bytes) of information. On hard disks, clusters may range in size from as little as 2K (2048) bytes to as much as 8K (8192) bytes. The minimum disk space that can be allocated to a file is one cluster.

For example, suppose your file contains only a single character (that is, one byte). When stored on a floppy disk, it will occupy one full cluster (1024 bytes), although a directory listing will show its size as only one byte. As you add characters to it, the actual disk space occupied will not increase until its size reaches 1025 bytes, at which time it will occupy two full clusters. Large files occupy many clusters.

DOS assigns each cluster a number during formatting. Ordinarily, the first two clusters (numbers 0 and 1) are assigned for specific purposes and do not contain user files. Hence, cluster 2 is normally the first one in the data area of the disk. DOS uses this cluster numbering scheme to locate files.

 **Disk Directory Essentials**

When you give the DIR command, DOS examines the directory area of the specified disk and provides an on-screen display such as the one shown in Figure 4-1.

```
C:\DIR A:

Volume in drive A has no label
Directory of  A:\

BARRIER  DOC     3488    8-02-87    1:06p
MORSE    LTR     1772   12-15-87    2:05p
PRNDBFS  TXT    37515    7-21-88    5:00p
README   DOC     9570    1-09-88    5:46p
RES      DBF    73446    5-22-88   12:43p
EDITOR   DOC     4446    4-21-88   10:38p
MANSCOPE DOC      956    1-20-88   11:07a
CONTRACT DOC     9084    7-31-88   11:51p
          8 File(s)    219136 bytes free
```

Figure 4-1. *Typical Directory Listing for a Floppy Disk*

The information displayed consists of disk drive identification, a disk label (if one exists), the name, extension, size (in bytes), and date and time of last update for each non-hidden file on the disk, the total number of files, and the remaining space on the disk. However, the display does not tell you where the files are stored in the data area of the disk, although the actual directory contains this vital information.

If you could see all the information stored in the directory, it would appear as shown in Figure 4-2.

```
BARRIER .DOC    3488  08/02/87  13:06:06  20  0002
MORSE   .LTR    1772  12/15/87  14:05:48  20  0006
PRNDBFS .TXT   37515  07/21/88  17:00:04  20  0008
README  .DOC    9570  01/09/88  17:46:00  20  002D
RES     .DBF   73446  05/22/88  12:43:28  20  0037
EDITOR  .DOC    4446  04/21/88  22:38:24  20  007F
MANSCOPE.DOC     956  01/20/88  11:07:58  20  0084
CONTRACT.DOC    9084  07/31/88  23:51:56  20  0085
```

Figure 4-2. *Complete Sample Directory Information for a Floppy Disk.*

Pay particular attention to the rightmost column. It contains the hex number of the cluster in which the file begins in the disk's data area. For an explanation of hex numbers, refer to Appendix D. We will show you how to examine disk directories in this way later.

 **FAT Essentials**

As you have seen, the disk directory provides only the starting location of each file. To find the remaining pieces, DOS must know where they are located and the order in which they are stored. This is what the File Allocation Table (FAT) shows. Think of the FAT as a table of rows and columns with a cell at each intersection. There is one cell for each disk cluster. Conceptually, the FAT is very simple. Each cell contains the number of the cluster containing the next piece of a file.

The total set of cells for a particular file form a file allocation chain. We may think of the cells as links in the chain. The last link contains a "file terminator."

Figure 4-3 shows a section of the FAT on our sample disk.

```
Clu     +0  +1  +2  +3    +4  +5  +6  +7    +8  +9  +A  +B    +C  +D  +E  +F
0000   FFD FFF 003 004   005 FFF 007 FFF   009 00A 00B 00C   00D 00E 00F 010
0010   011 012 013 014   015 016 017 018   019 01A 01B 01C   01D 01E 01F 020
0020   021 022 023 024   025 026 027 028   029 02A 02B 02C   FFF 02E 02F 030
0030   031 032 033 034   035 036 FFF 038   039 03A 03B 03C   03D 03E 03F 040
0040   041 042 043 044   045 046 047 048   049 04A 04B 04C   04D 04E 04F 050
0050   051 052 053 054   055 056 057 058   059 05A 05B 05C   05D 05E 05F 060
0060   061 062 063 064   065 066 067 068   069 06A 06B 06C   06D 06E 06F 070
0070   071 072 073 074   075 076 077 078   079 07A 07B 07C   07D 07E FFF 080
0080   081 082 083 FFF   FFF 086 087 088   089 08A 08B 08C   08D FFF 000 000
0090   000 000 000 000   000 000 000 000   000 000 000 000   000 000 000 000
```

Figure 4-3. Sample File Allocation Table (FAT) for a Floppy Disk

On a floppy disk, each FAT cell contains a 3-digit (12 bit) hexadecimal number. As you will see later, large hard disks have many more clusters than floppy disks and therefore require larger numbers to identify clusters.

Figure 4-3 shows the FAT in a format with 16 cells per line. The leftmost column contains the **number** of the first cell. The remaining 16 hex numbers on each line show the **contents** of the cells. For example, the first cell in the top line corresponds to cluster 0 and contains FFD hex. The next cell to the right corresponds to cluster 1 and contains FFF hex. These first two cells refer to clusters used by DOS. The next cell, corresponding to cluster 2, contains the number 3 which points to the next link in a chain.

Looking back at the last directory display (Figure 4-2), you will see a file BARRIER.DOC that starts in cluster 2. But since FAT cell 2 contains 3, DOS knows that the next piece of this file is in cluster 3. Moving similarly through the rest of the allocation chain, we see that cell 3 points to cell 4, cell 4 points to cell 5, and cell 5 contains FFF, the file terminator. Thus, DOS can find all the pieces of BARRIER.DOC.

A file that occupies only a single cluster has FFF in the corresponding FAT cell. For example, consider the file MANSCOPE.DOC in Figure 4-2. It contains only 956 bytes, less than one 1024-byte cluster. Its directory entry indicates that it starts in cluster 84. The fact that FAT cell 84 contains FFF indicates that the file also terminates there. In this case the file's allocation chain consists of a single link.

Our examples have involved only files having contiguous links in their allocation chains. Such files are said to be *unfragmented*. Later, we will discuss fragmented files and ones having various forms of allocation chain damage.

 # Hard Disk FATs

Although the structure and function of the FAT on a large capacity hard disk are the same as on a floppy disk, the details differ since the cells are larger. For example, on a 40-megabyte hard disk, a section of the directory might appear as shown in Figure 4-4 and a section of the FAT might appear as shown in Figure 4-5.

```
BARRIER  .DOC      3488   08/02/87   13:06:06   20   2DA4
MORSE    .LTR      1772   12/15/87   14:05:48   20   2DA6
PRNDBFS  .TXT     37515   07/21/88   17:00:04   20   2DA7
README   .DOC      9570   01/09/88   17:46:00   20   2DBA
RES      .DBF     73446   05/22/88   12:43:28   20   2DBF
EDITOR   .DOC      4446   04/21/88   22:38:24   20   2F26
MANSCOPE.DOC        956   01/20/88   11:07:58   20   2F29
CONTRACT.DOC       9084   07/31/88   23:51:56   20   2F2A
```

Figure 4-4. *Typical Partial Directory Information for a Hard Disk*

```
Clu     +0   +1   +2   +3      +4   +5   +6   +7      +8   +9   +A   +B
2D80  0000 2D83 FFFF 2D84    2D85 2D86 2D87 FFFF    2D89 2D8A 2D8B 2D8C
2D8C  FFFF 2D8E 2D92 2D90    2D91 FFFF 2D93 2D94    2D95 FFFF 0000 2D98
2D98  2D99 2D9A 2D9B FFFF    0000 0000 2D9F 2DA0    2DA1 2DA2 FFFF FFFF
2DA4  2DA5 FFFF FFFF 2DA8    2DA9 2DAA 2DAB 2DAC    2DAD 2DAE 2DAF 2DB0
2DB0  2DB1 2DB2 2DB3 2DB4    2DB5 2DB6 2DB7 2DB8    2DB9 FFFF 2DBB 2DBC
2DBC  2DBD 2DBE FFFF 2DC0    2DC1 2DC2 2DC3 2DC4    2DC5 2DC8 2DC7 FFFF
2DC8  2E39 FFFF 2DCB 2DCC    2DCD 2DCE 2DCF 2DD0    2DD1 2DD2 FFFF 2DD4
2DD4  2DD5 2DD6 2DD7 2DD8    2DD9 2DDA 2DDB 2DDC    2DDD 2DDE 2DDF 2DE0
2DE0  2DE1 2DE2 FFFF 2DE4    2DE5 2DE6 2DE7 2DE8    2DE9 2DEA 2DEB 2DEC
2DEC  2DED 2DEE 2DEF 2DF0    2DF1 2DF2 2DF3 2DF4    2DF5 2DF6 2DF7 2DF8
2DF8  2DF9 2DFA 2DFB 2DFC    2DFD 2DFE 2DFF 2E00    2E01 2E02 2E03 2E04
2E04  2E05 2E06 FFFF 2E08    FFFF FFFF 2E0B 2E0C    2E2D 2E0E 2E0F 2E10
2E10  2E11 2E12 2E13 2E14    2E15 2E16 2E17 2E18    2E19 2E1A 2E1B 2E1C
2E1C  2E1D 2E1E 2E1F 2E20    2E21 2E22 2E23 2E24    2E25 2E26 2E27 2E28
2E28  2E29 2E2A 2E2B 2E2C    FFFF 2E2E 2E2F 2E30    2E31 FFFF 2E33 FFFF
2E34  2E35 FFFF 2E37 FFFF    FFFF 2E3A 2E3E 2E3C    2E3D FFFF 2E3F 2E40
```

Figure 4-5. *Typical Partial FAT for a Hard Disk*

Note that the cell values are four digits (16 bits) rather then three because the FAT must accommodate more clusters.

In this example, the file BARRIER.DOC starts at cluster 2DA4 (as shown in the directory in Figure 4-4) and ends at cluster 2DA5 (as indicated by the FFFF terminator in its FAT cell). It occupies only two clusters. Figure 4-5 shows its allocation chain in boldface.

It should be clear by now that you can determine how many clusters a file occupies if you know its size and the disk's cluster size. For example, BAR-RIER.DOC consists of 3488 bytes. Dividing this by the size of a floppy disk cluster (1024) yields 3.4, indicating that BARRIER.DOC requires four clusters (as we saw above). In the 40-megabyte hard disk example where the cluster size is 2048 bytes, the division yields 1.7, indicating that the file requires only two clusters.

Before leaving this example, note that some FAT cells contain zero. It means they are not part of any file, either because no data has ever been written into them or because they were deallocated by file erasure or a similar process. In the latter case, the contents of the erased file are still in the data area of the disk, but they are extremely vulnerable since the next thing written to the disk may overwrite them. We will discuss erased files further when we deal with ZAP'd datafiles in Chapter 9.

5

File
Fragmentation

If you examine the File Allocation Table immediately after formatting a disk, you will see that all cells contain zero except the first two. DOS reserves them. Files written to the disk when it is in this state have logically contiguous allocation chains. That is, each link in every file's chain refers to its numerical successor. For example, cell 2 points to cell 3, cell 3 to cell 4, cell 4 to cell 5, and so forth until the file terminator (FFF) is reached. All other files do likewise. We say that they are unfragmented, as noted in Chapter 4.

Figure 5-1 shows a typical unfragmented file allocation chain on a floppy disk.

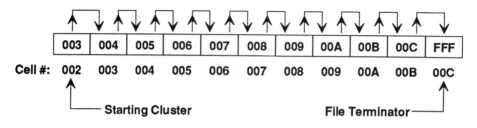

Figure 5-1. *Typical Unfragmented File Allocation Chain on a Floppy Disk*

As you use your disk, you will surely erase files, ZAP DBF datafiles, or do other things that deallocate (i.e., clear) FAT cells, informing DOS that their clusters are available for recording. Early versions of DOS (prior to 3.0) use the freed clusters immediately, but later versions try to find contiguous clusters (in previously unused areas) for new files. Even then, the time will come (as the disk fills) when DOS cannot find enough contiguous free clusters for a new file. In such cases, it uses whatever space it can find. The files then occupy non-contiguous clusters; we say they are *fragmented.*

In Figure 5-2, File 1 consists of two pieces (clusters 2 through 4 and A through C), whereas File 2 occupies contiguous clusters (5 through 9). File 1 is fragmented, but File 2 is not.

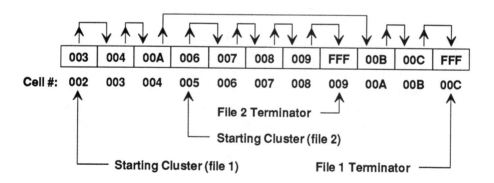

Figure 5-2. *Typical FAT Chains Showing Fragmentation*

There is another situation you should understand because of its effects on file recovery, particularly of ZAP'd DBF datafiles. This is the case of a backward-pointing pointer in the file allocation chain. Although some may argue that such pointers have nothing to do with fragmentation, the classification is unimportant as long as you understand the problem.

Consider the file allocation chain in Figure 5-3. It has a backward-pointing pointer in cell 9. The file thus consists of clusters in non-consecutive order despite the absence of any numerical gaps.

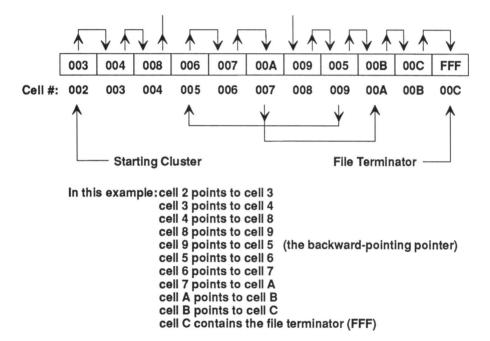

Figure 5-3. *File Allocation Chain with a Backward-Pointing Pointer*

Fragmentation is not the same as damage. One consequence of fragmentation is longer read times due to the extra head motion required to find all the file's pieces. The extra time may not even be noticeable until fragmentation becomes severe. Another consequence is the extra wear and tear on disk drives. Even more important, however, is that excessive fragmentation represents extra stress on your computer's hardware and operating software. It can therefore increase the likelihood of file damage.

Some fragmentation is unavoidable as you create and erase files. As it increases, however, disk performance degrades. With heavy disk usage and no corrective action, large files may be fragmented into fifty or more pieces. We have seen files split into more than two hundred pieces scattered all over a disk. Utilities such as Norton's Speed Disk or Mace's UnFrag can measure and correct file fragmentation.

6

The DOS
Utility CHKDSK

CHKDSK is a valuable DOS utility for detecting File Allocation Table problems that cause datafile damage. Although CHKDSK can play a key role in file recovery, many computer users never run it. Perhaps they worry about how it might affect their disks or what damage it could cause if they use it improperly. Others may not even be aware of its existence or function.

I believe firmly in the frequent use of CHKDSK, and I generally advise my clients to execute it each time they turn on their computers. Think of it as the computer equivalent of brushing your teeth or taking your vitamins. If File Allocation Table problems develop on your disk, it is better to know about them as soon as possible. You can then act before they become larger or more complicated. File Allocation

Table problems, like toothaches, don't go away by themselves. As with tooth-aches, the longer you wait to correct them, the worse they are likely to become.

To run CHKDSK, it must either be in the current directory or in one defined by the PATH command in your AUTOEXEC.BAT file. By placing the CHKDSK command directly in AUTOEXEC.BAT, you will ensure its execution each time your computer is turned on.

CHKDSK can check any valid disk drive. If you invoke it with no parameters, it will examine the FAT on the current disk drive (the one you are currently logged onto). If you run CHKDSK from drive C (your hard disk) and you want to examine the FAT of a floppy disk in drive A, give the command CHKDSK A:.

You can invoke CHKDSK with a "fix" option. Without it, CHKDSK merely reports disk status without taking any corrective action. If invoked with the "fix" option and if lost cluster problems exist, CHKDSK will force you to decide between two possible actions. Unfortunately, it does not provide a complete picture of disk status before requiring a decision, and you may not know what to do. So I advise users to run CHKDSK **without** the "fix" option initially. We will deal with the decision process later in this chapter.

To run CHKDSK with the "fix" option, add /F or /f to the command. For example, to run CHKDSK on the disk in drive A with the "fix" option, give the command CHKDSK A:/F.

If CHKDSK finds no problems on the target disk, it will simply display some information about it and about the status of memory in your computer. Figure 6-1 shows a typical display for a trouble-free floppy disk.

```
C:\CHKDSK A:

       362496 bytes total disk space
        38912 bytes in 2 user files
       323584 bytes available on disk
       655360 bytes total memory
       570512 bytes free
```

Figure 6-1. *Typical CHKDSK Display for a Trouble-Free Floppy Disk*

Suppose, however, that a file on the target disk has lost clusters (ones to which no links point) in its allocation chain. CHKDSK invoked without the /F option would produce a display like Figure 6-2.

```
C:\CHKDSK A:

Errors found, F parameter not specified.
Corrections will not be written to disk.

A:\SAMPLE.DBF
   Allocation error, size adjusted.

5 lost clusters found in 1 chains.
Convert lost chains to files  (Y/N)?
```

Figure 6-2. *Typical CHKDSK Display for a Floppy Disk with Lost Clusters.*

Since you invoked CHKDSK without the /F option, it does not matter how you answer the question in Figure 6-2 since CHKDSK will do nothing (as indicated by the message "Corrections will not be written to disk."). If you answer no, the response will be as shown in Figure 6-3.

```
Convert lost chains to files  (Y/N)? n
     5120 bytes disk space
          would be freed.

   362496 bytes total disk space
    33792 bytes in 2 user files
   323584 bytes available on disk

   655360 bytes total memory
   570512 bytes free
```

Figure 6-3. *Continued CHKDSK Display for a Floppy Disk with Lost Clusters.*

In response to our answer, CHKDSK reports that 5120 bytes (five 1024-byte clusters) of disk space could have been freed. We will discuss what this means later.

Now let's look at a case involving more complex damage to the File Allocation Table. Suppose the target disk contains both lost clusters and cross-linking. (Chapter 7 explains this terminology). CHKDSK responds with the display shown in Figure 6-4.

```
C:\CHKDSK A:

Errors found, F parameter not specified.
Corrections will not be written to disk.

A:\SAMPLE.DBF
    Allocation error, size adjusted.

8 lost clusters found in 1 chains.
Convert lost chains to files  (Y/N)?
```

Figure 6-4. *Typical CHKDSK Display for a Floppy*
Disk with Lost Clusters and Cross-Linking

Here again, since we invoked CHKDSK without the /F option, the answer does
not matter. CHKDSK will do nothing in any case. If we answer "N" for No, the
response will be as shown in Figure 6-5.

```
Convert lost chains to files  (Y/N)? N
     8192 bytes disk space
          would be freed.

A:\SAMPLE.DBF
    Is cross linked on cluster 24
A:\TECHNOTE.DOC
    Is cross linked on cluster 24

    362496 bytes total disk space
     30720 bytes in 2 user files
    323584 bytes available on disk

    655360 bytes total memory
    570512 bytes free
```

Figure 6-5. *Continued CHKDSK Display for a Floppy*
Disk with Lost Clusters and Cross-Linking

Note that CHKDSK did not report the cross-linking until **after** we decided about
converting lost chains to files. As you will see later, we must sometimes run
CHKDSK with the /F option, but the correct decision about chain-to-file conversion depends on the situation. This is why you should run CHKDSK initially
without the /F option.

◈ To Convert or Not to Convert: That is the Question

(Our apologies to W. Shakespeare, who never worried about dBASE files).

Sometimes, perhaps to recover a damaged DBF datafile, you must invoke CHKDSK with the /F option. You must therefore understand the consequences of your answer to CHKDSK's chain-to-file conversion question.

For example, consider the simple case of skipped (lost) clusters. Suppose, as shown in Figure 6-6, that cell 4 of the file allocation chain for DATAFILE originally pointed to cell 5 but was corrupted to point to cell 9. The chain thereby skips cells 5 through 8, producing a chain of four lost clusters.

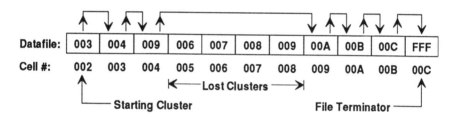

Figure 6-6. File Allocation Chain for a Datafile with Lost Clusters

When you invoke CHKDSK with the /F option, it reports four lost clusters in 1 chain and asks whether you want to convert it to a file.

If your answer is no, CHKDSK simply deallocates the lost clusters by clearing their FAT cells. The resulting chain then appears as shown in Figure 6-7.

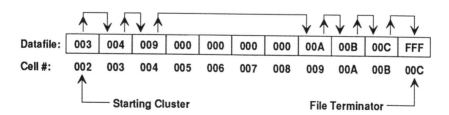

Figure 6-7. File Allocation Chain after Deallocation of Lost Clusters

It is very important to realize that, although FAT cells 5 through 8 have been deallocated, **nothing has changed in the data area of the disk**. Whatever data was in the clusters **still exists**. The **ONLY** changes are in the FAT and in the file size recorded in the disk directory. The new size reflects the number of clusters still associated with DATAFILE (that is, 7 instead of the original 11). The data in the four deallocated clusters is still there, but it is now extremely vulnerable since DOS thinks the clusters are unused. Therefore, it might use them to store the next file you write to the disk. Once this happens, of course, the original data will no longer exist and cannot be recovered.

If you answer yes to CHKDSK's chain-to-file conversion question, an entirely different sequence of actions occurs. In this case, CHKDSK assigns the lost clusters to a new entry in the disk's root directory. It calls the entry FILEnnnn.CHK where nnnn is the next available number starting with 0000. CHKDSK also writes a file size (into the directory) for the new entry, changes the recorded size of DATAF-ILE, and puts a terminator in the last link of the 4-cell FAT chain.

To illustrate, here is the situation before we run CHKDSK A:/F:

```
C:\DIR A:

 Volume in drive A has no label
 Directory of  A:\

DATAFILE DBF    10752   8-19-88   1:01a
TECHNOTE DOC    24689  10-02-87   9:46p
         2 File(s)    323584 bytes free
```

Afterward, we see:

```
C:\CHKDSK A:/F
A:\DATAFILE.DBF
   Allocation error, size adjusted.
4 lost clusters found in 1 chains.
Convert lost chains to files  (Y/N)?
```

When we answer yes to the question, CHKDSK proceeds as follows:

```
Convert lost chains to files  (Y/N)? Y

   362496 bytes total disk space
    32768 bytes in 2 user files
     4096 bytes in 1 recovered files
   325632 bytes available on disk

   655360 bytes total memory
   570512 bytes free
```

Now let's examine the disk directory again:

```
C:\DIR A:

 Volume in drive A has no label
 Directory of  A:\

 DATAFILE DBF     7168    8-19-88   3:51p
 TECHNOTE DOC    24689   10-02-87   9:46p
 FILE0000 CHK     4096    8-19-88   3:54p
         3 File(s)    325632 bytes free
```

Note that the directory shows a new file FILE0000.CHK with a size of 4096 bytes (four 1024-byte clusters). DATAFILE.DBF now has a size of 7168 bytes (seven 1024-byte clusters).

As in the previous case, **absolutely nothing has happened to the data area of the disk**. The FAT now appears as shown in Figure 6-8.

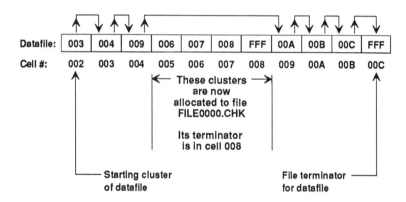

Figure 6-8. *File Allocation Chains after Chain-to-File Conversion*

The CHK file created by CHKDSK simply gives a name to the chain of lost clusters. The idea is to prevent DOS from overwriting them. Each chain of lost clusters protected in this way is assigned a filename of the form FILExxxx.CHK, where 'xxxx' is '0000' for the first such filename created, '0001' for the second, '0002' for the third, and so forth. As you will see later when we discuss the recovery of datafiles with lost cluster damage, we can recall data in CHK files and re-insert it into the correct positions in the damaged file.

As you will also see, in some situations you must answer yes to the chain-to-file conversion question, but in others you must answer no.

7

Lost Clusters

A healthy file allocation chain consists of a continuous (but not necessarily contiguous) set of cells, each pointing to its successor until the file terminator is reached. Many things can break a chain, causing a cell to point to the wrong place. The erroneous cell may point to the wrong cell in the file's own chain, to a cell in another file's chain, or to an unused cell. In any case, there will be cells to which no cell points. Such cells are called "lost clusters."

These errors dramatically affect the appearance of the data in a DBF file. We will illustrate the results in this chapter.

For simplicity, we will show only contiguous chains, but the discussion applies to non-contiguous ones also.

Lost (Skipped) Clusters

Figure 7-1 illustrates the case in which a cell points to the wrong cell later in the file's own chain. The file originally started in cluster 2 and ended in cluster C. But cell 4, which originally pointed to cell 5, was corrupted and now points to cell 9, a cluster much later in the file. Since the FAT now contains no pointer to cell 5, cells 5 through 8 form a chain not identified with any file. CHKDSK (discussed in Chapter 6) describes this situation as "4 lost clusters in 1 chain." The lost clusters are skipped in the file's allocation chain.

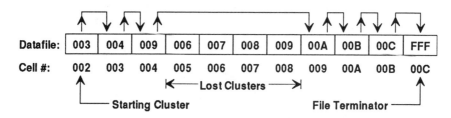

Figure 7-1. File Allocation Chain with Lost Clusters

A datafile having this kind of damage in its allocation chain (or a copy of such a file) would exhibit a discontinuity when viewed in the BROWSE mode since record boundaries and cluster boundaries do not coincide. Data beyond the point of discontinuity would be offset from the field boundaries as shown in Figure 7-2.

```
SURNAME-------- FNAME---------- STREET-----------------------------
Schaeffer       Evan J.         10 Vinton Rd.
Roof            Frederick E.    12 River St.
Reilly          Gerard J.       6841 County Rd. 32
Porravecchio    Harvey D.       4062 Standord
Peek            Jack            337 Avery Street
Orcutt          James G.        1612 Hennessey Rd.
Mench           John J.         5839 Chile Ave.
Mayberry       k lea Cr.                      Pittsford       VT0
               1826 C enter Road              Phoenix         AZ3
      A.       4014 F rancher Road            Philadelphia    PA2
               165 We stminster               Los Angeles     CA9
```

```
n L.    16 Rea donna Lane         Chicago       IL6
e S.    19 Gre enmoor Way         New York      NY1
m A.    95 Lin coln Street        Portland      ME0
        1430 E dgemere Drive      Pittsford     NY1
s.      42 Lar ksaur Lane         Stamford      CT0
        10 Rom mie Lane           St. Louis     MO4


BROWSE          |<A:>|Datafile          |Rec: 17/80          |
```
View and edit fields.

Figure 7-2.   BROWSE Display for a Datafile with Lost Clusters

Note that the first seven records shown in Figure 7-2 are normal. Beyond them, however, data lies in the wrong fields and even straddles field and record boundaries. The file is useless for dBASE operations.

Lost Clusters with Internal Cross-Linking

Figure 7-3 shows a more complex example of incorrect linking. Here the erroneous cell points to an *earlier* cell rather than a later one in the file's own chain. CHKDSK describes this situation as "3 lost clusters in 1 chain." CHKDSK also indicates the presence of "cross-linking." The problem is actually "internal cross-linking" since DATAFILE is cross-linked to itself.

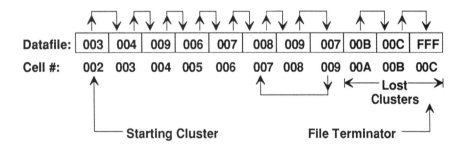

Figure 7-3.   File Allocation Chain with Internal Cross-Linking

A file having this kind of damage in its allocation chain would appear as shown in Figure 7-4 when viewed in the BROWSE mode. Repeated record groups, each one offset from its predecessor, indicate internal cross-linking.

```
SURNAME-------- FNAME---------- STREET----------------------------
Holmes          Philip O.      157 Barberry Terrace
Hatch           Richard A.     257 Clay Ave.
Gruber          Richard J.     5093 S. Lima Rd.
Gielberg        Robert         198 Avenue Road
     17 Mancini       Joseph A.       19 Greenmoor Way
     18 Liva          Kerney          104 Weld Street
     19 Learmout h    Louis D.        377 Maple Street
     20 Blessing ton  Michael         53 Cameron Street
     21 Koehler       Michael  A.     77 Woodsmeadow
     22 Kennett       Mohan S.        21 Barons St.
     23 Jankowsk i    Paul D.         196 Kenwood
     24 Holmes        Philip O.       157 Barberry Terrace
     25 Hatch         Richard  A.     257 Clay Ave.
     26 Gruber        Richard  J.     5093 S. Lima Rd.
     27 Gielberg      Robert          198 Avenue Road
 O.         17 M ancini    J oseph A.      19 Greenmoor Way
am G.       18 L iva       K erney         104 Weld Street
am A.       19 L earmouth  L ouis D.       377 Maple Street
an K.       20 B lessington M ichael       53 Cameron Street
ny M.       21 K oehler    M ichael A.     77 Woodsmeadow
            22 K ennett    M ohan S.       21 Barons St.
T.          23 J ankowski  P aul D.        196 Kenwood
t T.        24 H olmes     P hilip O.      157 Barberry Terrace
            25 H atch      R ichard A.     257 Clay Ave.
t E.        26 G ruber     R ichard J.     5093 S. Lima Rd.
t G.        27 G ielberg   R obert         198 Avenue Road
   Franz O.        17 Mancini      Joseph A.      19 Greenmoor W
   William G.      18 Liva         Kerney         104 Weld Stree
   William A.      19 Learmouth    Louis D.       377 Maple Stre
   Shrawan K.      20 Blessingt on Michael        53 Cameron Str
   Anthony M.      21 Koehler      Michael A.     77 Woodsmeadow
   Larry           22 Kennett      Mohan S.       21 Barons St.
   John T.         23 Jankowski    Paul D.        196 Kenwood
   Robert T.       24 Holmes       Philip O.      157 Barberry T
   Mable           25 Hatch        Richard A.     257 Clay Ave.
   Robert E.       26 Gruber       Richard J.     5093 S. Lima R
   Robert G.       27 Gielberg     Robert         198 Avenue Roa
ch       Franz  O.       17 Ma ncini     Joseph A.      19 Gree
         Willia m G.     18 Li va        Kerney         104 Wel
sky      Willia m A.     19 Le armouth   Louis D.       377 Map
         Shrawa n K.     20 Bl essington Michael        53 Came
ki       Anthon y M.     21 Ko ehler     Michael A.     77 Wood
rski     Larry           22 Ke nnett     Mohan S.       21 Baro
         John T .        23 Ja nkowski   Paul D.        196 Ken
er       Robert  T.      24 Ho lmes      Philip O.      157 Bar
         Mable           25 Ha tch       Richard A.     257 Cla
         Robert  E.      26 Gr uber      Richard J.     5093 S.
         Robert  G.      27 Gi elberg    Robert         198 Ave
```

Figure 7-4. *BROWSE Display of a File with Internal Cross-Linking*

Note how groups of records (starting with the one containing the name "Mancini" and ending with the one containing "Gielberg") repeat, each time with an offset. The link from cell 9 to cell 7 causes the repetition. That is, clusters 2 through 9 are read. Then clusters 7, 8, and 9 are read again and again until the total number of records displayed equals the count in the file header. The offsets occur because record and cluster boundaries do not coincide.

Lost Clusters with Cross-Linking to Another File

Figure 7-5 illustrates the case in which a cell in one file's chain points to a cell in another's chain. FILEONE originally started in cluster 2 and ended in cluster C. But cell 4, which originally pointed to cell 5 in FILEONE's chain, was corrupted and now points to cell 127, a cell in FILETWO's chain. Since the FAT now contains no pointer to cell 5, cells 5 through C form a chain not identified with any file. CHKDSK would describe this situation as "8 lost clusters in 1 chain." In addition, it would also indicate the presence of "cross-linking."

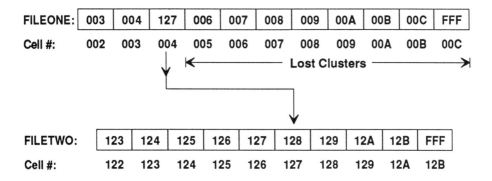

Figure 7-5. *File Allocation Chain with Cross-Linking to Another File*

For example, suppose that FILEONE is a DBF datafile and FILETWO is an ASCII text file. In the BROWSE mode, FILEONE appears to contain some text as shown in Figure 7-6 since DOS thinks FILEONE consists of clusters 2 through 4 and 127 through 12B. The display of Figure 7-6 is characteristic of cross-linking.

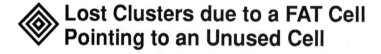

```
SURNAME-------- FNAME---------- STREET----------------------------
Mayberry       John P.         126 Fulton
Mancini        Joseph A.       19 Greenmoor Way
Liva           Kerney          104 Weld Street
Learmouth      Louis D.        377 Maple Street
Blessington    Michael         53 Cameron Street
Koehler        Michael A.      77 Woodsmeadow
Kennett        Mohan S.        21 Barons St.          whether or not
ata in a form s imilar to that  displayed by the EDIT command in d
displayed for e dit exactly as  it is stored in the datafile inclu
ASE EDIT mode.   In addition to  modifying record data, this edit
e database.  It  also provides  instant diagnosis of the current r
both horizontal  and  vertical  scrolling, any portion of any reco
nforms the user  of the cursor  position in the file both in terms
 in the current  record.  The u ser can switch back and forth betw
ed as a continu ous character s tring in  a window for full-screen
 block handling  including copy , move, delete, undelete and the w
```

Figure 7-6.   *BROWSE Display for a Datafile with Cross-Linking to a Text File*

If you examine FILETWO with a word processor, text editor, or DOS' TYPE command, it appears perfectly normal. You can always, therefore, determine the direction of the linking. The file that appears distorted is the one with the corrupted allocation chain. This information, which CHKDSK does not provide, is essential in the repair of cross-linking damage.

◈ Lost Clusters due to a FAT Cell Pointing to an Unused Cell

Figure 7-7 illustrates the case in which a cell in a file's chain points to an unused cell. File A originally started in cluster 2 and ended in cluster C. But cell 4, which originally pointed to cell 5 in File A's chain, was corrupted and now points to cell 37A, an unused cluster. Since the FAT now has no pointer to cell 5, cells 5 through C form a chain not identified with any file. CHKDSK describes this situation as "8 lost clusters in 1 chain."

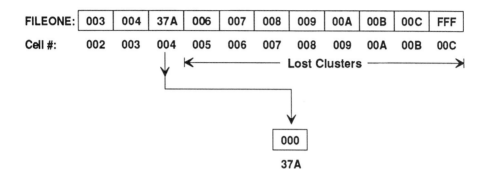

Figure 7-7. *File Allocation Chain with a Cell Pointing to an Unused Cell*

A file having this kind of damage in its allocation chain would appear as shown in Figure 7-8 when viewed in the BROWSE mode, assuming that nothing had ever been written into cluster 37A. The characters "Mayb" are the last four characters in cluster 4. The "÷" symbols (ASCII F6 hex) are the characters written into cluster 37A during formatting.

```
SURNAME-------- FNAME---------- STREET----------------------------
Smith          Donald S.       1040 Genesee Pk. Blvd.
Sherman        Edward L.       35 Brooklyn St.
Schaeffer      Evan J.         10 Vinton Rd.
Roof           Frederick E.    12 River St.
Reilly         Gerard J.       6841 County Rd. 32
Porravecchio   Harvey D.       4062 Standord
Peek           Jack            337 Avery Street
Orcutt         James G.        1612 Hennessey Rd.
Mench          John J.         5839 Chile Ave.
Mayb+++++++++++ +++++++++++++++ +++++++++++++++++++++++++++++++++++
+++++++++++++++ +++++++++++++++ +++++++++++++++++++++++++++++++++++
+++++++++++++++ +++++++++++++++ +++++++++++++++++++++++++++++++++++
+++++++++++++++ +++++++++++++++ +++++++++++++++++++++++++++++++++++
+++++++++++++++ +++++++++++++++ +++++++++++++++++++++++++++++++++++
+++++++++++++++ +++++++++++++++ +++++++++++++++++++++++++++++++++++
+++++++++++++++ +++++++++++++++ +++++++++++++++++++++++++++++++++++
```

Figure 7-8. *BROWSE Display for a Datafile*
with a Cell Pointing to an Unused Cell

◈ Multiple Cross-Linking

We have seen that cross-linking may involve a cell in one file's allocation chain pointing to a cell in another's chain or to an earlier cell in its own chain. However, cross-linking can assume even more bizarre forms. By identifying such rare situations, you may be able to recover a datafile that seemed to be hopelessly lost. Consider, for example, the multiple cross-linking shown in Figure 7-9.

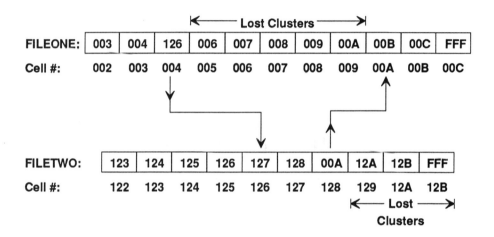

Figure 7-9.   File Allocation Chains with Multiple Cross-Linking

Here cell 4 in FILEONE's chain (which originally pointed to cell 5) has been corrupted so that it now points to cell 126 (a cell in FILETWO's chain). Cell 128 in FILETWO's chain (which originally pointed to cell 129) has also been corrupted so that it now points to cell A (a cell in FILEONE's chain). CHKDSK describes this situation as "8 lost clusters in 2 chains." It also indicates the presence of cross-linking and names the two files involved.

Suppose that FILEONE is a DBF datafile and FILETWO is an ASCII text file. In the BROWSE mode, FILEONE would appear to contain good data up to a certain point, followed by some text and followed, in turn, by the rest of the DBF datafile, with its data offset from the field boundaries. The datafile might appear as shown in Figure 7-10.

```
SURNAME-------- FNAME---------- STREET--------------------------
Schaeffer      Evan J.         10 Vinton Rd.
Roof           Frederick E.    12 River St.
Reilly         Gerard J.       6841 County Rd. 32
Porravecchio   Harvey D.       4062 Standord
Peek           Jack            337 Avery Street
Orcutt         James G.        1612 Hennessey Rd.
Mench          John J.         5839 Chile Ave.
Mayberry     l not open a fil e having this type of damage and wi
ge, no validity test of the da ta area of the file can be made wit
eader.  If the header is found  to be damaged, it will usually be
olves the creat ion of a new fi le that consists of a new header (i
ed with the exi sting data, an  offset may be detected by examinati
han the first c haracter of a r ecord.  If such an offset is detect
disk's File All ocation Table (FAT).  Each disk, whether floppy di
irst part of ea ch file is to b e found in the data area of the dis
This map is the  FAT and consis ts of one or more entries depending
e cluster or sm aller will have  only one entry in the FAT.  Large
gle FAT entry.   In such a case , each FAT entry will contain a "po
  in such a chai n is a  42 Gilm ore                       Provide
n        David          3900 Cu lver Rd.                San Fra
         Douglas  W.    21 Baro ns St.                  Demoine
g        Franz O .      596 Lis t Ave.                  Albuque
         James R .      769 Gar son Ave.                Miami
         John J.        230 Col umbia Ave.              Concord
         Michael  D.    1372 Ba y Shore Blvd.           Olympia
         Richard  K.    349 Gra nd Ave.                 Denver
         Robert   H.    435 Por tland Ave.              Baton R
         Shrawan  K.    1319 Mo nitor Rd.               Boston
         Tibor C .      21 Davy  Dr.                    Altoona
         William  P.    755 Lak e Ave.                  Pasaden
ski      Andrew  P.     14 Park  Circle Dr.             Los Ang
r        Betsy          8 Rockl ea Cr.                  Pittsfo
```

Figure 7-10. *BROWSE Display for a File with Multiple Cross-Linking*

Note that part of a text file appears in the middle of the datafile and the data beyond it shows offset. The offset occurs because the datafile's record boundaries do not coincide with the cluster boundaries.

If we invoke CHKDSK with the files in this condition, it reports the following:

```
Errors found, F parameter not specified.
Corrections will not be written to disk.

A:\FILEONE.DBF
  Allocation error, size adjusted.

8 lost clusters found in 2 chains.
Convert lost chains to files (Y/N)? N
    8192 bytes disk space
```

```
        would be freed.

A:\FILEONE.DBF
   Is cross linked on cluster 294

A:\FILETWO.DOC
   Is cross linked on cluster 294

   362496 bytes total disk space
    30720 bytes in 2 user files
   323584 bytes available on disk

   655360 bytes total memory
   570512 bytes free
```

Recall that CHKDSK displays cluster numbers in decimal. 294 decimal is 126 hex, the number of the FILETWO FAT cell involved in the cross-linking.

Please note that CHKDSK reports only cluster 294 and ignores the other cell (296 decimal or 128 hex) involved in the cross-linking. This emphasizes the importance of understanding the exact nature of the cross-linking before trying to repair or copy cross-linked files. For example, if you copy FILEONE to another disk, the copy would contain the data in clusters 2 through 4 (FILEONE's first three clusters), clusters 126 through 128 (three clusters in the middle of FILETWO), and clusters A through C (FILEONE's last three clusters). In other words, the copy would be a mess. Furthermore, if you copy FILETWO to another disk, the copy would contain clusters 122 through 128 (the first seven clusters of FILETWO) and clusters A through C (the last three clusters of FILEONE). This copy would also be a mess.

The DiskMinder sector editor (discussed in Chapter 8) is a powerful tool for determining the exact nature of cross-linking.

Later in this book, we will show how you can completely recover files with lost clusters (regardless of whether cross-linking exists), as long as the data has not been overwritten.

Copying Files with Damaged FATs

When you copy a file using DOS' COPY command (or dBASE's COPY or COPY FILE command), it will copy all clusters DOS recognizes as part of the file. If damage to the allocation chain creates lost clusters, however, their data will not be copied. If you copy such a file to another disk, all its data will still exist on the original disk (even though DOS may not recognize it as belonging to the file), but not on the destination disk. As you will see later, you can usually recover all the data from the original disk but not from the destination disk. You will also see that the "missing" data in a cross-linked file is generally recoverable.

This shows the importance of running CHKDSK before copying a valuable file. It detects lost clusters and cross-linking. You can thus avoid unpleasant surprises.

 **Summary**

A datafile having lost clusters will appear to contain data offset when you LIST or BROWSE it, and records will be missing. If cross-linking is present, the datafile will also appear to contain part of another file. Copies of such datafiles will look the same as the originals to dBASE. If the file is an original (i.e., not a copy), its records will usually be intact in the data area of the disk and can be recovered. When you make a copy, however, the missing data is not transferred to the destination file. Repair of the copy, therefore, is limited to removal of the offset. CHKDSK is an important tool for checking the integrity of the FAT, and you should run it before copying or repairing files.

8

Tools

You will need the proper software tools to examine and edit disk directories, data areas, and File Allocation Tables, and to diagnose and repair damaged datafiles. The wrong tool can cause inefficiency, aggravation, and often a ruined job. Imagine trying to repair your bathroom plumbing with a heart surgeon's implements. Or, even worse, imagine your dentist working on your teeth with an automobile mechanic's tools. Many software tools are available today. Their adequacy is measured by how well they do the job for you.

This chapter considers two types of tools: general purpose ones and ones specifically designed for recovering DBF datafiles. As examples of the former, we discuss DEBUG, IBM's Disk Repair, Westlake's DiskMinder, and the Norton

Utilities. As examples of the latter, we discuss Comtech Publishing's dSALV-AGE and dSALVAGE Professional and Paul Mace Software's dBFix.

Power and ease of use are important for any tool, but you should look for other features as well. With general purpose tools, the ability to portray directories and FATs in intelligible form is essential. So is the ability to switch easily among the directory, FAT, and data area of a disk, and to perform byte and string searches from a user-defined starting point in a file. File recovery tools must provide diagnostic, repair, and editing capabilities designed specifically for DBF datafiles. Their repair processes should be as automatic as possible, requiring user intervention only when human decision-making is essential, but allowing such intervention at any time. They should be able to rebuild file allocation chains and update directories when required to recover files having damage at the DOS level.

For examining and repairing small DBF datafiles having minor damage, the DOS DEBUG utility is often adequate. Besides, it comes free with DOS; the price is definitely right.

For examining and editing directories and FATs, however, DEBUG is inadequate. We will discuss three other tools, each of which has strengths and weaknesses. One of them, the Norton Utilities, is well known and widely used. It comes in two versions: standard and an Advanced Edition. The standard version, probably the more widespread, is not well-suited to working with directories and FATs because of the unintelligible way in which it displays their contents for editing. The Advanced Edition is much better, but displays FAT cell values in decimal rather than the traditional hex format. The hex format is more familiar to the serious computer user who has the knowledge and confidence to delve into directories and FATs in the first place. The Advanced Edition also has limited data search capabilities.

The second tool is a little-known and relatively hard-to-find utility called Disk Repair (or DR) from IBM. Until recently, it was my preferred tool for working with directories and FATs because of its excellent user interface, speed of response, display formats, and ability to move easily between display/edit screens.

The third product is DiskMinder (or DM) from Westlake Data Corporation. It is the best tool yet for the serious user for displaying and editing disk information, including directories, FATs, and data areas. Besides all the features one wants in a sector editor, DM also has the best search and replace features that I have seen in any tool.

Using the IBM Disk Repair Utility

The Disk Repair screen appears as shown in Figure 8-13 when viewing or editing the disk's data area that contains DATAFILE.

```
                      Disk Repair - BIOS Sector Mode

     Addr   +0       +4       +8       +C              ASCII

     00000  03580506 50000000 21029D00 00000000        ".X..P...!......."
     00010  00000000 00000000 00000000 00000000        "................"
     00020  5355524E 414D4500 00000043 05005764        "SURNAME....C..Wd"
     00030  0F000000 01000000 00000000 00000000        "................"
     00040  464E414D 45000000 00000043 14005764        "FNAME......C..Wd"
     00050  0F000000 01000000 00000000 00000000        "................"
     00060  53545245 45540000 00000043 23005764        "STREET.....C#.Wd"
     00070  23000000 01000000 00000000 00000000        "#..............."
     00080  43495459 00000000 00000043 46005764        "CITY.......CF.Wd"
     00090  12000000 01000000 00000000 00000000        "................"
     000A0  53544154 45000000 00000043 58005764        "STATE......CX.Wd"
     000B0  02000000 01000000 00000000 00000000        "................"
     000C0  5A495000 00000000 00000043 5A005764        "ZIP........CZ.Wd"
     000D0  05000000 01000000 00000000 00000000        "................"
     000E0  41434354 4E4F0000 0000004E 5F005764        "ACCTNO.....N_.Wd"
     000F0  05000000 01000000 00000000 00000000        "................"


            Drive Cylinder Head Sector Cluster        BIOS Sector Mode
            00    012      0    03     009F
     Command:
        F1 Help F2 Explain F3/F4 Sector F5 File F6 Mem F7 Dir F8 FAT F9 Param F10 INT
```

Figure 8-13. *Typical Data Area Displayed by Disk Repair*

Norton displays more information but Disk Repair shows addresses, so neither has a clear advantage here. Disk Repair has no search capability. On the other hand, it does maintain a status line near the bottom of the screen that indicates the location on disk (drive, cylinder, head, sector, and cluster) of the currently displayed data.

Using Westlake's DiskMinder

The file display/edit screen provided by DiskMinder is similar to Disk Repair's, as Figure 8-14 shows.

```
File Editing Mode                                          DiskMinder
[Esc] Displays Main Menu

       +0 +1 +2 +3 +4 +5 +6 +7 +8 +9 +A +B +C +D +E +F   0   4   8   C
 0000  03 58 05 06 50 00 00 00 21 02 9D 00 00 00 00 00   ♥X♣♠P...! ¥.....
 0010  00 00 00 00 00 00 00 00 00 00 00 00 00 00 00 00   ................
 0020  53 55 52 4E 41 4D 45 00 00 00 00 43 05 00 57 64   SURNAME....C♣.Wd
 0030  0F 00 00 00 01 00 00 00 00 00 00 00 00 00 00 00   ... ...........
 0040  46 4E 41 4D 45 00 00 00 00 00 00 43 14 00 57 64   FNAME......C .Wd
 0050  0F 00 00 00 01 00 00 00 00 00 00 00 00 00 00 00   ... ...........
 0060  53 54 52 45 45 54 00 00 00 00 00 43 23 00 57 64   STREET.....C#.Wd
 0070  23 00 00 00 01 00 00 00 00 00 00 00 00 00 00 00   #... ...........
 0080  43 49 54 59 00 00 00 00 00 00 00 43 46 00 57 64   CITY.......CF.Wd
 0090  12 00 00 00 01 00 00 00 00 00 00 00 00 00 00 00   ... ...........
 00A0  53 54 41 54 45 00 00 00 00 00 00 43 58 00 57 64   STATE......CX.Wd
 00B0  02 00 00 00 01 00 00 00 00 00 00 00 00 00 00 00   ... ...........
 00C0  5A 49 50 00 00 00 00 00 00 00 00 43 5A 00 57 64   ZIP........CZ.Wd
 00D0  05 00 00 00 01 00 00 00 00 00 00 00 00 00 00 00   ♣... ...........
 00E0  41 43 43 54 4E 4F 00 00 00 00 00 4E 5F 00 57 64   ACCTNO.....N_.Wd
 00F0  05 00 00 00 01 00 00 00 00 00 00 00 00 00 00 00   ♣... ...........

 Editing File A:\Datafile.DBF
 Offset        0 of 13,105                Cluster 009FH  Sector      326
```

DiskMinder — Copyright 1988 Westlake Data Corporation

Figure 8-14. *Typical Data Area Displayed by DiskMinder*

An advantage of DiskMinder is that the cursor's position always appears as an "Offset" near the bottom of the screen. Thus you know the exact byte location of the character under the cursor.

Another advantage is that DiskMinder's file search and search/replace processes can start anywhere. We can thus easily search for nulls in the record area without wasting time in the file header (which usually contains many of them). DiskMinder's search starts from the cursor's current position, so all we must do is move the cursor to the end of the header initially.

Tools Specifically Designed for DBF Datafile Recovery

DiskMinder, Disk Repair, and the Norton Utilities are general purpose tools for viewing and editing information on disk. They are particularly useful for correcting errors in disk directories, analyzing file allocation chains, and modifying File Allocation Tables. Although they are valuable supplements to datafile recovery software, they lack the specific features, processes, and functions that you generally need to diagnose and recover damaged DBF datafiles.

Tools specifically designed for the recovery of damaged DBF datafiles include dSALVAGE and dSALVAGE Professional (from Comtech Publishing) and dBFix (from Paul Mace Software). Note: The author of this book is also the developer of dSALVAGE and dSALVAGE Professional. I do not claim any objectivity whatsoever. I created these products to be the best tools obtainable for diagnosing and repairing dBASE files.

dSALVAGE

dSALVAGE (Standard Version) is a fully integrated software tool consisting of three major modules: a diagnostic module for assessing and reporting damage in a datafile, a recovery module for repairing it, and an editing module. The editing module (see Chapter 22) consists of an array of editors for examining and altering DBF datafiles in ways not normally possible. dSALVAGE is menu-driven for ease of use by the novice, but has features that sophisticated and knowledgeable users will find invaluable when dealing with datafiles. dSALVAGE will recover non-overwritten file data, regardless of how complex and severe the damage is. A unique feature of dSALVAGE is its ability to recover a ZAP'd datafile with a single keystroke even if the file is fragmented, contains backward-pointing pointers in its allocation chain, or is interlaced with deleted files. dSALVAGE's un-ZAP'ing capability also allows it to recover cross-linked files.

dSALVAGE lets some repairs be performed "in place" to reduce recovery time, but always allows the user to optionally specify a separate output file. It also allows the transplant of a healthy header onto a file having one that is damaged or missing. This may not be as newsworthy as a heart transplant, but it has saved some very sick databases. dSALVAGE is available in English, German, French, and Spanish versions.

The newer dSALVAGE Professional has the following additional features:

- Continue-from-here repair capability (particularly useful for large datafiles having scattered damage)

- Hex editor for advanced users

- Manually-assisted un-ZAP function for the recovery of ZAP'd files that have been partially overwritten

- Ability to create a DBF file structure, including a preview feature and user-customization of field names

- Cut-and-paste capability

- Foreign language switches for German, French, and Spanish

Both dSALVAGE and dSALVAGE Professional are compatible with all versions of dBASE.

dBFix

dBFix repairs many simple forms of damage during a single pass through a file. It always requires writing to a separate output file and provides a screen display of all records written there. Although it has no editors, cannot un-ZAP a file, and has no provision for directly replacing a damaged file header, it does allow the user to generate a header based on the data in the records. It automatically assigns arbitrary names to the fields.

 # Where to Obtain Tools

dBFix is available from Paul Mace Software, 400 Williamson Way, Ashland, OR 97520.

DiskMinder is available from Westlake Data Corporation, P.O. Box 1711, Austin, TX 78767 or from Comtech Publishing Ltd. as part of the dSALVAGE Professional package.

Disk Repair is included in the Professional Debugging Facility software available from IBM through any authorized dealer.

dSALVAGE and **dSALVAGE Professional** are available from Comtech Publishing Ltd., P.O. Box 456, Pittsford, NY 14534.

The **Norton Utilities** are available from Peter Norton Computing, Inc., 100 Wilshire Boulevard, 9th Floor, Santa Monica, CA 90401. They can also be obtained from most retailers and mail-order suppliers.

9

ZAP'd Datafiles

A special case of external file damage is the ZAP'd datafile. As a dBASE user, you know that the ZAP command removes all records from a datafile, leaving it empty. This section describes exactly what ZAP does since its actions are more extensive than you might think. We will then examine three different ZAP'd file situations in order of increasing difficulty of recovery.

Note that ZAP differs from random or careless damage. Usually, you ZAP a file intentionally to remove all the records. In such a case, you cannot say the datafile is damaged. But occasionally you may ZAP the wrong file or ZAP a file before you intended. Then you have a damaged file on your hands that must be recovered.

For years, users have been told that the data in a ZAP'd file is gone forever and that there is no chance for recovery. Many users still believe this to be true. But ZAP'd datafiles are recoverable, as you will see later.

 What ZAP Does

The ZAP command does the following:

1. Sets the record count to zero in the DBF file header.

2. Writes an end-of-file marker (Ctrl-Z) into the first character position after the end of the file header.

3. Clears links in the file's allocation chain beyond those that contain the DBF file header, thereby freeing the corresponding data clusters. It also writes a file terminator into the last FAT cell occupied by the file header.

4. Changes the file size in the disk directory to reflect only clusters occupied by the file header.

Note that ZAP does not affect the data area of the disk. The data in a ZAP'd file is still intact, but it is no longer accessible by dBASE since DOS no longer associates it with any file.

Note also that the file header of a ZAP'd file remains intact and that ZAP'ing a file is not the same as erasing it. An erased file no longer appears in a conventional directory listing; it gives no evidence of its presence unless you examine the directory with a disk analysis tool. The examination shows that neither the file size nor the starting cluster information has changed. A ZAP'd file, on the other hand, still appears in a conventional directory listing, but reduced in size.

The ease of recovering a ZAP'd datafile depends on how it was stored on disk and, in fact, on how other files on the same disk were stored. Here we examine the following four conditions, in order of increasing difficulty of recovery:

1. An unfragmented datafile

2. A fragmented datafile whose interstitial regions are occupied by active files

3. A fragmented datafile whose interstitial regions are occupied by erased files

4. A datafile that contains backward-pointing pointers in its allocation chain

 # Example Unfragmented Datafile

The file we use here is ZFILE.DBF. It is on a floppy disk in drive A together with another file, TECHNOTE.DOC. A directory listing of drive A appears as follows:

```
Volume in drive A has no label
Directory of  A:\

ZFILE    DBF    13106   5-06-88   5:55p
TECHNOTE DOC    24689  10-02-87   9:46p
         2 File(s)     323584 bytes free
```

Viewing the directory with DiskMinder shows that ZFILE.DBF starts in cluster 2, as you can see below.

```
Directory Editing Mode                                     DiskMinder
[Esc] Displays Main Menu

Filename.Ext    Size    Date      Time     Attr Clu  Reserved
ZFILE   .DBF    13106   05/06/88  17:55:10  20  0002  00000000000000000000
TECHNOTE.DOC    24689   10/02/87  21:46:48  20  000F  00000000000000000000
```

Examining the File Allocation Table (with ZFILE selected for display and shown in boldface) gives:

```
Fat Editing Mode                                          DiskMinder
[Esc] Displays Main Menu

Clu    +0  +1  +2  +3    +4  +5  +6  +7    +8  +9  +A  +B    +C  +D  +E  +F
0000   FFD FFF 003 004   005 006 007 008   009 00A 00B 00C   00D 00E FFF 010
0010   011 012 013 014   015 016 017 018   019 01A 01B 01C   01D 01E 01F 020
0020   021 022 023 024   025 026 027 FFF   000 000 000 000   000 000 000 000
0030   000 000 000 000   000 000 000 000   000 000 000 000   000 000 000 000
```

As you can see, the allocation chain (starting at cluster 2 and extending through cluster E) is continuous, indicating that ZFILE.DBF is not fragmented.

Now we will invoke dBASE, open ZFILE with the USE command, ZAP it, and examine the results.

After ZAPping, the directory listing shows:

```
Volume in drive A has no label
Directory of  A:\

ZFILE    DBF     1024    6-24-88   4:23p
TECHNOTE DOC    24689   10-02-87   9:46p
         2 File(s)    335872 bytes free
```

Observe that ZFILE.DBF has been reduced to 1024 bytes (a rapid weight loss indeed). This means that its header occupies only one cluster.

Examining the directory again with DiskMinder shows that ZFILE's starting cluster is the same as before (as expected) and its size is now 1024 bytes.

```
Directory Editing Mode                                  DiskMinder
[Esc] Displays Main Menu

 Filename.Ext     Size     Date      Time    Attr Clu   Reserved
 ZFILE   .DBF     1024   06/24/88  16:23:38   20  0002   0000000000000000000
 TECHNOTE.DOC    24689   10/02/87  21:46:48   20  000F   0000000000000000000
```

The File Allocation Table (with ZFILE selected for display and shown in boldface) now appears as follows:

```
Fat Editing Mode                                        DiskMinder
[Esc] Displays Main Menu

 Clu    +0  +1  +2  +3    +4  +5  +6  +7    +8  +9  +A  +B    +C  +D  +E  +F
 0000   FFD FFF FFF 000   000 000 000 000   000 000 000 000   000 000 000 010
 0010   011 012 013 014   015 016 017 018   019 01A 01B 01C   01D 01E 01F 020
 0020   021 022 023 024   025 026 027 FFF   000 000 000 000   000 000 000 000
 0030   000 000 000 000   000 000 000 000   000 000 000 000   000 000 000 000
```

Observe that cluster 2, the starting cluster, is the only one still identified with ZFILE. Its FAT cell now contains the FFF terminator rather than a pointer to another FAT cell. All other clusters that were in the ZFILE allocation chain (clusters 3 through E) now contain zero, indicating that they have been deallocated. The pointers in these FAT cells have been lost. If the ZFILE chain contained backward-pointing pointers, there is no longer any evidence of it. Remember, however, that ZFILE's data still exists in clusters 3 through E in the data area of the disk, but DOS no longer recognizes them as part of ZFILE.

Before leaving this example, we will also use DiskMinder to examine cluster 2 in the data area of the disk (see Figure 9-1).

```
DOS Sector Editing Mode                                    DiskMinder
[Esc] Displays Main Menu

        +0 +1 +2 +3 +4 +5 +6 +7 +8 +9 +A +B +C +D +E +F   0   4   8   C
 0000   03 58 06 18 00 00 00 00 21 02 9D 00 00 00 00 00   ♥X♠ ....! ¥.....
 0010   00 00 00 00 00 00 00 00 00 00 00 00 00 00 00 00   ...............
 0020   53 55 52 4E 41 4D 45 00 00 00 00 00 43 05 00 57 64   SURNAME....C♠.Wd
 0030   0F 00 00 00 00 01 00 00 00 00 00 00 00 00 00 00   ... .........
 0040   46 4E 41 4D 45 00 00 00 00 00 00 00 43 14 00 57 64   FNAME......C .Wd
 0050   0F 00 00 00 00 01 00 00 00 00 00 00 00 00 00 00   ... .........
 0060   53 54 52 45 45 54 00 00 00 00 00 00 43 23 00 57 64   STREET.....C#.Wd
 0070   23 00 00 00 00 01 00 00 00 00 00 00 00 00 00 00   #... .........
 0080   43 49 54 59 00 00 00 00 00 00 00 00 43 46 00 57 64   CITY.......CF.Wd
 0090   12 00 00 00 00 01 00 00 00 00 00 00 00 00 00 00   ... .........
 00A0   53 54 41 54 45 00 00 00 00 00 00 00 43 58 00 57 64   STATE......CX.Wd
 00B0   02 00 00 00 00 01 00 00 00 00 00 00 00 00 00 00   ... .........
 00C0   5A 49 50 00 00 00 00 00 00 00 00 00 43 5A 00 57 64   ZIP........CZ.Wd
 00D0   05 00 00 00 00 01 00 00 00 00 00 00 00 00 00 00   ♠... .........
 00E0   41 43 43 54 4E 4F 00 00 00 00 00 00 4E 5F 00 57 64   ACCTNO.....N_.Wd
 00F0   05 00 00 00 00 01 00 00 00 00 00 00 00 00 00 00   ♠... .........
 0100   50 41 49 44 55 50 00 00 00 00 00 00 4C 64 00 57 64   PAIDUP.....Ld.Wd
 0110   01 00 00 00 00 01 00 00 00 00 00 00 00 00 00 00   ... .........
 0120   42 41 4C 41 4E 43 45 00 00 00 00 00 4E 65 00 57 64   BALANCE....Ne.Wd
 0130   06 02 00 00 00 01 00 00 00 00 00 00 00 00 00 00   ♠ .. .........
 0140   4C 41 53 54 54 52 41 4E 00 00 00 00 44 6B 00 57 64   LASTTRAN...Dk.Wd
 0150   08 00 00 00 00 01 00 00 00 00 00 00 00 00 00 00   ... .........
 0160   43 41 54 45 47 4F 52 59 00 00 00 00 4E 73 00 57 64   CATEGORY...Ns.Wd
 0170   02 00 00 00 00 01 00 00 00 00 00 00 00 00 00 00   ... .........
 0180   41 52 45 41 43 4F 44 45 00 00 00 00 43 75 00 57 64   AREACODE...Cu.Wd
 0190   03 00 00 00 00 01 00 00 00 00 00 00 00 00 00 00   ♠... .........
 01A0   54 45 4C 00 00 00 00 00 00 00 00 00 43 78 00 57 64   TEL........Cx.Wd
 01B0   08 00 00 00 00 01 00 00 00 00 00 00 00 00 00 00   ... .........
 01C0   53 4C 4E 41 4D 45 00 00 00 00 00 00 43 80 00 57 64   SLNAME.....CÇ.Wd
 01D0   0F 00 00 00 00 01 00 00 00 00 00 00 00 00 00 00   ... .........
 01E0   53 46 4E 41 4D 45 00 00 00 00 00 00 43 8F 00 57 64   SFNAME.....CÅ.Wd
 01F0   0F 00 00 00 00 01 00 00 00 00 00 00 00 00 00 00   ... .........
 0000   4F 52 44 45 52 00 00 00 00 00 00 00 4E 9E 00 57 64   ORDER......NR.Wd
 0010   03 00 00 00 00 01 00 00 00 00 00 00 00 00 00 00   ♠... .........
 0020   0D 1A 5A 75 63 6B 65 72 6D 61 6E 20 20 20 20 20   ..Zuckerman
 0030   20 41 64 64 69 73 6F 6E 20 42 2E 20 20 20 20 20    Addison B.
 0040   34 31 36 20 47 61 72 66 69 65 6C 64 20 41 76 65   416 Garfield Ave
 0050   6E 75 65 20 20 20 20 20 20 20 20 20 20 20 20 20   nue
 0060   20 20 20 20 42 6F 73 74 6F 6E 20 20 20 20 20 20       Boston
 0070   20 20 20 20 20 4D 41 30 32 31 33 30 20 20 38 35        MA02130  85
 0080   31 54 20 20 30 2E 30 30 31 39 38 36 30 37 31 30   1T  0.0019860710
 0090   38 35 36 31 37 38 38 32 2D 38 32 36 34 5A 75 68   85617882-8264Zuh
 00A0   69 6B 65 20 20 20 20 20 20 20 20 20 20 57 69 6C 6C   ike        Will
 00B0   69 61 6D 20 50 2E 20 20 20 20 20 20 20 31 20 57   iam P.       1 W
```

Figure 9-1. *ZAP'd Datafile as Displayed by DiskMinder*

Please observe the two boldface areas in Figure 9-1. The first is the sequence starting at byte 4 (the first byte being byte 0) and extending through byte 7. It contains the record count which you can see has been set to zero. The second is the single value 1A (Ctrl-Z) immediately following the 0D hex that marks the end of the file header. It is the end-of-file marker.

Thus you have seen the results of the four actions ZAP takes. ZFILE.DBF is now extremely vulnerable. DOS may elect to use the space currently occupied by its data to store the next file you decide to save on the disk. ZFILE's data would then be overwritten and unrecoverable.

Example Fragmented Datafile with Interstitial Regions Occupied by Active Files

A directory display of our sample disk is as follows:

```
C:\DIR A:

    Volume in drive A has no label
    Directory of  A:\

    ZFILE     DBF     13106    5-06-88    5:55p
    DOCA      DOC      4096    8-21-88    7:01p
    DOCB      DOC      7100    8-21-88    7:01p
             3 File(s)     337920 bytes free
```

The disk's directory appears as follows when displayed by DiskMinder:

```
Directory Editing Mode                                        DiskMinder
[Esc] Displays Main Menu

 Filename.Ext      Size     Date      Time     Attr Clu   Reserved
 σONEFILE.TXT       512    08/21/88  19:01:16   20  0002   0000000000000000000
 ZFILE   .DBF     13106    05/06/88  17:55:10   20  0003   0000000000000000000
 DOCA    .DOC      4096    08/21/88  19:01:20   20  0004   0000000000000000000
 DOCB    .DOC      7100    08/21/88  19:01:36   20  000C   0000000000000000000
```

Note the presence of a fourth file that did not appear in the directory listing: namely, σONEFILE.TXT. The Greek letter sigma (ASCII 229 decimal) in the first character of the filename indicates that the file has been erased. However, the filename (less the first character), the starting cluster number, and the file size are still in the directory. A zero in cell 2 of the File Allocation Table, as shown below, further confirms that the file (which had occupied a single cluster) was erased.

Although you cannot tell from the directory listing, ZFILE.DBF is fragmented. Its links appear in boldface in the following FAT display.

```
Fat Editing Mode                                              DiskMinder
[Esc] Displays Main Menu

Clu     +0  +1  +2  +3    +4  +5  +6  +7    +8  +9  +A  +B    +C  +D  +E  +F
0000    FFD FFF 000 005   006 007 008 009   00A 00B FFF 00D   00E 00F 010 011
0010    012 013 014 015   016 017 018 019   FFF 01A FFF 000   000 000 000 000
0020    000 000 000 000   000 000 000 000   000 000 000 000   000 000 000 000
0030    000 000 000 000   000 000 000 000   000 000 000 000   000 000 000 000
```

For clarity, we show the allocation chains for DOCA.DOC and DOCB.DOC with their links in boldface.

Allocation chain of DOCA.DOC:

```
Fat Editing Mode                                              DiskMinder
[Esc] Displays Main Menu

Clu     +0  +1  +2  +3    +4  +5  +6  +7    +8  +9  +A  +B    +C  +D  +E  +F
0000    FFD FFF 000 005   006 007 008 009   00A 00B FFF 00D   00E 00F 010 011
0010    012 013 014 015   016 017 018 019   FFF 01A FFF 000   000 000 000 000
0020    000 000 000 000   000 000 000 000   000 000 000 000   000 000 000 000
0030    000 000 000 000   000 000 000 000   000 000 000 000   000 000 000 000
```

Allocation chain of DOCB.DOC:

```
Fat Editing Mode                                              DiskMinder
[Esc] Displays Main Menu

Clu     +0  +1  +2  +3    +4  +5  +6  +7    +8  +9  +A  +B    +C  +D  +E  +F
0000    FFD FFF 000 005   006 007 008 009   00A 00B FFF 00D   00E 00F 010 011
0010    012 013 014 015   016 017 018 019   FFF 01A FFF 000   000 000 000 000
0020    000 000 000 000   000 000 000 000   000 000 000 000   000 000 000 000
0030    000 000 000 000   000 000 000 000   000 000 000 000   000 000 000 000
```

The FAT displays show that DOCA.DOC and DOCB.DOC are also fragmented and fill the interstitial regions of ZFILE.DBF.

We will now invoke dBASE, open ZFILE with the USE command, ZAP it, and examine the results.

After ZAP, the directory listing shows:

```
C:\DIR A:

  Volume in drive A has no label
  Directory of  A:\

  ZFILE    DBF    1024    5-06-88    5:58p
  DOCA     DOC    4096    8-21-88    7:01p
  DOCB     DOC    7100    8-21-88    7:01p
          3 File(s)    337920 bytes free
```

The File Allocation Table (with ZFILE selected for display and shown in boldface) now appears as follows:

```
Fat Editing Mode                                            DiskMinder
[Esc] Displays Main Menu

Clu     +0  +1  +2  +3    +4  +5  +6  +7    +8  +9  +A  +B    +C  +D  +E  +F
0000   FFD FFF 000 FFF   006 000 008 000   00A 000 FFF 000   00E 000 010 000
0010   012 000 014 000   016 000 018 000   FFF 000 000 000   000 000 000 000
0020   000 000 000 000   000 000 000 000   000 000 000 000   000 000 000 000
0030   000 000 000 000   000 000 000 000   000 000 000 000   000 000 000 000
```

As in the preceding example, note that the only cluster still identified with ZFILE is cluster 3 (the starting cluster containing the file header). Its FAT cell now contains the FFF terminator rather than a pointer to another FAT cell. All other clusters that were in ZFILE's allocation chain now contain zero, indicating that they have been deallocated. The pointers in these FAT cells have been lost. If the ZFILE chain contained backward-pointing pointers, there is no longer any evidence of them.

Example Fragmented Datafile with Interstitial Regions Occupied by Erased Files

A directory display of our sample disk is as follows:

```
C:\DIR A:

  Volume in drive A has no label
  Directory of  A:\

  ZFILE    DBF    13106    5-06-88    5:55p
          1 File(s)    349184 bytes free
```

Although this listing indicates only one file, the following directory display shows that there were originally four files on the disk, three of which have been erased:

```
Directory Editing Mode                                    DiskMinder
[Esc] Displays Main Menu

Filename.Ext      Size    Date      Time    Attr Clu  Reserved
σONEFILE.TXT       512   08/21/88  19:01:16  20   0002 0000000000000000000
ZFILE    .DBF    13106   05/06/88  17:55:10  20   0003 0000000000000000000
σOCA     .DOC     4096   08/21/88  19:01:20  20   0004 0000000000000000000
σOCB     .DOC     7100   08/21/88  19:01:36  20   000C 0000000000000000000
```

A display of the FAT (with ZFILE.DBF selected and shown in boldface) is as follows:

```
Fat Editing Mode                                          DiskMinder
[Esc] Displays Main Menu

Clu    +0  +1  +2  +3   +4  +5  +6  +7   +8  +9  +A  +B   +C  +D  +E  +F
0000   FFD FFF 000 005  000 007 000 009  000 00B 000 00D  000 00F 000 011
0010   000 013 000 015  000 017 000 019  000 01A FFF 000  000 000 000 000
0020   000 000 000 000  000 000 000 000  000 000 000 000  000 000 000 000
0030   000 000 000 000  000 000 000 000  000 000 000 000  000 000 000 000
```

Note that the ZFILE clusters are as in the previous example, but all other FAT cells have been cleared, confirming that their associated files have been erased.

Once again, we invoke dBASE, open ZFILE, and ZAP it, leaving the disk directory as follows:

```
C:\DIR A:

 Volume in drive A has no label
 Directory of  A:\

ZFILE     DBF    1024   5-06-88   5:58p
        1 File(s)    361472 bytes free
```

The FAT now appears as follows. Observe that all cells have been cleared except the one containing ZFILE's header.

```
Fat Editing Mode                                              DiskMinder
[Esc] Displays Main Menu

 Clu     +0  +1  +2  +3    +4  +5  +6  +7    +8  +9  +A  +B    +C  +D  +E  +F
 0000   FFD FFF 000 FFF   000 000 000 000   000 000 000 000   000 000 000 000
 0010   000 000 000 000   000 000 000 000   000 000 000 000   000 000 000 000
 0020   000 000 000 000   000 000 000 000   000 000 000 000   000 000 000 000
 0030   000 000 000 000   000 000 000 000   000 000 000 000   000 000 000 000
```

The FAT now provides no evidence of the erased files or the ZAP'd parts of ZFILE. However, the data from the files is still in the data area of the disk and will stay there until it is overwritten. Since all chain pointers have been cleared, there is no way to identify fragmented files. We also cannot determine whether the original files contained backward-pointing pointers. All we know (from the directory) is the size and starting location of each erased file and the starting location (only) of the ZAP'd file.

Although this situation is the most difficult ZAP'd file to recover (short of one that has been partially overwritten), you will see later that complete recovery is possible. In the case of partial overwriting, we can recover the non-overwritten portion.

Example Datafile with Backward-Pointing Pointers in Its Allocation Chain

This condition does not require a separate example since the earlier ones suffice. As noted along the way, a file with backward-pointing pointers in its allocation chain is indistinguishable from one without such links after ZAPing. The evidence of backward-pointing pointers disappears when the file is ZAP'd.

Summary

When you ZAP a DBF datafile, its records are unaffected except for the end-of-file marker written into the first character position of the first record. Nothing else in the file is altered, except the header's record count which is set to zero. All other changes are made in the disk's directory and FAT. The file's data is completely intact and is recoverable as long as you do not overwrite it.

10

Un-Erasing Files: What You Get May Not Be What You Expect

As noted in Chapter 9, there is a major difference between ZAP'd files and erased files. Specifically, erasing a file has just two effects: (1) it replaces the first character of the file's name in the disk directory with the Greek letter sigma (ASCII 229 decimal); and (2) it clears all FAT cells containing links in the file's allocation chain. **No other changes are made on the disk.** Simple un-erasing programs merely:

1. Determine the starting cluster and the file size (both are still in the disk directory).

2. Rebuild the file's allocation chain. They begin at the known starting point and change consecutive cleared FAT cells until they have reassigned enough clusters to account for the known file size.

3. Write a file terminator (usually FFF hex) into the last reassigned cell.

4. Change the first character of the filename in the directory (usually by asking the user to enter it).

The un-erasing process has an important consequence that you should understand. It occurs for files that were fragmented and interleaved. A typical computer user, of course, is normally unaware of either characteristic since their presence can be determined only with specialized software (such as the DiskMinder sector editor discussed in Chapter 8). The result of un-erasing files that have both characteristics can be surprising.

Suppose, for example, you have two files (FILEA and FILEB) on your disk. A directory listing shows the following:

```
C:\DIR A:

Volume in drive A has no label
Directory of  A:\

FILEA            5102    8-27-88    6:00p
FILEB            5933    8-27-88    6:02p
        2 File(s)     351232 bytes free
```

Although you cannot tell from this listing, the files are both fragmented and interleaved. Their allocation chains are as follows:

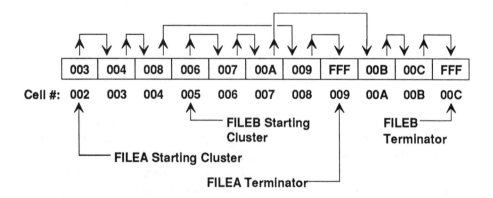

If we erase both files, FAT cells 2 through C appear as follows:

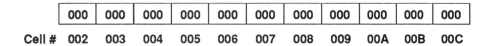

000	000	000	000	000	000	000	000	000	000	000

Cell # 002 003 004 005 006 007 008 009 00A 00B 00C

Now that the links have all been cleared, an un-erasing program has no way of knowing which allocation chain (if any) a cell belonged to, much less its order in the chain. The un-erasing program knows only the following, based on information in the disk directory:

- FILEA starts in cluster 2.

- FILEA's size and, therefore, the number of clusters it occupied

- FILEB starts in cluster 5.

- FILEB's size and, therefore, the number of clusters it occupied

In the following un-erasing process, we use the automatic (un-assisted) form of the Norton Utilities. As you will appreciate soon, the non-automatic features of Norton's un-erase are very important, although seldom used. Even with their help, reconstructing fragmented and interleaved files that are not human-readable (such as COM, EXE, or other non-ASCII files) is virtually impossible.

The disk's directory and File Allocation Table, viewed with the DiskMinder sector editor, appear as follows before the files are erased:

```
Directory Editing Mode                                        DiskMinder
[Esc] Displays Main Menu

 Filename.Ext      Size    Date      Time     Attr Clu  Reserved
 FILEA    .        5102  08/27/88  18:00:20    20  0002  00000000000000000000
 FILEB    .        5933  08/27/88  18:02:58    20  0005  00000000000000000000
```

FILEA's chain is in boldface:

```
Fat Editing Mode                                              DiskMinder
[Esc] Displays Main Menu

 Clu     +0  +1  +2  +3    +4  +5  +6  +7    +8  +9  +A  +B    +C  +D  +E  +F
 0000   FFD FFF 003 004   008 006 007 00A   009 FFF 00B 00C   FFF 000 000 000
 0010   000 000 000 000   000 000 000 000   000 000 000 000   000 000 000 000
```

We will now erase both files, after which the FAT appears as follows. All cells
have been cleared.

```
Fat Editing Mode                                              DiskMinder
[Esc] Displays Main Menu

Clu     +0  +1  +2  +3    +4  +5  +6  +7    +8  +9  +A  +B    +C  +D  +E  +F
0000    FFD FFF 000 000   000 000 000 000   000 000 000 000   000 000 000 000
0010    000 000 000 000   000 000 000 000   000 000 000 000   000 000 000 000
```

Remember, no changes have been made in the data area of the disk.

Now let us un-erase FILEA with the automatic mode of the Norton Utilities and
examine the results. The resulting DIR listing of the disk shows:

```
C:\DIR A:

Volume in drive A has no label
Directory of  A:\

FILEA             5102   8-27-88    6:00p
        1 File(s)     357376 bytes free
```

Unless we look deeper, we might think that we have recovered FILEA successfully. The sector editor now displays the directory as follows:

```
Directory Editing Mode                                       DiskMinder
[Esc] Displays Main Menu

Filename.Ext      Size      Date      Time    Attr Clu   Reserved
FILEA     .       5102   08/27/88  18:00:20    20  0002   0000000000000000000
σILEB     .       5933   08/27/88  18:02:58    20  0005   0000000000000000000
```

but the FAT appears (with the un-erased FILEA shown in boldface) as follows:

```
Fat Editing Mode                                             DiskMinder
[Esc] ·Displays Main Menu

Clu     +0  +1  +2  +3    +4  +5  +6  +7    +8  +9  +A  +B    +C  +D  +E  +F
0000    FFD FFF 003 004   005 006 FF8 000   000 000 000 000   000 000 000 000
0010    000 000 000 000   000 000 000 000   000 000 000 000   000 000 000 000
```

Please examine this display carefully. You will see that the un-erase program has
incorrectly assigned cells 5 and 6 to FILEA **even though the directory indicates**

that cluster 5 belongs to the erased FILEB. The un-eraser has assigned five clusters to FILEA as it should, but **two of them are wrong**.

Now we will un-erase FILEB. Afterward, a DIR listing shows:

```
C:\DIR A:

     Volume in drive A has no label
               Directory of  A:\

  FILEA             5102    8-27-88    6:00p
  FILEB             5933    8-27-88    6:02p
          2 File(s)      351232 bytes free
```

The sector editor displays the directory as:

```
Directory Editing Mode                                  DiskMinder
[Esc] Displays Main Menu

Filename.Ext      Size      Date       Time    Attr Clu   Reserved
FILEA     .       5102    08/27/88   18:00:20   20  0002   00000000000000000000
FILEB     .       5933    08/27/88   18:02:58   20  0007   00000000000000000000
```

But now look at the FAT (here the FILEB allocation chain appears in boldface):

```
Fat Editing Mode                                        DiskMinder
[Esc] Displays Main Menu

Clu     +0  +1  +2  +3    +4  +5  +6  +7     +8  +9  +A  +B    +C  +D  +E  +F
0000   FFD FFF 003 004   005 006 FF8 008    009 00A 00B 00C   FF8 000 000 000
0010   000 000 000 000   000 000 000 000    000 000 000 000   000 000 000 000
```

Note that the un-erase program ignored the original directory information about FILEB's starting cluster. Instead, it simply took the next six free clusters.

The end result is that FILEA now consists of three clusters of FILEA data and two of FILEB data. FILEB, on the other hand, now consists of one cluster of FILEB followed by two of FILEA, and followed, in turn, by the rest of FILEB. In other words, both files are damaged.

If the erased fragmented and interleaved files are human-readable, you can recover them both correctly, as I will now show using the sector editor. I cannot overemphasize the importance of examining a disk meticulously **before** executing an un-erase procedure. You can then map the locations of all parts of your erased files, so you can proceed with confidence.

Let's begin with a disk whose directory shows:

```
C:\DIR A:

 Volume in drive A has no label
 Directory of  A:\

 BELGRADE DOC      1280    5-21-88   7:18p
 GARDEN   DOC      5464    3-14-89   3:45p
 CHAINSAW DOC      2086    3-14-89   3:51p
 FISH     DOC      1436    8-27-88   2:14p
          4 File(s)     349184 bytes free
```

The directory as seen by the sector editor is:

```
Directory Editing Mode                                    DiskMinder
[Esc] Displays Main Menu

 Filename.Ext       Size     Date       Time    Attr Clu   Reserved
 BELGRADE.DOC       1280   05/21/88   19:18:05   20  0002  00000000000000000000
 GARDEN  .DOC       5464   03/14/89   15:45:17   20  0004  00000000000000000000
 CHAINSAW.DOC       2086   03/14/89   15:51:17   20  0006  00000000000000000000
 FISH    .DOC       1436   08/27/88   14:14:09   20  000D  00000000000000000000
         .             0   00/00/80   00:00:00   00  0000  00000000000000000000
```

The file allocation chain for GARDEN.DOC starts in cell 4 and extends through cells 5, 9, A, B, and C. The allocation chain for CHAINSAW.DOC consists of cells 6, 7, and 8. GARDEN.DOC is fragmented. Its chain appears in boldface in the following display:

```
Fat Editing Mode                                          DiskMinder
[Esc] Displays Main Menu

 Clu    +0  +1  +2  +3    +4  +5  +6  +7    +8  +9  +A  +B    +C  +D  +E  +F
 0000  FFD FFF 003 FFF   005 009 007 008   FFF 00A 00B 00C   FFF 00E FFF 000
 0010  000 000 000 000   000 000 000 000   000 000 000 000   000 000 000 000
 0020  000 000 000 000   000 000 000 000   000 000 000 000   000 000 000 000
 0030  000 000 000 000   000 000 000 000   000 000 000 000   000 000 000 000
```

Now we erase both GARDEN.DOC and CHAINSAW.DOC, after which a directory listing shows:

```
C:\DIR A:

Volume in drive A has no label
Directory of  A:\

BELGRADE DOC      1280   5-21-88   7:18p
FISH     DOC      1436   8-27-88   2:14p
         2 File(s)    358400 bytes free
```

The listing is as follows when displayed with the sector editor:

```
Directory Editing Mode                                  DiskMinder
[Esc] Displays Main Menu

Filename.Ext     Size    Date      Time    Attr Clu   Reserved
BELGRADE.DOC     1280    05/21/88  19:18:05  20  0002  0000000000000000000
σARDEN  .DOC     5464    03/14/89  15:45:17  20  0004  0000000000000000000
σHAINSAW.DOC     2086    03/14/89  15:51:17  20  0006  0000000000000000000
FISH    .DOC     1436    08/27/88  14:14:09  20  000D  0000000000000000000
        .           0    00/00/80  00:00:00  00  0000  0000000000000000000
```

Note the Greek sigma characters in the file names, indicating erasure.

The FAT now contains nine consecutive cleared cells extending from cell 4 through cell C. We know (from the directory display) that GARDEN.DOC starts in cluster 4, but we can't tell where it goes from there. It might occupy clusters 4, 5, 7, 8, 9, and A. Or perhaps 4, 5, 8, 9, A, and B. Or 4, C, 5, 8, 9, and A (in that order). Or one of many other possible sequences. We cannot tell. It clearly does not occupy cluster 6 since the directory indicates 6 as the starting cluster for CHAINSAW.DOC.

```
Fat Editing Mode                                        DiskMinder
[Esc] Displays Main Menu

Clu     +0  +1  +2  +3   +4  +5  +6  +7   +8  +9  +A  +B   +C  +D  +E  +F
0000    FFD FFF 003 FFF  000 000 000 000  000 000 000 000  000 00E FFF 000
0010    000 000 000 000  000 000 000 000  000 000 000 000  000 000 000 000
```

Before starting the unerase process, we must determine exactly where the erased files are located. We will examine clusters 4 through C using DiskMinder's sector editing mode. It allows us to view (and even edit) any cluster in the data area of the disk, even if the corresponding FAT cell has been cleared.

In cluster 4, we see the start of the GARDEN file:

```
DOS Sector Editing Mode                                              DiskMinder
[Esc] Displays Main Menu

        +0 +1 +2 +3 +4 +5 +6 +7 +8 +9 +A +B +C +D +E +F    0    4    8    C
  0000  53 6F 69 6C 20 50 72 65 70 61 72 61 74 69 6F 6E    Soil Preparation
  0010  3A 20 20 50 72 65 70 61 72 65 20 74 68 65 20 73    :   Prepare the s
  0020  6F 69 6C 20 66 6F 72 20 6C 61 77 6E 73 20 6F 66    oil for lawns of
  0030  20 64 69 63 68 6F 6E 64 72 61 20 61 74 0D 0A 6C     dichondra at  l
  0040  65 61 73 74 20 74 77 6F 20 6D 6F 6E 74 68 73 20    east two months
  0050  62 65 66 6F 72 65 20 73 6F 77 69 6E 67 20 73 65    before sowing se
  0060  65 64 2E 20 20 53 70 72 65 61 64 20 6D 61 6E 75    ed.   Spread manu
  0070  72 65 2C 20 63 6F 6D 70 6F 73 74 2C 0D 0A 6C 65    re, compost,   le
  0080  61 66 6D 6F 6C 64 2C 20 70 65 61 74 20 6D 6F 73    afmold, peat mos
  0090  73 20 6F 72 20 61 20 63 6F 6D 62 69 6E 61 74 69    s or a combinati
  00A0  6F 6E 20 6F 66 20 74 68 65 73 65 20 6F 6E 20 74    on of these on t
  00B0  68 65 20 73 6F 69 6C 2E 20 20 50 6C 6F 77 0D 0A    he soil.    Plow
  00C0  75 6E 64 65 72 20 74 6F 20 61 20 64 65 70 74 68    under to a depth
    .     .   .   .   .   .   .   .   .   .   .   .   .   .   .   .   .
    .     .   .   .   .   .   .   .   .   .   .   .   .   .   .   .   .
    .     .   .   .   .   .   .   .   .   .   .   .   .   .   .   .   .
  0180  68 69 67 68 2E 0D 0A 0D 0A 54 68 65 20 62 65 73    high.      The bes
  0190  74 20 74 69 6D 65 20 74 6F 20 73 6F 77 20 61 20    t time to sow a
  01A0  6C 61 77 6E 20 69 73 20 74 68 65 20 65 6E 64 20    lawn is the end
  01B0  6F 66 20 53 65 70 74 65 6D 62 65 72 20 74 6F 20    of September to
  01C0  74 68 65 20 6D 69 64 64 6C 65 0D 0A 6F 66 20 4E    the middle  of N
  01D0  6F 76 65 6D 62 65 72 2E 20 20 54 68 65 20 6E 65    ovember.  The ne
  01E0  78 74 20 62 65 73 74 20 74 69 6D 65 20 69 73 20    xt best time is
  01F0  74 68 65 20 65 6E 64 20 6F 66 20 4D 61 72 63 68    the end of March

Editing Logical Sector 17 of 720
        Drive            A:                              Cluster 0004H
```

DiskMinder -- Copyright 1988 Westlake Data Corporation

end of cluster 004

Cluster 5 starts with the following (a continuation of the text at the end of cluster 4), indicating that it contains the next piece of the GARDEN file:

```
  0000  20 75 6E 74 69 6C 20 74 68 65 0D 0A 6C 61 73 74    until the  last
  0010  20 6F 66 20 4D 61 79 2E 20 20 48 75 6D 69 64 69    of May.  Humidi
  0020  74 79 20 69 73 20 68 69 67 68 20 61 6E 64 20 74    ty is high and t
  0030  65 6D 70 65 72 61 74 75 72 65 73 20 63 6F 6F 6C    emperatures cool
  0040  65 72 20 64 75 72 69 6E 67 0D 0A 74 68 65 73 65    er during  these
  0050  20 6D 6F 6E 74 68 73 2E 20 20 49 74 20 69 73 20    months.  It is
    .     .   .   .   .   .   .   .   .   .   .   .   .   .   .   .   .
    .     .   .   .   .   .   .   .   .   .   .   .   .   .   .   .   .
    .     .   .   .   .   .   .   .   .   .   .   .   .   .   .   .   .
  01A0  61 74 65 72 69 6E 67 3A 20 20 41 66 74 65 72 20    atering:  After
  01B0  6C 61 77 6E 20 69 73 20 65 73 74 61 62 6C 69 73    lawn is establis
  01C0  68 65 64 2C 20 77 61 74 65 72 20 6C 65 73 73 20    hed, water less
  01D0  6F 66 74 65 6E 2E 20 20 44 65 65 70 0D 0A 70 65    often.  Deep  pe
  01E0  6E 65 74 72 61 74 69 6F 6E 2C 20 68 6F 77 65 76    netration, howev
  01F0  65 72 2C 20 69 73 20 69 6D 70 6F 72 74 61 6E 74    er, is important

Editing Logical Sector 19 of 720
        Drive            A:                              Cluster 0005H
```

DiskMinder -- Copyright 1988 Westlake Data Corporation

end of cluster 005

At the beginning of cluster 6, we recognize text known to be at the start of the CHAINSAW file:

```
DOS Sector Editing Mode                                    DiskMinder
[Esc] Displays Main Menu

       +0 +1 +2 +3 +4 +5 +6 +7 +8 +9 +A +B +C +D +E +F    0   4   8   C
0000   4F 6E 20 74 68 65 20 63 61 72 65 20 61 6E 64 20    On the care and
0010   75 73 65 20 6F 66 20 63 68 61 69 6E 73 61 77 73    use of chainsaws
0020   3A 0D 0A 2D 2D 2D 2D 2D 2D 2D 2D 2D 2D 2D 2D 2D    : --------------
0030   2D 2D 2D 2D 2D 2D 2D 2D 2D 2D 2D 2D 2D 2D 2D 2D    ----------------
0040   2D 2D 2D 2D 0D 0A 0D 0A 41 2E 20 4B 65 65 70 20    ----   A. Keep
0050   63 68 61 69 6E 20 73 68 61 72 70 2E 0D 0A 0D 0A    chain sharp.
0060   42 2E 20 47 61 73 6F 6C 69 6E 65 3A 20 20 4D 69    B. Gasoline:  Mi
0070   6E 20 6F 63 74 61 6E 65 20 39 30 20 52 4F 5A 20    n octane 90 ROZ
0080   28 70 72 65 66 65 72 61 62 6C 79 20 75 6E 6C 65    (preferably unle
0090   61 64 65 64 20 72 65 67 75 6C 61 72 2C 20 62 75    aded regular, bu
00A0   74 20 70 72 65 6D 69 75 6D 20 6F 6B 29 0D 0A 20    t premium ok)
00B0   20 20 46 75 65 6C 20 6D 69 78 74 75 72 65 20 61     Fuel mixture a
00C0   67 65 73 2E 20 20 4D 69 78 20 69 6E 20 73 6D 61    ges.  Mix in sma
00D0   6C 6C 20 71 75 61 6E 74 69 74 69 65 73 2E 0D 0A    ll quantities.
00E0   20 20 20 43 68 61 6E 67 65 20 66 69 6C 74 65 72       Change filter
00F0   20 65 6C 65 6D 65 6E 74 20 69 6E 20 66 75 65 6C    element in fuel

Editing Logical Sector 20 of 720
        Drive         A:                           Cluster 0006H

         DiskMinder -- Copyright 1988 Westlake Data Corporation
```

Continuing through clusters 7 and 8, we see a continuation of the CHAINSAW file. Its end lies in cluster 8 as shown next:

```
DOS Sector Editing Mode                                    DiskMinder
[Esc] Displays Main Menu

       +0 +1 +2 +3 +4 +5 +6 +7 +8 +9 +A +B +C +D +E +F    0   4   8   C
0000   6C 79 20 69 6E 20 63 6C 65 61 6E 20 67 61 73 6F    ly in clean gaso
0010   6C 69 6E 65 20 6F 6E 63 65 20 61 20 77 65 65 6B    line once a week
0020   2E 0D 0A 0D 0A 1A 20 20 20 20 20 20 20 20 20 20    .
0030   20 20 20 20 20 20 20 20 20 20 20 20 20 20 20 20
0040   20 20 20 20 20 20 20 20 20 20 20 20 20 20 20 20
0050   20 20 20 20 20 20 20 20 20 20 20 20 20 20 20 20
0060   20 20 20 20 20 20 20 20 20 20 20 20 20 20 20 20
0070   20 20 20 20 20 20 20 20 20 20 20 20 20 20 20 20
0080   20 20 20 20 20 20 20 20 20 20 20 20 20 20 20 20
0090   20 20 20 20 20 20 20 20 20 20 20 20 20 20 20 20
00A0   20 20 20 20 20 20 20 20 20 20 20 20 20 20 20 20
00B0   20 20 20 20 20 20 20 20 20 20 20 20 20 20 20 20
00C0   20 20 20 20 20 20 20 20 20 20 20 20 20 20 20 20
00D0   20 20 20 20 20 20 20 20 20 20 20 20 20 20 20 20
00E0   20 20 20 20 20 20 20 20 20 20 20 20 20 20 20 20
00F0   20 20 20 20 20 20 20 20 20 20 20 20 20 20 20 20

Editing Logical Sector 24 of 720
        Drive         A:                           Cluster 0008H

         DiskMinder -- Copyright 1988 Westlake Data Corporation
```

end of CHAINSAW file in cluster 008

In cluster 9, we see a continuation of the GARDEN file (resuming from where it left off in cluster 5).

```
DOS Sector Editing Mode                                      DiskMinder
[Esc] Displays Main Menu

       +0 +1 +2 +3 +4 +5 +6 +7 +8 +9 +A +B +C +D +E +F   0    4    8    C
  0000 2E 20 20 4F 6E 65 20 67 6F 6F 64 20 73 6F 61 6B   .  One good soak
  0010 69 6E 67 20 69 73 20 62 65 74 74 65 72 0D 0A 74   ing is better  t
  0020 68 61 6E 20 6D 61 6E 79 20 6C 69 67 68 74 20 73   han many light s
  0030 70 72 69 6E 6B 6C 69 6E 67 73 2E 20 20 73 68 61   prinklings.  sha
  0040 6C 6C 6F 77 20 77 61 74 65 72 69 6E 67 20 63 61   llow watering ca
  0050 75 73 65 73 20 61 20 73 68 61 6C 6C 6F 77 0D 0A   uses a shallow
  0060 72 6F 6F 74 20 73 79 73 74 65 6D 2E 20 20 54 6F   root system.  To
  0070 6F 20 6D 75 63 68 20 77 61 74 65 72 20 63 61 75   o much water cau
  0080 73 65 73 20 62 72 6F 77 6E 20 73 70 6F 74 20 6F   ses brown spot o
  0090 72 20 62 72 6F 77 6E 20 70 61 74 63 68 2E 0D 0A   r brown patch.
  00A0 0D 0A 50 65 73 74 73 3A 20 20 54 68 65 72 65 20     Pests:  There
  00B0 61 72 65 20 74 77 6F 20 6D 61 6A 6F 72 20 6C 61   are two major la
  00C0 77 6E 20 70 65 73 74 73 3A 20 73 6F 64 20 77 65   wn pests: sod we
  00D0 62 77 6F 72 6D 20 61 6E 64 20 63 75 74 20 77 6F   bworm and cut wo
  00E0 72 6D 2E 20 0D 0A 54 68 65 79 20 65 61 74 20 74   rm.  They eat t
  00F0 68 65 20 67 72 61 73 73 20 72 6F 6F 74 73 20 61   he grass roots a

Editing Logical Sector 26 of 720
        Drive          A:                          Cluster 0009H
```

DiskMinder -- Copyright 1988 Westlake Data Corporation

Continuing through clusters A and B, we see a continuation of the GARDEN file and its end in cluster C.

```
DOS Sector Editing Mode                                      DiskMinder
[Esc] Displays Main Menu

       +0 +1 +2 +3 +4 +5 +6 +7 +8 +9 +A +B +C +D +E +F   0    4    8    C
  0100 65 70 74 61 63 6C 65 73 2C 20 61 6E 64 0D 0A 77   eptacles, and  w
  0110 6F 6F 64 20 73 74 6F 72 61 67 65 2E 20 20 49 74   ood storage.  It
  0120 20 73 68 6F 75 6C 64 20 62 65 20 72 65 61 64 69    should be readi
  0130 6C 79 20 61 63 63 65 73 73 69 62 6C 65 20 74 6F   ly accessible to
  0140 20 74 68 65 20 6B 69 74 63 68 65 6E 0D 0A 64 6F    the kitchen  do
  0150 6F 72 2E 0D 0A 0D 0A 1A 00 00 00 00 00 00 00 00   or.  ........
  0160 00 00 00 00 00 00 00 00 00 00 00 00 00 00 00 00   ................
  0170 00 00 00 00 00 00 00 00 00 00 00 00 00 00 00 00   ................
  0180 00 00 00 00 00 00 00 00 00 00 00 00 00 00 00 00   ................
  0190 00 00 00 00 00 00 00 00 00 00 00 00 00 00 00 00   ................
  01A0 00 00 00 00 00 00 00 00 00 00 00 00 00 00 00 00   ................
  01B0 00 00 00 00 00 00 00 00 00 00 00 00 00 00 00 00   ................
  01C0 00 00 00 00 00 00 00 00 00 00 00 00 00 00 00 00   ................
  01D0 00 00 00 00 00 00 00 00 00 00 00 00 00 00 00 00   ................
  01E0 00 00 00 00 00 00 00 00 00 00 00 00 00 00 00 00   ................
  01F0 00 00 00 00 00 00 00 00 00 00 00 00 00 00 00 00   ................

Editing Logical Sector 32 of 720
        Drive          A:                          Cluster 000CH
```

DiskMinder -- Copyright 1988 Westlake Data Corporation

end of GARDEN file in cluster C

Our examination has found that the GARDEN file starts in cluster 4, continues through clusters 5, 9, A, and B, and terminates in cluster C. We have also found that the CHAINSAW file starts in cluster 6, continues through cluster 7, and terminates in cluster 8. It is now simple to un-erase both of them. The only steps necessary are:

1. Enter the directory editing mode of the sector editor, use the arrow keys to move the cursor to the "σ" in σARDEN, and press "G" to restore the file name. Do the same for the σHAINSAW file, changing the "σ" to "C". Write the changes to disk with the Update command.

2. Enter the FAT editing mode of the sector editor, position the cursor at the first "0" in cell 4, and type the sequence: 005 009 007 008 FFF 00A 00B 00C FFF to rebuild the chains. You must type the leading zeroes for compatibility with the FAT format. Write the changes to disk with the Update command and you are done.

 # Summary

Erasing a file changes only the FAT and directory. It does not affect the data area of the disk.

Un-erase programs have no way of knowing which clusters belong to an erased file. However, they can determine a file's starting cluster from the disk directory. In practice, as we have seen, they may ignore this vital information.

Automatic mode un-erasers are unreliable since they pick up the wrong data in fragmented files that are interleaved with other erased files. Without careful analysis, you cannot tell whether fragmentation and interleaving are present. Even such examination will not help unless the files are human-readable. To un-erase a file, first determine manually which clusters its data occupies and in what order. Then rebuild the allocation chains accordingly. This procedure can be done with a sector editor, as we have seen, or with un-erase software that has a manually-assisted mode.

11

PACK'd
Datafiles

The dBASE PACK command physically removes deleted records from a datafile. In most cases, the data is unrecoverable since the deleted records are overwritten. Sometimes, however, it is recoverable. To understand when and why, we must explain what the PACK command actually does.

To illustrate the effects of packing a datafile in dBASE, we will use the sample file PFILE.DBF on drive A. It contains 683 records, but every third one (3, 6, 9, 12, etc) has been marked for deletion. A directory listing shows the following:

```
C:\DIR A:

 Volume in drive A has no label
 Directory of  A:\

PFILE    DBF    29184   1-09-89   3:35p
        1 File(s)    332800 bytes free
```

The structure of PFILE is as follows:

```
Structure for database: A:pfile.dbf
Number of data records:    683
Date of last update   : 01/09/89
Field  Field Name  Type        Width    Dec
    1  SURNAME     Character     15
    2  FNAME       Character     15
    3  TEL         Character      8
    4  ORDER       Numeric        3
** Total **                      42
```

A partial LISTing of the file shows:

```
Record#  SURNAME          FNAME           TEL      ORDER
      1  Zuckerman        Addison B.      882-8264     1
      2  Wood             Anthony G.      827-3741     2
      3  *Tomlinson       Blake           733-8729     3
      4  Werner           Bradley A.      929-2873     4
      5  Swartwout        David B.        828-7371     5
      6  *Steenburg       Denise R.       119-8282     6
      7  Smith            Donald S.       929-4188     7
      8  Sherman          Edward L.       237-2724     8
      9  *Roof            Frederick E.    254-9992     9
     10  Reilly           Gerard J.       882-7874    10
     11  Porravecchio     Harvey D.       249-1592    11
     12  *Peek            Jack            292-9494    12
     13  Mench            John J.         834-8269    13
     14  Mayberry         John P.         923-9199    14
     15  *Mancini         Joseph A.       482-8342    15
     16  Liva             Kerney          499-1873    16
     17  Blessington      Michael         727-8273    17
     18  *Koehler         Michael A.      749-2946    18
     19  Kennett          Mohan S.        827-6419    19
      .   .    .     .     .    .    .     .    .    .     .
      .   .    .     .     .    .    .     .    .    .     .
      .   .    .     .     .    .    .     .    .    .     .
```

Let's now invoke DEBUG to examine PFILE.DBF by giving the command

```
DEBUG A:PFILE.DBF
```

Examining the CPU registers with DEBUG's R (Register) command shows

```
-R
AX=0000  BX=0000  CX=7200  DX=0000  SP=FFEE  BP=0000  SI=0000  DI=0000
DS=33D4  ES=33D4  SS=33D4  CS=33D4  IP=0100    NV UP EI PL NZ NA PO NC
```

As noted in Appendix B, registers BX and CX contain the length of the file just loaded. Here the length is 7200 hex (29184 decimal), which agrees with the directory listing.

Although we could use DEBUG's Search command to find the end-of-file marker, let's first calculate its location manually as an exercise. Since there are four fields per record and 683 records of 42 bytes each, we have

		Decimal	**Decimal**	**Hex**
Header size	= $4 \times 32 + 33$ =	161 =	A1
Size of record area	= 683×42 =	28686 =	700E
End-of-file marker	= 1 =	1 =	1
Total file size	=	**28848** =	**70B0**

Note that the actual size of a DBF datafile may differ from the size recorded in the directory. In our sample case, the actual size is 28848 bytes, whereas the directory indicates a size of 29184.

To our total (70B0 hex), we must add FF hex since DEBUG loads the file starting at address 0100. 70B0 + FF = 71AF hex. This address should contain the end-of-file marker. Let's check it by using the Search command. We will search memory from address 0100 to 72FF by giving the DEBUG command

```
S 100 72FF 1A
```

DEBUG returns the answer 33D4:71AF, confirming that it found the marker at address 71AF.

A display of memory addresses 0100 through 71AF using the DEBUG Dump command shows:

```
-D 100 71AF
33D4:0100  03 59 01 09 AB 02 00 00-A1 00 2A 00 00 00 00 00   .Y........*.....
33D4:0110  00 00 00 00 00 00 00 00-00 00 00 00 00 00 00 00   ................
33D4:0120  53 55 52 4E 41 4D 45 00-00 00 00 43 05 00 53 68   SURNAME....C..Sh
33D4:0130  0F 00 00 00 01 00 00 00-00 00 00 00 00 00 00 00   ................
33D4:0140  46 4E 41 4D 45 00 00 00-00 00 00 43 14 00 53 68   FNAME......C..Sh
33D4:0150  0F 00 00 00 01 00 00 00-00 00 00 00 00 00 00 00   ................
33D4:0160  54 45 4C 00 00 00 00 00-00 00 00 43 23 00 53 68   TEL........C#.Sh
33D4:0170  08 00 00 00 01 00 00 00-00 00 00 00 00 00 00 00   ................
```

```
33D4:0180  4F 52 44 45 52 00 00 00-00 00 00 4E 2B 00 53 68   ORDER......N+.Sh
33D4:0190  03 00 00 00 01 00 00 00-00 00 00 00 00 00 00 00   ................
33D4:01A0  0D 20 5A 75 63 6B 65 72-6D 61 6E 20 20 20 20 20   . Zuckerman
33D4:01B0  20 41 64 64 69 73 6F 6E-20 42 2E 20 20 20 20 20    Addison B.
33D4:01C0  38 38 32 2D 38 32 36 34-20 20 31 20 57 6F 6F 64   882-8264  1 Wood
33D4:01D0  20 20 20 20 20 20 20 20-20 20 20 41 6E 74 68 6F              Antho
33D4:01E0  6E 79 20 47 2E 20 20 20-20 20 38 32 37 2D 33 37   ny G.     827-37
33D4:01F0  34 31 20 20 32 2A 54 6F-6D 6C 69 6E 73 6F 6E 20   41  2*Tomlinson
33D4:0200  20 20 20 20 20 42 6C 61-6B 65 20 20 20 20 20 20        Blake
33D4:0210  20 20 20 20 37 33 33 2D-38 37 32 39 20 20 33 20       733-8729  3
33D4:0220  57 65 72 6E 65 72 20 20-20 20 20 20 20 20 20 42   Werner         B
33D4:0230  72 61 64 6C 65 79 20 41-2E 20 20 20 20 20 39 32   radley A.     92
33D4:0240  39 2D 32 38 37 33 20 20-34 20 53 77 61 72 74 77   9-2873  4 Swartw
33D4:0250  6F 75 74 20 20 20 20 20-20 44 61 76 69 64 20 42   out      David B
33D4:0260  2E 20 20 20 20 20 20 20-38 32 38 2D 37 33 37 31   .        828-7371
33D4:0270  20 20 35 2A 53 74 65 65-6E 62 75 72 67 20 20 20     5*Steenburg
33D4:0280  20 20 20 44 65 6E 69 73-65 20 52 2E 20 20 20 20      Denise R.
33D4:0290  20 20 31 31 39 2D 38 32-30 32 20 20 36 20 53 6D     119-8202  6 Sm
33D4:02A0  69 74 68 20 20 20 20 20-20 20 20 20 20 44 6F 6E   ith          Don
33D4:02B0  61 6C 64 20 53 2E 20 20-20 20 20 20 39 32 39 2D   ald S.       929-
33D4:02C0  34 31 38 38 20 20 37 20-53 68 65 72 6D 61 6E 20   4188  7 Sherman
33D4:02D0  20 20 20 20 20 20 20 45-64 77 61 72 64 20 4C 2E          Edward L.
33D4:02E0  20 20 20 20 20 20 32 33-37 2D 32 37 32 34 20 20         237-2724
33D4:02F0  38 2A 52 6F 6F 66 20 20-20 20 20 20 20 20 20 20   8*Roof
```

```
 .    .   .   .   .   .   .   .   .   .   .   .   .   .   .
 .    .   .   .   .   .   .   .   .   .   .   .   .   .   .
 .    .   .   .   .   .   .   .   .   .   .   .   .   .   .
```

```
33D4:7100  38 31 39 36 36 37 39 20-46 6C 65 69 73 63 68 6D   8196679 Fleischm
33D4:7110  61 6E 6E 20 20 20 20 20-52 6F 62 65 72 74 20 48 2E   ann    Robert H.
33D4:7120  20 20 20 20 20 20 34 32-33 2D 38 37 31 38 36 38         423-871868
33D4:7130  30 2A 4E 6F 72 74 6F 6E-20 20 20 20 20 20 20 20   0*Norton
33D4:7140  20 4A 61 6D 65 73 20 4C-2E 20 20 20 20 20 20 20    James L.
33D4:7150  38 37 36 2D 39 31 35 39-36 38 31 20 4B 6F 66 66   876-9159681 Koff
33D4:7160  20 20 20 20 20 20 20 20-20 20 20 4D 69 63 68 61              Micha
33D4:7170  65 6C 20 41 2E 20 20 20-20 20 39 32 39 2D 34 38   el A.     929-48
33D4:7180  33 37 36 38 32 20 46 6F-69 73 79 20 20 20 20 20   37682 Foisy
33D4:7190  20 20 20 20 20 52 6F 62-65 72 74 20 47 2E 20 20        Robert G.
33D4:71A0  20 20 20 20 38 36 34 2D-31 32 30 32 36 38 33 1A       864-1202683.
```

Observe the asterisks (ASCII 2A hex) located at addresses 01F5, 0273, 02F1, and 7131 at the beginning of the "Tomlinson", "Steenburg", "Roof", and "Norton" records, indicating that they have been marked for deletion. Fortunately, the Norton is "James", not "Peter"; we surely would not want to lose Peter Norton and his famous narrow ties.

Also observe the end-of-file marker (1A hex) at address 71AF.

PFILE.DBF starts in disk cluster 2 as indicated by the directory display of the DiskMinder sector editor:

```
Directory Editing Mode                              DiskMinder
[Esc] Displays Main Menu

┌─────────────────────────────────────────────────────────────────────┐
│Filename.Ext      Size     Date      Time   Attr Clu  Reserved        │
│PFILE   .DBF     29184  01/09/89  16:15:29   20  0002  0000000000000000000000│
│        .             0  00/00/80  00:00:00   00  0000  0000000000000000000000│
│        .             0  00/00/80  00:00:00   00  0000  0000000000000000000000│
└─────────────────────────────────────────────────────────────────────┘
```

The file is unfragmented, as you can see from its allocation chain (in boldface):

```
Fat Editing Mode                                    DiskMinder
[Esc] Displays Main Menu

┌─────────────────────────────────────────────────────────────────────┐
│Clu   +0  +1  +2  +3    +4  +5  +6  +7    +8  +9  +A  +B    +C  +D  +E  +F │
│0000 FFD FFF 003 004   005 006 007 008   009 00A 00B 00C   00D 00E 00F 010│
│0010 011 012 013 014   015 016 017 018   019 01A 01B 01C   01D 01E FFF 000│
│0020 000 000 000 000   000 000 000 000   000 000 000 000   000 000 000 000│
└─────────────────────────────────────────────────────────────────────┘
```

Although PACK does not care whether the DBF file is fragmented, we are using an unfragmented file to simplify the illustrations.

We will now PACK the file (thereby removing the 227 records marked for deletion) and examine it again.

A directory listing of the file now shows:

```
C:\DIR A:

 Volume in drive A has no label
 Directory of  A:\

 PFILE     DBF     19456    1-09-89    4:22p
         1 File(s)      343040 bytes free
```

Note that the new file size is 19456 bytes rather than the 19650 that you would expect from removing 9534 bytes (227 records at 42 bytes per record) from the original 29184. The reason is that removing 227 records from the file allows it to fit into 19 disk clusters instead of the 29 it previously occupied. dBASE computes file size as an integral number of clusters (i.e., 19 times 1024 or 19456), and writes the value into the disk's directory.

The revised allocation chain for the file appears as follows (in boldface):

```
Fat Editing Mode                                    DiskMinder
[Esc] Displays Main Menu

┌─────────────────────────────────────────────────────────────────────┐
│Clu   +0  +1  +2  +3    +4  +5  +6  +7    +8  +9  +A  +B    +C  +D  +E  +F │
│0000 FFD FFF 003 004   005 006 007 008   009 00A 00B 00C   00D 00E 00F 010│
│0010 011 012 013 014   FFF 000 000 000   000 000 000 000   000 000 000 000│
│0020 000 000 000 000   000 000 000 000   000 000 000 000   000 000 000 000│
│0030 000 000 000 000   000 000 000 000   000 000 000 000   000 000 000 000│
└─────────────────────────────────────────────────────────────────────┘
```

As expected, a listing of the file structure shows only 456 records versus the original 683.

```
Structure for database: A:pfile.dbf
Number of data records:    456
Date of last update   : 01/09/89
Field  Field Name  Type        Width     Dec
    1  SURNAME     Character     15
    2  FNAME       Character     15
    3  TEL         Character      8
    4  ORDER       Numeric        3
** Total **                      42
```

Let's now examine the packed file with DEBUG.

The CPU registers contain:

```
AX=0000  BX=0000  CX=4C00  DX=0000  SP=FFEE  BP=0000  SI=0000  DI=0000
DS=33D4  ES=33D4  SS=33D4  CS=33D4  IP=0100   NV UP EI PL NZ NA PO NC
```

The BX/CX registers contain 4C00, indicating the new file size of 4C00 hex (exactly 19 clusters).

By finding the end-of-file marker with the Search command, we see that it has moved forward 9534 (decimal) bytes from its original address of 71AF to 4C71. The the PACK operation "squeezed" 227 records out of the file by moving non-deleted ones forward.

```
S 100 4CFF 1A
33D4:4C71
```

For brevity, we will now examine just part of the packed PFILE.DBF file:

```
33D4:0100  03 59 01 09 C8 01 00 00-A1 00 2A 00 00 00 00 00   .Y........*.....
33D4:0110  00 00 00 00 00 00 00 00-00 00 00 00 00 00 00 00   ................
33D4:0120  53 55 52 4E 41 4D 45 00-00 00 00 43 05 00 53 68   SURNAME....C..Sh
33D4:0130  0F 00 00 00 01 00 00 00-00 00 00 00 00 00 00 00   ................
33D4:0140  46 4E 41 4D 45 00 00 00-00 00 00 43 14 00 53 68   FNAME......C..Sh
33D4:0150  0F 00 00 00 01 00 00 00-00 00 00 00 00 00 00 00   ................
33D4:0160  54 45 4C 00 00 00 00 00-00 00 00 43 23 00 53 68   TEL........C#.Sh
33D4:0170  08 00 00 00 01 00 00 00-00 00 00 00 00 00 00 00   ................
33D4:0180  4F 52 44 45 52 00 00 00-00 00 00 4E 2B 00 53 68   ORDER......N+.Sh
33D4:0190  03 00 00 00 00 00 00 00-00 00 00 00 00 00 00 00   ................
33D4:01A0  0D 20 5A 75 63 6B 65 72-6D 61 6E 20 20 20 20 20   . Zuckerman
33D4:01B0  20 41 64 64 69 73 6F 6E-20 42 2E 20 20 20 20 20    Addison B.
33D4:01C0  38 38 32 2D 38 32 36 34-20 20 31 20 57 6F 6F 64   882-8264  1 Wood
33D4:01D0  20 20 20 20 20 20 20 20-20 20 20 41 6E 74 68 6F              Antho
33D4:01E0  6E 79 20 47 2E 20 20 20-20 20 38 32 37 2D 33 37   ny G.      827-37
33D4:01F0  34 31 20 20 32 20 57 65-72 6E 65 72 20 20 20 20   41   2 Werner
33D4:0200  20 20 20 20 20 42 72 61-64 6C 65 79 20 41 2E 20        Bradley A.
33D4:0210  20 20 20 20 20 39 32 39-2D 32 38 37 33 20 20 34        929-2873   4
```

```
33D4:0220  53 77 61 72 74 77 6F 75-74 20 20 20 20 20 20 44    Swartwout       D
33D4:0230  61 76 69 64 20 42 2E 20-20 20 20 20 20 20 38 32    avid B.       82
33D4:0240  38 2D 37 33 37 31 20 20-35 20 53 6D 69 74 68 20    8-7371  5 Smith
33D4:0250  20 20 20 20 20 20 20 20-20 44 6F 6E 61 6C 64 20             Donald
33D4:0260  53 2E 20 20 20 20 20 20-39 32 39 2D 34 31 38 38    S.       929-4188
33D4:0270  20 20 37 20 53 68 65 72-6D 61 6E 20 20 20 20 20     7 Sherman
33D4:0280  20 20 20 45 64 77 61 72-64 20 4C 2E 20 20 20 20       Edward L.
33D4:0290  20 20 32 33 37 2D 32 37-32 34 20 20 38 20 52 65      237-2724  8 Re
33D4:02A0  69 6C 6C 79 20 20 20 20-20 20 20 20 20 47 65 72    illy         Ger
33D4:02B0  61 72 64 20 4A 2E 20 20-20 20 20 20 38 38 32 2D    ard J.       882-
33D4:02C0  37 38 37 34 20 31 30 20-50 6F 72 72 61 76 65 63    7874 10 Porravec
33D4:02D0  63 68 69 6F 20 20 20 48-61 72 76 65 79 20 44 2E    chio    Harvey D.
33D4:02E0  20 20 20 20 20 20 32 34-39 2D 31 35 39 32 20 31          249-1592 1
33D4:02F0  31 20 4D 65 6E 63 68 20-20 20 20 20 20 20 20 20    1 Mench

      .    .    .    .    .     .    .    .    .     .    .    .    .    .    .    .
      .    .    .    .    .     .    .    .    .     .    .    .    .    .    .    .
      .    .    .    .    .     .    .    .    .     .    .    .    .    .    .    .
33D4:4C00  20 20 20 52 6F 62 65 72-74 20 48 2E 20 20 20 20       Robert H.
33D4:4C10  20 20 34 32 33 2D 38 37-31 38 36 38 30 20 4B 6F      423-8718680 Ko
33D4:4C20  66 66 20 20 20 20 20 20-20 20 20 20 20 4D 69 63    ff           Mic
33D4:4C30  68 61 65 6C 20 41 2E 20-20 20 20 20 39 32 39 2D    hael A.       929-
33D4:4C40  34 38 33 37 36 38 32 20-46 6F 69 73 79 20 20 20    4837682 Foisy
33D4:4C50  20 20 20 20 20 20 20 20-52 6F 62 65 72 74 20 47 2E         Robert G.
33D4:4C60  20 20 20 20 20 20 38 38-36 2D 31 32 30 32 36 38          864-120268
33D4:4C70  33 1A                                              3.
```

Note that the "Werner" record (originally the fourth one in the file and shown in boldface in the above display) now begins immediately after the end of record 2 ("Wood"). It starts where the old record 3 ("Tomlinson") started previously (address 01F5). This clearly shows that the data formerly in record 3 has been overwritten by record 4's data and all subsequent records have moved forward. The "Tomlinson" record no longer exists. Since its data has been overwritten, it cannot be recovered. This is also true of all records marked for deletion. "...here today and gone tomorrow", as the illustrious Aphra Behn (whoever he was) once wrote.

But there are cases worth examining where the outlook for recovery is not so bleak. They involve DELETE REST or DELETE ALL followed by PACK.

Case 1: DELETE REST
Followed by PACK

Starting again with our original PFILE.DBF datafile, let us give the following commands in dBASE and examine the consequences:

```
GOTO 3
DELETE REST
PACK
```

The first command moves the file pointer to record 3. The second one marks record 3 and everything after it for deletion. The third command packs the file.

After we enter this series of commands and exit from dBASE, a directory listing of the disk appears as follows:

```
C:\DIR A:

    Volume in drive A has no label
    Directory of  A:\

    PFILE     DBF        512   1-09-89    4:37p
            1 File(s)      361472 bytes free
```

or, as displayed by the sector editor, as follows:

```
Directory Editing Mode                                    DiskMinder
[Esc] Displays Main Menu

  Filename.Ext       Size     Date      Time    Attr Clu   Reserved
  PFILE   .DBF        512   01/09/89  16:37:19   20  0002   00000000000000000000
         .              0   00/00/80  00:00:00   00  0000   00000000000000000000
         .              0   00/00/80  00:00:00   00  0000   00000000000000000000
```

Examining the FAT reveals that the file, now containing only the header and the first two records, occupies just one disk cluster. Its allocation chain, therefore, consists of a single link (cell 2) as shown in boldface below:

```
Fat Editing Mode                                          DiskMinder
[Esc] Displays Main Menu

  Clu    +0  +1  +2  +3    +4  +5  +6  +7    +8  +9  +A  +B    +C  +D  +E  +F
  0000  FFD FFF FFF 000   000 000 000 000   000 000 000 000   000 000 000 000
  0010  000 000 000 000   000 000 000 000   000 000 000 000   000 000 000 000
  0020  000 000 000 000   000 000 000 000   000 000 000 000   000 000 000 000
  0030  000 000 000 000   000 000 000 000   000 000 000 000   000 000 000 000
```

As far as DOS is concerned, PFILE now contains only the data in cluster 2. But, as you will soon see, all the data is still intact in the data area of the disk. Since the FAT no longer tells us where the rest of the file is located, however, DEBUG is not useful here. Instead we will use the sector-read feature of the DiskMinder sector editor to examine cluster 2 as well as the unassigned clusters beyond it, paying particular attention to the data at the beginning of cluster 3.

Cluster 2 in the data area contains the following:

```
03 59 01 09 02 00 00 00 A1 00 2A 00 00 00 00 00     ♥Y  ...í.*.....
00 00 00 00 00 00 00 00 00 00 00 00 00 00 00 00     ................
53 55 52 4E 41 4D 45 00 00 00 00 43 05 00 4E 7F     SURNAME....C♣.N
0F 00 00 00 01 00 00 00 00 00 00 00 00 00 00 00     ... ...........
46 4E 41 4D 45 00 00 00 00 00 00 43 14 00 4E 7F     FNAME......C .N
0F 00 00 00 01 00 00 00 00 00 00 00 00 00 00 00     ... ...........
54 45 4C 00 00 00 00 00 00 00 00 43 23 00 4E 7F     TEL........C#.N
08 00 00 00 01 00 00 00 00 00 00 00 00 00 00 00     ... ...........
4F 52 44 45 52 00 00 00 00 00 00 4E 2B 00 4E 7F     ORDER......N+.N
03 00 00 00 01 00 00 00 00 00 00 00 00 00 00 00     ♥... ...........
0D 20 5A 75 63 6B 65 72 6D 61 6E 20 20 20 20 20     . Zuckerman
20 41 64 64 69 73 6F 6E 20 42 2E 20 20 20 20 20     Addison B.
38 38 32 2D 38 32 36 34 20 20 31 20 57 6F 6F 64     882-8264  1 Wood
20 20 20 20 20 20 20 20 20 20 20 41 6E 74 68 6F     Antho
6E 79 20 47 2E 20 20 20 20 20 38 32 37 2D 33 37     ny G.   827-37
34 31 20 20 32 1A 54 6F 6D 6C 69 6E 73 6F 6E 20     41  2→Tomlinson
20 20 20 20 20 42 6C 61 6B 65 20 20 20 20 20 20     Blake
20 20 20 20 37 33 33 2D 38 37 32 39 20 20 33 2A     733-8729  3*
57 65 72 6E 65 72 20 20 20 20 20 20 20 20 20 42     Werner        B
72 61 64 6C 65 79 20 41 2E 20 20 20 20 20 39 32     radley A.     92
39 2D 32 38 37 33 20 20 34 2A 53 77 61 72 74 77     9-2873  4*Swartw
6F 75 74 20 20 20 20 20 20 44 61 76 69 64 20 42     out      David B
2E 20 20 20 20 20 20 20 38 32 38 2D 37 33 37 31     .       828-7371
20 20 35 2A 53 74 65 65 6E 62 75 72 67 20 20 20     5*Steenburg
20 20 44 65 6E 69 73 65 20 52 2E 20 20 20 20 20     Denise R.
20 20 31 31 39 2D 38 32 38 32 20 20 36 2A 53 6D     119-8282  6*Sm
69 74 68 20 20 20 20 20 20 20 20 20 20 44 6F 6E     ith       Don
61 6C 64 20 53 2E 20 20 20 20 20 20 39 32 39 2D     ald S.      929-
34 31 38 38 20 20 37 2A 53 68 65 72 6D 61 6E 20     4188  7*Sherman
20 20 20 20 20 20 20 45 64 77 61 72 64 20 4C 2E     Edward L.
20 20 20 20 20 20 32 33 37 2D 32 37 32 34 20 20     237-2724
38 2A 52 6F 6F 66 20 20 20 20 20 20 20 20 20 20     8*Roof
20 46 72 65 64 65 72 69 63 6B 20 45 2E 20 20 20     Frederick E.
32 35 34 2D 39 39 39 32 20 20 39 2A 52 65 69 6C     254-9992 9*Reil
6C 79 20 20 20 20 20 20 20 20 20 47 65 72 61 72     ly       Gerar
64 20 4A 2E 20 20 20 20 20 20 38 38 32 2D 37 38     d J.      882-78
37 34 20 31 30 2A 50 6F 72 72 61 76 65 63 63 68     74 10*Porravecch
69 6F 20 20 20 48 61 72 76 65 79 20 44 2E 20 20     io   Harvey D.
20 20 20 20 32 34 39 2D 31 35 39 32 20 31 31 2A     249-1592 11*
50 65 65 6B 20 20 20 20 20 20 20 20 20 20 20 4A     Peek         J
61 63 6B 20 20 20 20 20 20 20 20 20 20 20 32 39     ack         29
32 2D 39 34 39 34 20 31 32 2A 4D 65 6E 63 68 20     2-9494 12*Mench
20 20 20 20 20 20 20 20 4A 6F 68 6E 20 4A 2E        John J.
20 20 20 20 20 20 38 33 34 2D 38 32 36 39           834-8269
20 31 33 2A 4D 61 79 62 65 72 72 79 20 20 20 20     13*Mayberry
20 20 20 4A 6F 68 6E 20 50 2E 20 20 20 20 20 20     John P.
20 20 39 32 33 2D 39 31 39 39 20 31 34 2A 4D 61     923-9199 14*Ma
6E 63 69 6E 69 20 20 20 20 20 20 20 20 4A 6F 73     ncini       Jos
65 70 68 20 41 2E 20 20 20 20 20 34 38 32 2D         eph A.     482-
38 33 34 32 20 31 35 2A 4C 69 76 61 20 20 20 20     8342 15*Liva
20 20 20 20 20 20 34 39 39 2D 31 38 37 33 20 31     499-1873 1
36 2A 42 6C 65 73 73 69 6E 67 74 6F 6E 20 20 20     6*Blessington
20 4D 69 63 68 61 65 6C 20 20 20 20 20 20 20 20     Michael
37 32 37 2D 38 32 37 33 20 31 37 2A 4B 6F 65 68     727-8273 17*Koeh
6C 65 72 20 20 20 20 20 20 20 20 20 4D 69 63 68 61  ler      Micha
65 6C 20 41 2E 20 20 20 20 20 20 37 34 39 2D 32 39  el A.      749-29
34 36 20 31 38 2A 4B 65 6E 6E 65 74 74 20 20 20     46 18*Kennett
20 20 20 20 20 4D 6F 68 61 6E 20 53 2E 20 20 20     Mohan S.
```

```
20 20 20 20 38 32 37 2D 36 34 31 39 20 31 39 2A        827-6419 19*
4A 61 6E 6B 6F 77 73 6B 69 20 20 20 20 20 20 50     Jankowski       P
61 75 6C 20 44 2E 20 20 20 20 20 20 20 20 38 33     aul D.          83
32 2D 38 33 34 37 20 32 30 2A 48 61 74 63 68 20     2-8347 20*Hatch
20 20 20 20 20 20 20 20 20 52 69 63 68 61 72 64              Richard
```

```
      < end of Cluster 2 >
```

Before proceeding, please note the end-of-file marker (shown above in boldface just ahead of the "T" in "Tomlinson"). PACK put it immediately after the end of record 2.

Also note the asterisks at the beginning of each subsequent record. They are the record deletion markers produced by the DELETE REST command.

As we now move into cluster 3, you will see that the original file's data is still intact **even though the FAT entry has been cleared**.

```
      < beginning of Cluster 3 >
```

```
20 41 2E 20 20 20 20 20 39 37 35 2D 37 32 34 39     A.       975-7249
20 32 31 2A 47 72 75 62 65 72 20 20 20 20 20 20     21*Gruber
20 20 20 52 69 63 68 61 72 64 20 4A 2E 20 20 20       Richard J.
20 20 36 34 36 2D 31 32 39 39 20 32 32 2A 47 69     646-1299 22*Gi
65 6C 62 65 72 67 20 20 20 20 20 20 52 6F 62     elberg      Rob
65 72 74 20 20 20 20 20 20 20 20 20 38 33 35 2D     ert         835-
37 32 33 37 20 32 33 2A 46 72 69 64 61 79 20 20     7237 23*Friday
20 20 20 20 20 20 20 52 6F 62 65 72 74 20 45 2E            Robert E.
20 20 20 20 20 20 38 32 37 2D 34 38 37 32 20 32         827-4872 2
34 2A 45 64 77 61 72 64 73 20 20 20 20 20 20 20     4*Edwards
20 52 6F 67 65 72 20 4A 2E 20 20 20 20 20 20 20       Roger J.
34 38 31 2D 36 38 31 35 20 32 35 2A 44 65 20 50     481-6815 25*De P
69 65 74 72 6F 20 20 20 20 20 20 53 68 69 72 6C     ietro       Shirl
65 79 20 4A 2E 20 20 20 20 20 32 37 32 2D 37 32     ey J.       272-72
34 38 20 32 36 2A 43 6F 6F 6B 20 20 20 20 20 20     48 26*Cook
20 20 20 20 20 54 65 72 72 61 6E 63 65 20 20 20          Terrance
20 20 20 20 38 32 38 2D 32 34 33 36 20 32 37 2A         828-2436 27*
42 75 72 6B 65 79 20 20 20 20 20 20 20 20 20 54     Burkey           T
68 6F 6D 61 73 20 4A 2E 20 20 20 20 20 20 31 38     homas J.        18
37 2D 33 36 31 38 20 32 38 2A 41 7A 61 72 20 20     7-3618 28*Azar
20 20 20 20 20 20 20 20 20 57 69 6C 6C 69 61 6D              William
20 47 2E 20 20 20 20 20 20 39 35 37 2D 33 35 37 36     G.       957-3576
20 32 39 2A 57 61 72 64 65 6E 20 20 20 20 20 20     29*Warden
20 20 20 20 43 61 72 6F 6C 20 4B 2E 20 20 20 20       Carol K.
20 20 32 34 37 2D 37 37 33 38 20 33 30 2A 53 69     247-7738 30*Si
6E 67 65 72 20 20 20 20 20 20 20 20 20 45 64 64     nger         Edd
69 65 20 20 20 20 20 20 20 20 20 20 38 38 32 2D     ie            882-
37 33 33 37 20 33 31 2A 50 68 69 70 70 73 20 20     7337 31*Phipps
20 20 20 20 20 20 20 48 6F 77 61 72 64 20 4D 2E            Howard M.
20 20 20 20 20 20 31 39 31 2D 39 31 35 34 20 33         191-9154 3
32 2A 4B 6C 6F 63 6B 65 6E 62 72 69 6E 6B 20 20     2*Klockenbrink
20 4D 69 63 68 61 65 6C 20 46 2E 20 20 20 20 20       Michael F.
39 32 38 2D 32 38 34 36 20 33 33 2A 47 72 6F 61     928-2846 33*Groa
6E 66 69 65 6C 64 20 20 20 20 20 52 69 63 68 61     nfield      Richa
```

```
72 64 20 4C 2E 20 20 20 20 20 39 37 35 2D 36 35    rd L.      975-65
39 37 20 33 34 2A 44 65 73 61 69 20 20 20 20 20    97 34*Desai
20 20 20 20 20 53 69 64 6E 65 79 20 4C 2E 20 20         Sidney L.
20 20 20 20 38 37 32 2D 33 36 37 34 20 33 35 2A        872-3674 35*
53 79 76 65 72 73 65 6E 20 20 20 20 20 20 20 44    Syversen       D
61 76 69 64 20 20 20 20 20 20 20 20 20 20 33 38    avid         38
33 2D 36 32 34 38 20 33 36 2A 52 6F 75 6E 64 69    3-6248 36*Roundi
6E 67 20 20 20 20 20 20 20 20 46 72 61 6E 7A 20 4F    ng       Franz O
2E 20 20 20 20 20 20 20 35 31 35 2D 33 32 38 32    .       515-3282
20 33 37 2A 4E 65 6C 73 6F 6E 20 20 20 20 20 20     37*Nelson
20 20 20 4A 61 6D 65 73 20 52 2E 20 20 20 20 20        James R.
20 20 37 33 30 2D 32 34 39 37 20 33 38 2A 4D 65       730-2497 38*Me
6C 72 6F 73 65 20 20 20 20 20 20 20 20 20 4A 6F 68    lrose       Joh
6E 20 4A 2E 20 20 20 20 20 20 20 20 20 36 39 39 2D    n J.       699-
31 38 32 38 20 33 39 2A 4B 6E 6F 78 20 20 20 20    1828 39*Knox
20 20 20 20 20 20 20 4D 69 63 68 61 65 6C 20 44           Michael D
2E 20 20 20 20 20 36 31 32 2D 39 32 34 38 20 34    .     612-9248 4
30 2A 46 6C 75 67 65 6C 20 20 20 20 20 20 20 20    0*Flugel
20 52 6F 62 65 72 74 20 48 2E 20 20 20 20 20 20     Robert H.
34 37 30 2D 32 38 37 34 20 34 31 2A 43 65 73 61    470-2874 41*Cesa
72 65 20 20 20 20 20 20 20 20 20 53 68 72 61 77    re         Shraw
61 6E 20 4B 2E 20 20 20 20 20 37 32 33 2D 38 37    an K.     723-87
32 38 20 34 32 2A 42 6F 75 6C 65 79 20 20 20 20    28 42*Bouley
20 20 20 20 20 54 69 62 6F 72 20 43 2E 20 20 20         Tibor C.
20 20 20 20 37 34 33 2D 36 32 38 33 20 34 33 2A        743-6283 43*
41 6C 6C 65 6E 20 20 20 20 20 20 20 20 20 20 57    Allen          W
69 6C 6C 69 61 6D 20 50 2E 20 20 20 20 20 31 30    illiam P.     10
32 2D 33 35 33 35 20 34 34 2A 57 65 72 73 74 6C    2-3535 44*Werstl
65 72 20 20 20 20 20 20 20 20 42 65 74 73 79 20 20    er       Betsy
20 20 20 20 20 20 20 20 20 33 38 32 2D 38 32 38 39            382-8289
```

```
< end of Cluster 3 and start of Cluster 4 >
```

```
20 34 35 2A 54 68 6F 6D 70 73 6F 6E 20 20 20 20     45*Thompson
20 20 20 44 61 6E 69 65 6C 20 20 20 20 20 20 20        Daniel
20 20 34 38 32 2D 33 37 36 34 20 34 36 2A 4D 61       482-3764 46*Ma
72 63 68 65 73 65 20 20 20 20 20 20 20 4A 6F 73    rchese       Jos
65 70 68 20 41 2E 20 20 20 20 20 20 38 32 33 2D    eph A.      823-
37 32 31 39 20 34 37 2A 47 69 62 73 6F 6E 20 20    7219 47*Gibson
20 20 20 20 20 20 20 52 6F 62 65 72 74 20 20 20           Robert
20 20 20 20 20 20 33 38 32 2D 37 31 39 39 20 34          382-7199 4
38 2A 42 6F 6F 6B 65 72 20 20 20 20 20 20 20 20    8*Booker
20 56 61 6C 65 72 69 65 20 53 2E 20 20 20 20 20     Valerie S.
32 33 34 2D 31 32 33 34 20 34 39 2A 42 61 72 74    234-1234 49*Bart
6F 6E 20 20 20 20 20 20 20 20 20 57 69 6C 6C 69    on         Willi
61 6D 20 41 2E 20 20 20 20 20 20 31 38 37 2D 36 32    am A.      187-62
35 34 20 35 30 2A 41 64 6F 6C 66 20 20 20 20 20    54 50*Adolf
20 20 20 20 20 57 69 6C 6C 69 73 20 20 20 20 20         Willis
20 20 20 20 35 34 31 2D 34 33 35 35 20 35 31 2A        541-4355 51*
```

If we proceed similarly through consecutive clusters including cluster 1E, we would see that **all** the file data is intact. PACK has not overwritten any records. As you will appreciate later in this book, we can recover the file completely by ZAP'ing it and then un-ZAP'ing it, as long as nothing else has been written to the disk.

Case 2: DELETE ALL Followed by Pack

The state of a datafile following the dBASE commands DELETE ALL and PACK is the same as its state after the ZAP command. Hence, all its data is completely recoverable if nothing else is written to the disk first.

Summary

We can draw the following important conclusions:

- Deleted records are lost forever after a PACK if they are scattered throughout the file.

- If **all** records from a point onward in a file are deleted, they remain intact after a PACK and are recoverable.

12

Internal and External
Datafile Damage

In diagnosing and treating DBF datafiles, we need standard terminology to clearly differentiate types of damage. I have chosen to separate damage into two principal categories and to further subdivide one of them by class and the other by descriptive name. Specifically, I will call the principal categories *internal* and *external*.

A datafile having only internal damage is recognized by DOS and the CHKDSK utility as a healthy file. There is no disruption of its allocation chain in the File Allocation Table. But it may contain extra end-of-file markers in the records, regions of discontinuity (data offset), a corrupted or missing file header, nulls (characters with ASCII value zero) in its data area, or other characteristics that prevent dBASE from handling it normally.

External damage, on the other hand, is characterized by FAT problems, including lost clusters and cross-linking. A special case is the ZAP'd datafile. Technically, you would not consider it as damaged if the ZAP were intentional. But an accidentally ZAP'd file represents a difficult recovery problem as we saw in Chapter 9.

In some cases, internal and external damage may produce identical symptoms when the file is viewed in dBASE. Then you must apply other tools to determine the underlying cause. Incorrect diagnosis of a problem can lead to the wrong corrective action with resulting failure to recover the file.

To make matters worse, a datafile may have both internal and external damage. In such a case, the internal damage might not be detectable until the external damage is repaired.

We divide internal damage into five classes, as follows:

Class 1:   The file header is intact, but spurious data has been written into data records. The damaged records are not necessarily consecutive. No records have been displaced. The spurious data may include control characters (ASCII values between 0 and 31 decimal) or graphics characters (ASCII values greater than 127 decimal).

Class 2:   Extra end-of-file markers in the records, making it appear that some have been lost.

Class 3:   Overwritten or partially overwritten file header, but the total space originally allocated to it is unchanged. No damage has occurred to the records themselves.

Class 4:   The file header is intact, but the records have been displaced. There may be several points of discontinuity. In terms of symptoms (such as appearance when viewed in the BROWSE mode of dBASE), the file is indistinguishable from one having external damage involving lost clusters. Class 4 damage usually occurs in a copy of a file having lost cluster damage.

Class 5:   The file header is partially or totally missing. If it is totally missing, initial records may also be missing, making the file appear to start in the middle of a record.

DBF datafiles having Class 1, 2, or 4 internal damage can be opened in dBASE with the USE command, but they will not appear normal. Those having Class 3 or 5 damage cannot be opened, and dBASE will display the "not a dBASE database" message if you try. An exception to this is minor Class 3 damage. In such a case, however, the file will not normally be usable and you will see strange things if you display its structure or records.

Datafiles having external damage of the lost cluster type can generally be opened in dBASE, but will usually exhibit data offset or displacement identical in appearance to Class 4 internal damage. Files having external damage of the cross-linking type will appear abnormal in that parts of other files will appear in them. ZAP'd files, of course, appear to contain no record data at all, and a STRUCTURE listing indicates no records.

 ## Summary

File damage can involve disruption of the FAT, problems internal to the file, or both. You cannot reliably determine the nature of damage by examining the file in dBASE because symptoms can be misleading. Incorrect analysis can lead to unnecessary loss of data. Accurate diagnosis of file damage is essential before attempting repair.

13

Diagnosing
the Damage

If a DBF datafile has been damaged, it displays symptoms when viewed in dBASE. In many cases, the symptoms indicate the nature of the damage, but sometimes they are misleading. Usually the damage will be of a single type, but multiple forms may occur. In such cases, you may see the symptoms of the more severe damage but not those of secondary damage. The most common situation is a combination of Class 2 damage (extra end-of-file markers) with a more severe form. For example, the symptom of a damaged or destroyed file header is that dBASE refuses to open the file, saying that it is "not a dBASE database." This major damage may be accompanied by secondary Class 2 damage. Until the major damage is repaired, you will see no evidence of the secondary damage.

Unfortunately, symptoms do not always provide a clear understanding of the nature of the damage since different underlying causes can produce identical symptoms. It is imperative, however, that you determine the true cause before starting repair procedures. Failure to do this can result in additional damage or loss of data. This section examines typical symptoms and explores their root causes.

◈ Spurious Characters in a File (Class 1 Damage)

Although dBASE II cannot access (and therefore edit) certain control characters in the record area of the file, later versions of dBASE let you access and remove them in the EDIT or BROWSE modes. There is one character, however, that even the later versions cannot handle. It is the null (the character with ASCII value zero). dBASE will not let you intentionally write a null into a record. If one exists, dBASE III PLUS will not allow you to place the cursor on it in any editing mode. dBASE IV, similarly, will not display the data in a field containing a null while you are in the BROWSE mode. Nor will it allow you to place the cursor in such a field in the EDIT mode. Hence, within the dBASE environment, you can see evidence of nulls but you can neither access them nor remove them through editing.

In the next example, we use the EDIT mode of dBASE III PLUS to examine a datafile containing nulls. As you can see below, record 1 is healthy, but records 2 and 3 show evidence of nulls. Record 4 and all its successors are healthy.

```
Record No.      1
SURNAME     Zuckerman
FNAME       Addison B.
STREET      416 Garfield Avenue
CITY        Boston
STATE       MA    ZIP        02130
ACCTNO       851
PAIDUP      T
BALANCE       0.00
LASTTRAN    07/10/87
CATEGORY    85
AREACODE    617
TEL         882-8264
SLNAME      Zuhike
SFNAME      William P.
ORDER         1
```

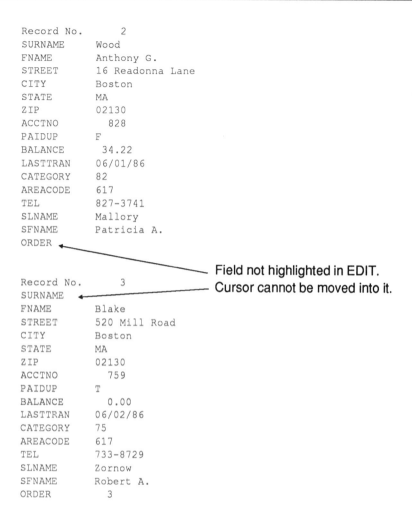

```
Record No.       2
SURNAME    Wood
FNAME      Anthony G.
STREET     16 Readonna Lane
CITY       Boston
STATE      MA
ZIP        02130
ACCTNO         828
PAIDUP     F
BALANCE      34.22
LASTTRAN   06/01/86
CATEGORY   82
AREACODE   617
TEL        827-3741
SLNAME     Mallory
SFNAME     Patricia A.
ORDER
```

Field not highlighted in EDIT.
Cursor cannot be moved into it.

```
Record No.       3
SURNAME
FNAME      Blake
STREET     520 Mill Road
CITY       Boston
STATE      MA
ZIP        02130
ACCTNO         759
PAIDUP     T
BALANCE       0.00
LASTTRAN   06/02/86
CATEGORY   75
AREACODE   617
TEL        733-8729
SLNAME     Zornow
SFNAME     Robert A.
ORDER          3
```

The symptoms indicate the presence of nulls near the end of record 2 and the beginning of record 3.

By this time, you are probably wondering how the nulls got into the file since neither a dBASE user nor dBASE itself could have put them there. One possibility is that dBASE was corrupted on the user's hard disk. After all, dBASE is just another file as far as your computer is concerned and is as susceptible to damage as anything else. Other possibilities include a hardware malfunction or a power disturbance while the disk head was writing data. In any case, nulls create problems in the record area of a DBF datafile.

Extra End-of-File Markers (Class 2 Damage)

This is a common form of file damage and is the easiest one to correct. The symptom of an extra EOF marker is that dBASE will display (for example, during a LISTing) fewer records than the header specifies. Consider the following example.

dBASE shows the structure of our sample file (XFILE.DBF) as follows:

```
Structure for database: C:xfile.dbf
Number of data records:      80
Date of last update   : 05/06/88
Field  Field Name  Type         Width    Dec
    1   SURNAME     Character      15
    2   FNAME       Character      15
    3   STREET      Character      35
    4   CITY        Character      18
    5   STATE       Character       2
    6   ZIP         Character       5
    7   ACCTNO      Numeric         5
    8   PAIDUP      Logical         1
    9   BALANCE     Numeric         6       2
   10   LASTTRAN    Date            8
   11   CATEGORY    Numeric         2
   12   AREACODE    Character       3
   13   TEL         Character       8
   14   SLNAME      Character      15
   15   SFNAME      Character      15
   16   ORDER       Numeric         3
** Total **                      157
```

The STRUCTURE display indicates 80 records. We now display the SUR-NAME and FNAME fields in all of them with the following result:

```
. disp all surname,fname
Record#  surname         fname
      1  Zuckerman       Addison B.
      2  Wood            Anthony G.
      3  Tomlinson       Blake
.
```

After displaying the third record, dBASE returns to the dot prompt as though it had reached the end of the file. If we view the file in the BROWSE mode, we see:

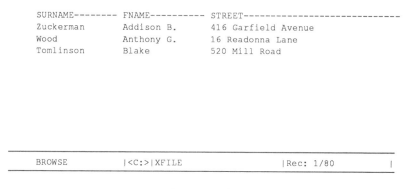

```
SURNAME-------- FNAME---------- STREET----------------------------
Zuckerman      Addison B.      416 Garfield Avenue
Wood           Anthony G.      16 Readonna Lane
Tomlinson      Blake           520 Mill Road
```

```
BROWSE          |<C:>|XFILE                  |Rec: 1/80            |
```

View and edit fields.

If we now use the Down Arrow to move beyond the third record, we see the fifth record:

```
SURNAME-------- FNAME---------- STREET----------------------------
Zuckerman      Addison B.      416 Garfield Avenue
Wood           Anthony G.      16 Readonna Lane
Tomlinson      Blake           520 Mill Road
Vavrick        Charles E.      14 Flamingo Dr.
```

```
BROWSE          |<C:>|XFILE                  |Rec: 5/80            |
```

View and edit fields.

Note that record 5 appears immediately after record 3. Record 4 is nowhere to be found, giving evidence of an extra end-of-file marker at its beginning.

It is important to understand that the marker (1A hex) must be at a particular position in a record for dBASE to treat it as an end-of-file. Specifically, it must be in the record's first byte (that is, the one reserved by dBASE for the delete status flag). A 1A hex anywhere else will be treated as just another character and will not confuse dBASE. If you copy such a file to SDF format, however, and view the result with your word processor, it might treat this 1A hex as a true end-of-file and not read beyond it.

Extra end-of-file markers are often the result of re-booting a computer with an open database file or removing a disk from a floppy drive without properly closing an open datafile on it.

Missing or Damaged Header (Class 3 or Class 5 Damage)

There is no uncertainty about the nature of the damage when dBASE tells you that a file is "not a dBASE database." This is clear evidence of a missing or damaged header.

When you ask dBASE to open a datafile by issuing the USE command, it checks the file's first byte, date of last update, header size, and a few other things. If the first byte is 02, dBASE will tell you that your file is a dBASE II file. If it is not 03 or 83 hex (for dBASE III or III PLUS), or 03 or 8B hex (for dBASE IV), or if the date of last update is invalid, you will get the "not a dBASE database" message. The issue of the header-size bytes is trickier. Some incorrect values trigger the message, but others allow the file to be opened. A file opened in this condition will appear to have data offset at the very beginning.

The example that follows is a dBASE III PLUS or dBASE IV datafile containing 16 fields per record. The correct header size is therefore $16 \times 32 + 33$ or 545 decimal or 221 hex. But the header has been damaged so that the header-size bytes now contain 225 hex (549 decimal). dBASE will open this file, but in the BROWSE mode the records will appear to be displaced relative to the field boundaries (starting from the very beginning of the file) and will appear as follows:

```
SURNAME-------- FNAME---------- STREET---------------------------
erman          Addi son B.     416  Garfield Avenue          Bost
               Anth ony G.      16 R eadonna Lane             Bost
inson          Blak e           520  Mill Road                Bost
er             Brad ley A.       36 C hamberlain              Bost
ick            Char les E.       14 F lamingo Dr.             Bost
twout          Davi d B.        189  Conkey Avenue            Bost
nburg          Deni se R.       7418 Redman Rd.               Bost
h              Dona ld S.       1040 Genesee Pk. Blvd.        Bost
man            Edwa rd L.        35 B rooklyn St.             Bost
effer          Evan  J.          10 V inton Rd.               Bost
               Fred erick E.     12 R iver St.                Bost
ly             Gera rd J.       6841 County Rd. 32            Bost
avecchio       Harv ey D.       4062 Standord                 Bost
               Jack            337  Avery Street              Bost
tt             Jame s G.        1612 Hennessey Rd.            Bost
h              John  J.         5839 Chile Ave.               Bost
erry           John  P.         126  Fulton                   Bost
```

```
BROWSE         |<C:>|X1                    |Rec: 1/80          |
```

View and edit fields.

The most frequent cause of header damage is re-booting the computer while a file is open. Sometimes this is a result of operator error, but it may be unavoidable. Suppose, for example, you are maintaining datafiles with a dBASE program that has SET ESCAPE OFF, opened datafiles, and entered a DO WHILE...ENDDO loop to process the records in one file. However, the programmer forgot to put a SKIP command (or any exit mechanism) in the loop. The result is that dBASE processes the same record over and over forever. As a user, you cannot halt the operation with the Esc key, so your only alternative is to re-boot the computer. In such a case, the probability of header damage is high.

 # Data Offset or Data Displacement (Class 4 or External)

We have just seen a case of apparent data displacement or offset, but it was special and rather unusual. The displacement was not real, but appeared only because of a problem in the header. The record area of the file was healthy. In a typical case of offset, there is a point of discontinuity in the record area. A file exhibiting such offset might appear as follows:

```
SURNAME-------- FNAME---------- STREET----------------------------
Koehler         Michael A.      77 Woodsmeadow
Kennett         Mohan S.        21 Barons St.
Jankowski       Paul D.         196 Kenwood
Holmes          Philip O.       157 Barberry Terrace
Hatch           Richard A.      257 Clay Ave.
Gruber          Richard J.      5093 S. Lima Rd.
Gielberg        Robert          198 Avenue Road
Friday          Robert E.       4511 Whitehall Drive
Finein          Robert 460 3612 9248Tomlinson     Earle F.
     1  228F  21.711 5 860608 260 3 741 2971Werner      Germaine M.
     1  171T   0.001 4 860602 760 3 470 2874Wensley     James G.
     1  114F  14.381 7 860612 160 3 723 8728Wendler     Robert H.
     1   57T   0.001 2 860602 560 3 743 6283Wendel      Kenneth N.
     1    7T   0.001 1 860602 060 3 102 3535Wells       Robert C.
     3  832T   0.001 9 860603 380 2 982 7264Wells       William R.
     3  806T   0.001 5 860621 080 2 382 8289Webster     Ronald B.
     3  754T   0.001 6 860622 580 2 482 3764Pestka      Richard M.

  BROWSE          |<C:>|XFILE             |Rec: 29/807       |
```
View and edit fields.

From this symptom alone, you cannot determine the nature of the file damage because it can have two different underlying causes. As discussed in Chapter 7, a file having skipped links in its allocation chain can exhibit this symptom. In such a case, the data in the skipped links still exists in the data area of the disk and can be recovered. A copy of such a file made with the DOS or dBASE COPY command, however, will also exhibit the offset, but, since the skipped clusters were not copied, the missing data is no longer there to be recovered. This is Class 4 internal damage.

In any case, if you run CHKDSK or examine the file allocation chain with a disk analysis tool, you can usually determine whether you are dealing with an original file having skipped clusters. A surer test, however, is the diagnosis provided by dSALVAGE (see Chapter 8) or dSALVAGE Professional. It will make the determination for you and will clearly identify the exact nature of the file damage.

Datafile Contains Parts of Another File

The presence of cross-linking is obvious when you LIST a datafile or view it in the BROWSE mode. A typical case appears as follows:

```
SURNAME-------- FNAME---------- STREET----------------------------
Mayberry        John P.         126 Fulton
Mancini         Joseph A.       19 Greenmoor Way
Liva            Kerney          104 Weld Street
Learmouth       Louis D.        377 Maple Street
Blessington     Michael         53 Cameron Street
Koehler         Michael A.      77 Woodsmeadow
Kennett         Mohan S.        21 Barons St.       whether or not
ata in a form s imilar to that  displayed by the EDIT command in d
displayed for e dit exactly as  it is stored in the datafile inclu
ASE EDIT mode.   In addition to  modifying record data, this edit
e database.  It  also provides  instant diagnosis of the current r
both horizontal  and  vertical  scrolling, any portion of any reco
nforms the user  of the cursor  position in the file both in terms
 in the current  record.  The u ser can switch back and forth betw
ed as a continu ous character s tring in  a window for full-screen
```

The datafile seems to contain part of a document file. The problem is cross-linking as discussed in Chapter 7. Here the datafile is cross-linked into the document.

Lost clusters and cross-linking often are caused by operating system problems, disk problems, conflicting software (such as terminate-and-stay resident or disk-caching software), defective software, abnormal shutdown of your computer (especially while a file is being written to disk), or a combination. Since these difficulties can occur at any time, you should run CHKDSK daily and check your files with dSALVAGE Professional before backing them up.

14

Repair of Class 1 Damage: Control or Graphics Characters in the Datafile

A datafile exhibiting Class 1 damage contains control characters (ASCII values below 32 decimal) or graphics characters (ASCII values above 127 decimal) in its records. Both types may appear legitimately in the file header. Furthermore, graphics characters may even be legitimate in the records. The popular SBT accounting software, for example, has a file that contains graphics characters for drawing windows, boxes, and arrows.

We are dealing with Class 1 damage at length here, not because it is exceptional but because it is a useful vehicle for explaining how to use software tools.

Nulls (ASCII value zero) are commonplace in the header of a dBASE datafile. In fact, every field name that is less than ten characters long is padded with nulls. They are a problem only in the record area.

Consider the file NULFILE.DBF whose structure is as follows:

```
Structure for database: C:nulfile.dbf
Number of data records:      19
Date of last update   : 09/02/88
Field  Field Name  Type         Width     Dec
   1   SURNAME     Character       15
   2   FNAME       Character       15
   3   LASTTRAN    Date             8
   4   TEL         Character        8
** Total **                        47
```

A LISTing of NULFILE shows:

```
Record#  SURNAME        FNAME          LASTTRAN  TEL
      1  Zuckerman      Addison B.     07/10/86  882-8264
      2  Wood           Anthony G.     06/01/86  827-3741
      3  Tomlinson      Blake          06/02/86  733-8729
      4  Werner         Bradley A.     06/02/86  929-2873
      5  Vavrick        Charles E.     06/03/86  684
      6                 David B.        06/01/86  828-7371
      7  Steenburg      Denise R.      06/11/86  119-8282
      8  Smith          Donald S.      07/10/86  929-4188
      9  Sherman        Edward L.      06/28/86  237-2724
      .      .              .             .         .
      .      .              .             .         .
      .      .              .             .         .
```

When we view NULFILE in the BROWSE mode, we see:

```
SURNAME-------- FNAME---------- LASTTRAN TEL-----
Zuckerman       Addison B.      07/10/86 882-8264
Wood            Anthony G.      06/01/86 827-3741
Tomlinson       Blake           06/02/86 733-8729
Werner          Bradley A.      06/02/86 929-2873
Vavrick         Charles E.      06/03/86 684
          David B.       06/01/86 828-7371
Steenburg       Denise R.       06/11/86 119-8282
Smith           Donald S.       07/10/86 929-4188
Sherman         Edward L.       06/28/86 237-2724
     .              .              .        .
     .              .              .        .
     .              .              .        .

 BROWSE          |<E:>|NULFILE              |Rec: 1/19

              View and edit fields.
```

Pay particular attention to records 5 and 6 in the displays. There appears to be either missing data or a localized offset. In the BROWSE mode of dBASE III PLUS, the highlighted area on the screen is distorted. For example, the region immediately left of "David" in record 6 does not contain the usual highlighting. Furthermore, you cannot move the cursor there. This is a clear indication of nulls. Since you cannot position the cursor on them, you cannot replace them with other characters.

 # Repair by Replacement Using DEBUG

If the file is small, you can repair it with DEBUG. We must start by finding the nulls. To search the record area, we must first determine where it begins. After DEBUG loads the file into memory, we can locate the end of the header (and, therefore, the beginning of the records) by visual inspection (or, of course, by calculation since we know how many fields each record contains). Using the DEBUG D (Dump) command, we find the end of the header at address 01A0 as follows (the last byte is in boldface):

```
C:\DEBUG NULFILE.DBF
-D 100 1BF
2F90:0100   03 58 09 02 13 00 00 00-A1 00 2F 00 00 00 00 00   .X......./.....
2F90:0110   00 00 00 00 00 00 00 00-00 00 00 00 00 00 00 00   ..............
2F90:0120   53 55 52 4E 41 4D 45 00-00 00 00 43 0D 00 EB 81   SURNAME....C....
2F90:0130   0F 00 00 00 01 00 00 00-00 00 00 00 00 00 00 00   ..............
2F90:0140   46 4E 41 4D 45 00 00 00-00 00 00 43 1C 00 EB 81   FNAME......C....
2F90:0150   0F 00 00 00 01 00 00 00-00 00 00 00 00 00 00 00   ..............
2F90:0160   4C 41 53 54 54 52 41 4E-00 00 00 44 2B 00 EB 81   LASTTRAN...D+...
2F90:0170   08 00 00 00 01 00 00 00-00 00 00 00 00 00 00 00   ..............
2F90:0180   54 45 4C 00 00 00 00 00-00 00 00 43 33 00 EB 81   TEL........C3...
2F90:0190   08 00 00 00 01 00 00 00-00 00 00 00 00 00 00 00   ..............
2F90:01A0   0D 20 5A 75 63 6B 65 72-6D 61 6E 20 20 20 20 20   . Zuckerman
2F90:01B0   20 41 64 64 69 73 6F 6E-20 42 2E 20 20 20 20 20   Addison B.
```

Checking the CPU registers with the DEBUG R (Register) command gives:

```
AX=0000  BX=0000  CX=0600  DX=0000  SP=FFEE  BP=0000  SI=0000  DI=0000
DS=3152  ES=3152  SS=3152  CS=3152  IP=0100     NV UP EI PL NZ NA PO NC
```

The BX/CX registers show the file size to be 600 hex. Hence, since the file starts at address 0100, it cannot extend beyond address 06FF. Therefore, we will search from address 01A1 to 06FF for nulls using the S (Search) command as follows:

```
-S 1A1 6FF 00
3152:0287
3152:0288
3152:0289
3152:028A
3152:028B
3152:028C
3152:028D
3152:028E
3152:028F
3152:0290
3152:0291
3152:0292
3152:0293
3152:0294
3152:0295
3152:0296
3152:0297
3152:0298
3152:0299
3152:029A
3152:029B
```

DEBUG reports 21 consecutive addresses containing nulls.

Although it is unnecessary, we can examine the data near these addresses using the Dump command as follows:

```
-D 240 2DF
4D59:0240  61 64 6C 65 79 20 41 2E-20 20 20 20 20 31 39 38  adley A.    198
4D59:0250  36 30 36 30 32 39 32 39-2D 32 38 37 33 20 56 61  60602929-2873 Va
4D59:0260  76 72 69 63 6B 20 20 20-20 20 20 20 43 68 61     vrick       Cha
4D59:0270  72 6C 65 73 20 45 2E 20-20 20 20 20 31 39 38 36  rles E.     1986
4D59:0280  30 36 30 33 36 38 34 00-00 00 00 00 00 00 00 00  0603684.........
4D59:0290  00 00 00 00 00 00 00 00-00 00 00 00 44 61 76 69  ............Davi
4D59:02A0  64 20 42 2E 20 20 20 20-20 20 20 31 39 38 36 30  d B.        19860
4D59:02B0  36 30 31 38 32 38 2D 37-33 37 31 20 53 74 65 65  601828-7371 Stee
4D59:02C0  6E 62 75 72 67 20 20 20-20 20 20 44 65 6E 69 73  nburg     Denis
4D59:02D0  65 20 52 2E 20 20 20 20-20 20 31 39 38 36 30 36  e R.      198606
```

Sure enough, we see the string of 21 nulls in addresses 0287 through 029B. They are the source of the problem. The simplest way to repair the file is to replace them with spaces (or legitimate data if you know what it should be). To overwrite the nulls with spaces, use the DEBUG F (Fill) command as follows:

```
F 0287 029B 20
```

The command fills 21 memory locations with the space character (20 hex), starting at address 0287. Then write the corrected file back to disk with the W (Write) command and exit from DEBUG with the Q (Quit) command. The job is done.

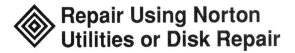

Repair Using Norton Utilities or Disk Repair

If Disk Repair had a search feature or if the Norton Utilities let you start a search at a particular location within a file, you could use them conveniently to repair the damage. Of course, you could have the Norton Utilities search for "David" or some other string near the damage. However, this is clumsy and time-consuming for a large file containing many instances of the search string. You could also scan the entire file visually for nulls, but this is also tedious and time-consuming for a large datafile.

As an example, let us use the Norton Utilities (Advanced Edition) to search for nulls in file PPD.DBF. After you specify the target file, Norton asks for the "Search data" on the following screen. Since you cannot use character format to specify a null, you must enter it in hex as shown in boldface below:

```
Menu 1.4.2
                          Text to Search For



        Search data, in character format:



      Tab switches between the character and hex windows



        Search data, in hexadecimal format:
        00


            1 character in search string


 Text to Search For                        Where to search
                                           ppd.dbf
```

Upon a successful find, the following screen appears:

```
Menu 1.4.3
                             Searching for data




                        Searching the file ppd.dbf


                                 Found!


                        Press any key to continue...




Text to Search For                               Where to search
                                                 ppd.dbf
```

When you press a key, the following screen appears. Norton has found the first null in the file (shown in boldface below). It is one of the many legitimate nulls in the header.

```
ppd.dbf                                                      Hex format
  Cluster 43, Sectors 94-95                       File offset 6, hex 6
03580915 27020000 E1014100 00000000 00000000 00000000  ♥X.§′ ..ß A...........
00000000 00000000 5055425F 49440000 00000043 01000000  ........PUB_ID.....C ...
03000000 00000000 00000000 4D414E5F 49440000  ♥..............MAN_ID..
00000043 04000000 03000000 00000000 00000000 00000000  ...♥♦...♥............
4D4B545F 49440000 00000043 07000000 03000000 00000000  MKT_ID.....C ...♥.......
00000000 00000000 50524F44 5F494400 00000043 0A000000  ........PROD_ID..C....
03000000 00000000 00000000 00000000 51315F45 58500000  ♥..............Q1_EXP..
0000004E 0D000000 07000000 00000000 00000000 00000000  ...N... ............
51315F50 41474553 0000004E 14000000 03000000 00000000  Q1_PAGES...N ...♥.......
00000000 00000000 51325F45 58500000 0000004E 17000000  ........Q2_EXP.....N ...
07000000 00000000 00000000 00000000 51325F50 41474553   ..............Q2_PAGES
0000004E 1E000000 03000000 00000000 00000000 00000000  ...N ...♥...............
51335F45 58500000 0000004E 21000000 07000000 00000000  Q3_EXP.....N!... .......
00000000 00000000 51335F50 41474553 0000004E 28000000  ........Q3_PAGES...N(...
03000000 00000000 00000000 00000000 51345F45 58500000  ♥..............Q4_EXP..
0000004E 2B000000 07000000 00000000 00000000 00000000  ...N+... ...............
51345F50 41474553 0000004E 32000000 03000000 00000000  Q4_PAGES...N2...♥.......
00000000 00000000 414C4C51 45000000 0000004E 35000000  ........ALLQE......N5...
08000000 00000000 00000000 00000000 414C4C51 50000000   ..............ALLQP...
0000004E 3D000000 04000000 00000000 00000000 00000000  ...N=...♦...............
0D202020 31202031 20203120 20312020 20202020 30202030  .   1  1   1   1        0  0
20202020 20203020           Press Enter to continue        0
1Help   2Hex   3Text   4Dir   5FAT   6Partn  7      8      9Undo   10QuitNU
```

To find nulls in the record area, you must repeat the search until you eventually pass beyond the header. In our case, the header has 438 nulls, so the process takes a long time and many keystrokes. It's like searching for "the" or "and" in a document. You could also compare it to riding the local bus from Los Angeles to New York - 438 stops are somewhat annoying.

 ## Repair Using DiskMinder

In the Directory Editing Mode of DiskMinder, a display like the one below appears.

```
Directory Editing Mode                                         DiskMinder
[Esc] Displays Main Menu

 Filename.Ext    Size    Date      Time    Attr Clu  Reserved
 R6      .FOX   13694  08/27/88  12:01:16   20  0002  000000000000000000000
 R6      .PRG   26803  08/27/88  12:00:14   20  0010  000000000000000000000
 PPD     .DBF   36297  09/21/88  11:06:10   20  002B  000000000000000000000
         .          0  00/00/80  00:00:00   00  0000  000000000000000000000
         .          0  00/00/80  00:00:00   00  0000  000000000000000000000
         .          0  00/00/80  00:00:00   00  0000  000000000000000000000
         .          0  00/00/80  00:00:00   00  0000  000000000000000000000
         .          0  00/00/80  00:00:00   00  0000  000000000000000000000
         .          0  00/00/80  00:00:00   00  0000  000000000000000000000
         .          0  00/00/80  00:00:00   00  0000  000000000000000000000
         .          0  00/00/80  00:00:00   00  0000  000000000000000000000
         .          0  00/00/80  00:00:00   00  0000  000000000000000000000

 Editing Directory A:\
         Entry    3 of 112                  Cluster  n/aH  Sector        5
```

DiskMinder -- Copyright 1988 Westlake Data Corporation

After we use the arrow keys to highlight the PPD line and select the File Editing Mode, DM provides the following edit screen with the first byte of the file highlighted (shown here in boldface). The "offset" counter at the bottom verifies that the cursor is on the first byte.

```
File Editing Mode                                            DiskMinder
[Esc] Displays Main Menu

        +0 +1 +2 +3 +4 +5 +6 +7 +8 +9 +A +B +C +D +E +F    0   4   8   C
  0000  03 58 09 15 27 02 00 00 E1 01 41 00 00 00 00 00   ♥X.∧'..ß A.....
  0010  00 00 00 00 00 00 00 00 00 00 00 00 00 00 00 00   ...............
  0020  50 55 42 5F 49 44 00 00 00 00 00 43 01 00 00 00   PUB_ID.....C ...
  0030  03 00 00 00 00 00 00 00 00 00 00 00 00 00 00 00   ♥..............
  0040  4D 41 4E 5F 49 44 00 00 00 00 00 43 04 00 00 00   MAN_ID.....C♦...
  0050  03 00 00 00 00 00 00 00 00 00 00 00 00 00 00 00   ♥..............
  0060  4D 4B 54 5F 49 44 00 00 00 00 00 43 07 00 00 00   MKT_ID.....C ...
  0070  03 00 00 00 00 00 00 00 00 00 00 00 00 00 00 00   ♥..............
  0080  50 52 4F 44 5F 49 44 00 00 00 00 43 0A 00 00 00   PROD_ID....C....
  0090  03 00 00 00 00 00 00 00 00 00 00 00 00 00 00 00   ♥..............
  00A0  51 31 5F 45 58 50 00 00 00 00 00 4E 0D 00 00 00   Q1_EXP.....N....
  00B0  07 00 00 00 00 00 00 00 00 00 00 00 00 00 00 00   ...............
  00C0  51 31 5F 50 41 47 45 53 00 00 00 4E 14 00 00 00   Q1_PAGES...N ...
  00D0  03 00 00 00 00 00 00 00 00 00 00 00 00 00 00 00   ♥..............
  00E0  51 32 5F 45 58 50 00 00 00 00 00 4E 17 00 00 00   Q2_EXP.....N ...
  00F0  07 00 00 00 00 00 00 00 00 00 00 00 00 00 00 00   ...............

Editing File A:\PPD.DBF
Offset        0 of 36,296                 Cluster 002BH  Sector      94
```

DiskMinder -- Copyright 1988 Westlake Data Corporation

After we press the PgDn key to display the next 256 bytes of the file, we see the end of the header (0D) at address 01E0, as you can see below. Using the arrow keys, we move the cursor to the first byte of the first record (at offset 481, shown in boldface), the point at which we will start searching for nulls.

```
File Editing Mode                                            DiskMinder
[Esc] Displays Main Menu

        +0 +1 +2 +3 +4 +5 +6 +7 +8 +9 +A +B +C +D +E +F    0   4   8   C
  0100  51 32 5F 50 41 47 45 53 00 00 00 4E 1E 00 00 00   Q2_PAGES...N ...
  0110  03 00 00 00 00 00 00 00 00 00 00 00 00 00 00 00   ♥..............
  0120  51 33 5F 45 58 50 00 00 00 00 00 4E 21 00 00 00   Q3_EXP.....N!...
  0130  07 00 00 00 00 00 00 00 00 00 00 00 00 00 00 00   ♥..............
  0140  51 33 5F 50 41 47 45 53 00 00 00 4E 28 00 00 00   Q3_PAGES...N(...
  0150  03 00 00 00 00 00 00 00 00 00 00 00 00 00 00 00   ♥..............
  0160  51 34 5F 45 58 50 00 00 00 00 00 4E 2B 00 00 00   Q4_EXP.....N+...
  0170  07 00 00 00 00 00 00 00 00 00 00 00 00 00 00 00   ♥..............
  0180  51 34 5F 50 41 47 45 53 00 00 00 4E 32 00 00 00   Q4_PAGES...N2...
  0190  03 00 00 00 00 00 00 00 00 00 00 00 00 00 00 00   ♥..............
  01A0  41 4C 4C 51 45 00 00 00 00 00 00 4E 35 00 00 00   ALLQE......N5...
  01B0  08 00 00 00 00 00 00 00 00 00 00 00 00 00 00 00   ...............
  01C0  41 4C 4C 51 50 00 00 00 00 00 00 4E 3D 00 00 00   ALLQP......N=...
  01D0  04 00 00 00 00 00 00 00 00 00 00 00 00 00 00 00   ♦..............
  01E0  0D 20 20 20 31 20 20 31 20 20 31 20 20 31 20 20   .   1  1  1  1
  01F0  20 20 20 20 30 20 20 30 20 20 20 20 20 20 30 20      0  0      0

Editing File A:\PPD.DBF
Offset      481 of 36,296                 Cluster 002BH  Sector      94
```

DiskMinder -- Copyright 1988 Westlake Data Corporation

We now select the "Find" option. DM produces the following display near the center of the screen, allowing us to specify the search character. Since the default is nulls, we need only press the Enter key to start.

```
Data to find:
00 00 00 00 00 00 00 00    ........
00 00 00 00 00 00 00 00    ........
00 00 00 00 00 00 00 00    ........
00 00 00 00 00 00 00 00    ........
```

DiskMinder moves the cursor to the first byte in the record area of the file that contains a null (shown in boldface below). It displays the appropriate region of the file for editing.

```
File Editing Mode                                              DiskMinder
[Esc] Displays Main Menu

      +0 +1 +2 +3 +4 +5 +6 +7 +8 +9 +A +B +C +D +E +F   0    4    8    C
0000  20 20 20 20 20 20 20 20 20 20 20 20 30 20 20 20                  0
0010  30 20 20 31 31 20 20 32 20 20 32 20 20 31 20 20   0   11   2    2   1
0020  20 20 20 20 20 20 20 20 20 20 20 20 20 20 20 20
0030  20 20 20 20 20 20 20 20 20 20 20 20 20 20 20 20
0040  20 20 20 20 20 20 00 20 20 20 20 20 30 20 20           .         0
0050  20 30 20 20 31 32 20 20 32 20 20 32 20 20 31 20   0   12   2    2   1
0060  20 20 20 20 20 20 20 20 20 20 20 20 20 20 20 20
0070  20 20 20 20 20 20 20 20 20 20 20 20 20 20 20 20
0080  20 20 20 20 20 20 20 20 20 20 20 20 20 20 30 20                   0
0090  20 20 30 20 20 31 33 20 20 32 20 20 31 20 20 31   0   13   2    1   1
00A0  20 20 20 20 20 20 20 20 20 20 20 20 20 20 20 20
00B0  20 20 20 20 20 20 20 20 20 20 20 20 20 20 20 20
00C0  20 20 20 20 20 20 20 20 20 20 20 20 20 20 20 30                   0
00D0  20 20 20 30 20 20 31 34 20 20 32 20 20 32 20 20       0   14   2   2
00E0  31 20 20 20 20 20 20 20 20 20 20 20 20 20 20 20   1
00F0  20 20 20 20 20 20 20 20 20 20 20 20 20 20 20 20

Editing File A:\PPD.DBF
Offset        3,654 of 36,296              Cluster 002EH  Sector      101
```

DiskMinder -- Copyright 1988 Westlake Data Corporation

We can now replace the null with a space simply by typing "20" over the "00." An alternative is to switch the cursor to the right side of the screen (over the boldface dot) and press the space bar.

Alternatively, we could use DiskMinder's Search and Replace feature to find all the nulls in the file's records and replace them with spaces.

In summary, with the Norton Utilities, you must select "Continue the Search" many times to work your way through the header before you can start searching for nulls in the file's records. With DiskMinder, you can place the cursor on the first byte of the first record and start the search there.

Repair Using dSALVAGE Professional

The simplest, fastest way to diagnose and repair a datafile containing nulls is with dSALVAGE Professional's built-in recovery procedures. The program automatically diagnoses the file damage, locates the nulls, and converts them to spaces with a single keystroke. You can also use its editors to do the repair. We will demonstrate both approaches, since the latter is sometimes faster for large continuous regions of nulls.

Nulls Restricted to One or Two Consecutive Records

We start with a file that has nulls in just one or two records, as in the NULFILE example. After invoking dSALVAGE Professional, selecting NULFILE, and asking the program to check it for damage, we get the following diagnostic report:

```
┌─────────────────────────────────────────────────────────────────────┐
│ INPUT FILE........ NULFILE.DBF      dBASE VERSION..... DBASE-III+ / IV │
│ HEADER SIZE....... 161              LAST UPDATED...... 9-2-88          │
│ FIELDS PER RECORD. 4                TOTAL RECORDS..... 19              │
│ FILE SIZE......... 1536             RECORD SIZE....... 47              │
│                                     CLUSTER SIZE...... 2048            │
│ CURRENT DIRECTORY. C:\                                                 │
│ OUTPUT WRITTEN TO. C:\NULFILE.DBF                                      │
│ DIRECTORY FILTER.. *.DBF            RECOMMENDED REPAIR: none           │
├──────────────────── Diagnosis & Repair Menu ────────────────────────┤
│                                                                       │
│    F1  Help                         F3  Internal Damage Repair        │
├───────────────────────────────────────────────────────────────────────┤
│ File contains record damage (Class 1 or Class 4).                     │
│ 17 records match header pattern out of expected 19                    │
│ Record(s) contain binary (less than hex 20) data.                     │
│ Deleted flag in record(s) invalid (not * or space).                   │
│ CLASS 1 repair is recommended:  Press Enter, then F3, then F2         │
│   or Press Enter then F5 to Execute Recommended Repair                 │
│ No dBASE header errors detected.                                       │
│ No unwanted EOF's detected in file.                                   │
│                                                                       │
│                                                                       │
└──────────────────── Press Enter to Continue ───────────────────────┘
```

Note that dSALVAGE Professional analyzes the damage in detail and recommends Class 1 repair. If we follow the recommendation by pressing Enter and F5, the file is positioned at the first record containing damage. The following screen appears:

```
 _____ Class 1 Repair Commands _____
| F1 Help                                 ALT-T      Check Record      |
| F2 Count Good Records  F10  Hide/Show Menu  HOME/END   First/Last Record  |
| F4 Fix Record          PgUp Prev Record   ^PgUp/^PgDn Vert Screen Scroll  |
| F5 Continue From Here  PgDn Next Record   ^HOME/^END  Horiz Screen Scroll |
|_____ Press ESC to Return to Internal Repair Menu _____|

 _____
| DELETEFLAG :                                                       |
|    SURNAME : Vavrick                                               |
|      FNAME : Charles E.                                            |
|   LASTTRAN : 19860603                                             |
|        TEL : 684                                                  |
|            :                                                       |
|            :                                                       |
|            :                                                       |
|            :                                                       |
|            :                                                       |
|            :                                                       |
|            :                                                       |
|            :                                                       |
|            :                                                       |
|            :                                                       |
|_____|
            binary   Record 5           file position 350
```

The illustration above does not depict the blank cell (just after the "4" of "684" in the TEL field) that you see on the screen.

At this point, all we must do is press the F4 key to repair the record. However, we will use the opportunity to illustrate additional features of dSALVAGE Professional.

The missing characters in the TEL field, the record number indicator, and the word "binary" at the bottom of the screen indicate that record 5 contains control or graphics characters. Since we do not see any strange characters (aside from a non-highlighted blank immediately after the "4" in the TEL field), we press the F1 key for Help to see the available options. The second page of the Help screen (shown next) reveals that pressing Alt-T analyzes the displayed record for damage.

```
───────────────── Class 1 Repair Commands ─────────────
 F1 Help                                   ALT-T      Check Record
 F2 Count Good Records   F10  Hide/Show Menu   HOME/END    First/Last Record
 F4 Fix Record           PgUp Prev Record      ^PgUp/^PgDn Vert Screen Scroll
 F5 Continue From Here   PgDn Next Record      ^HOME/^END  Horiz Screen Scroll
  ───────────── Press ESC to Return to Internal Repair Menu ──────────
```

```
 DELETEFLAG :
    SURNAME : Vavrick
      FNAME : Charles E.
   LASTTRAN : 19860603
        TEL : 684
            :
            :
```

```
                the Right and Left Arrow keys.  If the field extends beyond the
                righthand window boundary, the window is scrolled horizontally.

 ALT-T          Provides a diagnosis of the record currently being displayed.

 PgUp/PgDn      Move to previous/next record in the file.

 HOME/END       Move to the first/last record in the file.

 ^PgUp/^PgDn    CTRL-PgUp/CTRL-PgDn scrolls fields one screen-full at a time.
  ───────── Pg-Up,Pg-Dn,↑,↓, for rest of message, press Enter to Continue ───────
```

After pressing Alt-T, we see the following diagnostic message at the bottom:

```
───────────────── Class 1 Repair Commands ─────────────
 F1 Help                                   ALT-T      Check Record
 F2 Count Good Records   F10  Hide/Show Menu   HOME/END    First/Last Record
 F4 Fix Record           PgUp Prev Record      ^PgUp/^PgDn Vert Screen Scroll
 F5 Continue From Here   PgDn Next Record      ^HOME/^END  Horiz Screen Scroll
  ───────────── Press ESC to Return to Internal Repair Menu ──────────
```

```
 DELETEFLAG :
    SURNAME : Vavrick
      FNAME : Charles E.
   LASTTRAN : 19860603
        TEL : 684
            :
            :
```

```
 File contains record damage (Class 1 or Class 4).
 Record(s) contain binary (less than hex 20) data.




  ───────────────── Press Enter to Continue ──────────
```

After pressing the Enter key to clear the diagnostic, we only have to press the F4 key to convert the troublesome characters to spaces, thereby repairing the record. Then we press the PgDn key to move to the next record, which we also suspect contains nulls. Alternatively, we could select the Continue-from-Here option to automatically locate and repair additional damaged records. The absence of data in the SURNAME field of the next record, together with non-highlighted areas in the display, suggests the presence of additional nulls. Furthermore, the "error" message at the bottom of the screen indicates damage in this record. Pressing Alt-T again to diagnose the record, we see:

```
┌───────────────────── Class 1 Repair Commands ─────────────────────┐
│ F1 Help                                ALT-T      Check Record     │
│ F2 Count Good Records  F10  Hide/Show Menu  HOME/END    First/Last Record  │
│ F4 Fix Record          PgUp Prev Record   ^PgUp/^PgDn Vert Screen Scroll  │
│ F5 Continue From Here  PgDn Next Record   ^HOME/^END  Horiz Screen Scroll  │
└──────────────── Press ESC to Return to Internal Repair Menu ───────┘
┌───────────────────────────────────────────────────────────────────┐
│ DELETEFLAG :                                                       │
│    SURNAME :                                                       │
│      FNAME : David B.                                              │
│   LASTTRAN : 19860601                                             │
│        TEL : 828-7371                                             │
│            :                                                       │
│            :                                                       │
└───────────────────────────────────────────────────────────────────┘
┌───────────────────────────────────────────────────────────────────┐
│ File contains record damage (Class 1 or Class 4).                 │
│ Record(s) contain binary (less than hex 20) data.                 │
│ Deleted flag in record(s) invalid (not * or space).               │
│                                                                    │
│                                                                    │
│                                                                    │
│                                                                    │
│                                                                    │
└────────────────────── Press Enter to Continue ────────────────────┘
```

We now have confirmation of control characters in the record. Once more, we press Enter to clear the message and F4 to fix the record. Continuing to advance through the next record or two, we see no further damage, at least in this area of the file. Hence, we can return to the Diagnosis and Repair menu and check the file for damage again. dSALVAGE gives it a clean bill of health, indicating that it contains no further damage.

In this example, we performed non-essential actions to show the Help screen and the individual record diagnoses. You would normally bypass them in an actual recovery situation.

Nulls Occupying a Larger Region

Let's now look at a file that contains a large block of nulls. Our sample file NULFILE2 contains 80 records. When viewed in the dBASE III PLUS BROWSE mode, it appears as:

```
SURNAME-------- FNAME---------- LASTTRAN TEL-----
Tomlinson       Blake           06/02/86 733-8729
Werner          Bradley A.      06/02/86 929-2873
Vavrick         Cha




                06/01/86 482-8342
     Liva       Kerney          06/18/86 499-1873
```

```
     BROWSE          |<C:>|NULFILE2          |Rec: 19/80
                       View and edit fields.
```

Note the large blank area. Pressing the down arrow key repeatedly moves the cursor down from record to record normally. But once it reaches the line starting with "06/01/86", we cannot move it up again to earlier records. A LISTing of the file shows:

```
. list
Record#  SURNAME       FNAME          LASTTRAN TEL
      1  Zuckerman     Addison B.     07/10/86 882-8264
      2  Wood          Anthony G.     06/01/86 827-3741
      3  Tomlinson     Blake          06/02/86 733-8729
      4  Werner        Bradley A.     06/02/86 929-2873
      5  Vavrick       Cha            01/.)/00
      6                               01/.)/00
      7                               01/.)/00
      8                               01/.)/00
      9                               01/.)/00
     10                               01/.)/00
     11                               01/.)/00
     12                               01/.)/00
     13                               01/.)/00
     14                               01/.)/00
     15                               01/.)/00
     16                               01/.)/00
     17                               01/.)/00
     18                               06/01/86 482-8342
     19  Liva          Kerney         06/18/86 499-1873
     20  Learmouth     Louis D.       06/19/86 919-2838
     21  Blessington   Michael        06/01/86 727-8273
     22  Koehler       Michael A.     06/02/86 749-2946
     23  Kennett       Mohan S.       06/15/86 827-6419
      .        .             .             .        .
      .        .             .             .        .
      .        .             .             .        .
```

Note that the listing appears normal from the 19th record on.

We now run dSALVAGE Professional to check the file for damage. We see the same diagnostic message as before:

```
INPUT FILE........ NULFILE2.DBF      dBASE VERSION..... DBASE-III+ / IV
HEADER SIZE....... 161               LAST UPDATED...... 9-4-88
FIELDS PER RECORD. 4                 TOTAL RECORDS..... 80
FILE SIZE......... 3922              RECORD SIZE....... 47
                                     CLUSTER SIZE...... 2048
CURRENT DIRECTORY. C:\
OUTPUT WRITTEN TO. C:\NULFILE2.DBF
DIRECTORY FILTER.. *.DBF             RECOMMENDED REPAIR: none

─────────────────── Diagnosis & Repair Menu ───────────────────

     F1  Help                        F3  Internal Damage Repair

File contains record damage (Class 1 or Class 4).
66 records match header pattern out of expected 80
Record(s) contain binary (less than hex 20) data.
Deleted flag in record(s) invalid (not * or space).
CLASS 1 repair is recommended:  Press Enter, then F3, then F2
   or Press Enter then F5 to Execute Recommended Repair
No dBASE header errors detected.
No unwanted EOF's detected in file.

──────────────────── Press Enter to Continue ────────────────────
```

Instead of using dSALVAGE's automatic repair here, we will use the Hex Editor to illustrate another way to repair the damage. After selecting the file and invoking the Editor Menu, we see the following screen:

```
INPUT FILE........ NULFILE2.DBF      dBASE VERSION..... DBASE-III+ / IV
HEADER SIZE....... 161               LAST UPDATED...... 9-4-88
FIELDS PER RECORD. 4                 TOTAL RECORDS..... 80
FILE SIZE......... 3922              RECORD SIZE....... 47
                                     CLUSTER SIZE...... 512
CURRENT DIRECTORY. C:\
OUTPUT WRITTEN TO. C:\NULFILE2.DBF
DIRECTORY FILTER.. *.DBF             RECOMMENDED REPAIR: none

───────────────────────── Editor Menu ─────────────────────────

   F1   Help            F3   Record Editor         F5   Hex Editor
   F2   Header Editor   F4   Byte-Stream Editor

────────────────── Press ESC to return to Main Menu ──────────────────
```

Upon pressing the F5 function key to select the Hex Editor, we see the following screen:

```
──────────────────── Hex Editor Commands ────────────────────
 F1       Help          PgUp  Prev Screen          HOME  Beginning of File
 F10      Hide/Show Menu PgDn  Next Screen          END   End of File
 ALT-S    Search         Arrow keys to move cursor  TAB   Hex  ASCII Display
 ALT-A    Repeat Search
──────────────── Press ESC to Return to Editor Menu ─────────────────
```

```
03 59 01 0E 50 00 00 00 A1 00 2F 00 00 00 00 00   ♥Y P     i /
00 00 00 00 00 00 00 00 00 00 00 00 00 00 00 00
53 55 52 4E 41 4D 45 00 00 00 00 00 43 11 00 3B 4C   SURNAME    C ;L
0F 00 00 00 01 00 00 00 00 00 00 00 00 00 00 00
46 4E 41 4D 45 00 00 00 00 00 00 43 20 00 3B 4C   FNAME      C  ;L
0F 00 00 00 01 00 00 00 00 00 00 00 00 00 00 00
4C 41 53 54 54 52 41 4E 00 00 00 44 71 00 3B 4C   LASTTRAN   Dq ;L
08 00 00 00 01 00 00 00 00 00 00 00 00 00 00 00
54 45 4C 00 00 00 00 00 00 00 00 00 43 7E 00 3B 4C   TEL        C~ ;L
08 00 00 00 01 00 00 00 00 00 00 00 00 00 00 00
0D 20 5A 75 63 6B 65 72 6D 61 6E 20 20 20 20 20   . Zuckerman
20 41 64 64 69 73 6F 6E 20 42 2E 20 20 20 20 20    Addison B.
31 39 38 36 30 37 31 30 38 38 32 2D 38 32 36 34   19860710882-8264
20 57 6F 6F 64 20 20 20 20 20 20 20 20 20 20 20    Wood
41 6E 74 68 6F 6E 79 20 47 2E 20 20 20 20 20 31   Anthony G.      1
39 38 36 30 36 30 31 38 32 37 2D 33 37 34 31 20   9860601827-3741
```

```
                    Record 1            file position 162
```

Although the header is displayed and is available for editing, the cursor (not shown above) is initially positioned at the first byte of the first record, as you can see from the Record and File Position counters at the bottom of the screen. You can reach the offending nulls either by searching the file with the editor's Search feature or by simple paging. In either case, you will see the following screen:

```
──────────────────── Hex Editor Commands ────────────────────
 F1·      Help          PgUp  Prev Screen          HOME  Beginning of File
 F10      Hide/Show Menu PgDn  Next Screen          END   End of File
 ALT-S    Search         Arrow keys to move cursor  TAB   Hex  ASCII Display
 ALT-A    Repeat Search
──────────────── Press ESC to Return to Editor Menu ─────────────────
```

```
54 6F 6D 6C 69 6E 73 6F 6E 20 20 20 20 20 20 42   Tomlinson      B
6C 61 6B 65 20 20 20 20 20 20 20 20 20 20 31 39   lake          19
38 36 30 36 30 32 37 33 33 2D 38 37 32 39 20 57   860602733-8729 W
65 72 6E 65 72 20 20 20 20 20 20 20 20 20 42 72   erner         Br
61 64 6C 65 79 20 41 2E 20 20 20 20 20 31 39 38   adley A.     198
36 30 36 30 32 39 32 39 2D 32 38 37 33 20 56 61   60602929-2873 Va
76 72 69 63 6B 20 20 20 20 20 20 20 20 43 68 61   vrick        Cha
00 00 00 00 00 00 00 00 00 00 00 00 00 00 00 00
00 00 00 00 00 00 00 00 00 00 00 00 00 00 00 00
00 00 00 00 00 00 00 00 00 00 00 00 00 00 00 00
00 00 00 00 00 00 00 00 00 00 00 00 00 00 00 00
00 00 00 00 00 00 00 00 00 00 00 00 00 00 00 00
00 00 00 00 00 00 00 00 00 00 00 00 00 00 00 00
00 00 00 00 00 00 00 00 00 00 00 00 00 00 00 00
00 00 00 00 00 00 00 00 00 00 00 00 00 00 00 00
00 00 00 00 00 00 00 00 00 00 00 00 00 00 00 00
```

```
                    Record 5            file position 369
```

The easiest way to replace the nulls with spaces or valid data is to press the Tab key to switch from the hex display (on the left) to the ASCII display (on the right). Then type legitimate characters (such as spaces) over the nulls.

We can also use dSALVAGE's Byte Stream Editor (see Chapter 22) to repair the damage. Upon selecting the Byte Stream Editor, we see the following screen:

```
┌──────────────────── Byte Stream Editor Commands ────────────────────┐
│ F1     Help        │ALT-B Mark Block │ALT-W Write Block│ALT-F Write File│
│ F10    Hide/Show Menu│ALT-M Move Block │ALT-G Goto Byte  │PgUp/PgDn       │
│ ALT-S Search       │ALT-C Copy Block │ALT-U Undelete   │HOME Top of File│
│ ALT-A Repeat Search│ALT-D Delete Block│ALT-P Paste File │END  End of File│
└──────────────────── Press ESC to Return to Editor Menu ─────────────┘

┌─────────────────────────────────────────────────────────────────┐
│   Zuckerman      Addison B.    19860710882-8264 Wood          A  │
│ nthony G.      19860601827-3741 Tomlinson      Blake         198 │
│ 60602733-8729 Werner        Bradley A.    19860602929-2873 Vav   │
│ rick         Cha                                                 │
│                                                                  │
│                                                                  │
│                                                                  │
│                                                                  │
│                                                                  │
│                                                                  │
│                                                              19  │
│ 860601482-8342 Liva        Kerney        19860618499-1873 Le     │
│ armouth       Louis D.    19860619919-2838 Blessington    Mich  │
│ ael        19860601727-8273 Koehler      Michael A.     198606  │
└─────────────────────────────────────────────────────────────────┘
                    Record 1        file position 162
```

The easiest way to replace the nulls with spaces or valid data is to move the cursor to the first character position beyond "Cha" and type legitimate characters (such as spaces). Continue until you reach the location just left of the "19" on the fourth line from the end of the window. The repair is done, and the file will appear normal when examined with dBASE.

As an alternative, you could mark the region of nulls as a block (in the Byte Stream Editor) and then delete it. This would, of course, create an offset in the file (unless the number of deleted characters happened to be an integral multiple of the record size).

 Summary

Class 1 damage is characterized by control or graphics characters in a datafile's records. A particularly troublesome form involves nulls in the records. You must find and remove them to restore file integrity. DiskMinder's Search or Search and Replace features are useful for this purpose after you have diagnosed the problem. dSALVAGE Professional has the advantage of combining diagnosis and repair.

15

Repair of Class 2 Damage: Extra End-of-File Markers

The most common form of damage involves extra end-of-file markers in the record area of the file. It is also one of the simplest forms to diagnose and repair. Chapter 13 describes the symptom of this type of damage. If you can afford to lose the records containing the markers, you can repair the file within dBASE. Although this solution is generally unacceptable, we include it here for completeness. If you cannot afford to lose a single record, there are alternatives.

If the file is small, you can repair the damage with DEBUG. If it is large, other tools are better, depending on the number of markers. In choosing among tools, the issues are efficiency and speed. The Norton Utilities, for example, let you find markers one at a time and change them to spaces manually. DiskMinder provides a search-and-replace feature that proceeds through the file, stopping at each marker and changing it to a space upon your authorization. dSALVAGE automatically finds all end-of-file markers in the file's records. It can also convert them all (excluding the legitimate one at the true end of the file) to spaces in a single operation upon your authorization.

Remember that a record containing an extra end-of-file marker also still contains the original data. It need not be lost in the recovery process.

Remember also that end-of-file markers (ASCII value 1A hex or 26 decimal) may appear legitimately in the file header. For example, a field having a width of 26 or a date of last update containing 26 (such as March 26, 1989) will produce an end-of-file marker in the header.

 # Recovery Using dBASE

We will first consider the case in which you are willing to sacrifice a record. Presumably it is not your oldest, largest, and fastest-paying customer.

It is usually easy to determine whether a file contains extra end-of-file markers since there are telltale signs. The most obvious is a discrepancy between the number of records indicated in the file structure and the number displayed in a listing. An attempt to GOTO the next record number following a LISTing produces a "Record is out of range" error message. If, however, you give a SKIP command, dBASE will position the file pointer at the first record beyond the one containing the extra marker. The GOTO command can also move the pointer beyond the troublesome record.

Let's say your file contains 500 records, but it has an end-of-file marker just after record 200. If you LIST STRUCTURE, the display will indicate 500 records in the file. LIST, however, will display only 200. If you give a GOTO 201 command after the listing, dBASE reports, "Record is out of range." But if you give the command SKIP or GOTO 202, dBASE moves the file pointer to record 202 and displays the dot prompt. If you give the LIST REST command after the initial 200 record display, you will see the rest of the file data except for record 201. Whatever you do, you cannot see the data in the record containing the marker (although its record number will appear).

Regardless of file size, repairing this kind of damage is easy. As we mentioned, you can do it from within dBASE if you don't mind losing a record. Merely copy the records before the one with the marker to a new file, copy the ones after it to a second file, and then combine the two files with the dBASE APPEND command. You will lose one record in the process.

Let's examine this procedure for the case described above. We call the file BADFILE.DBF. Enter the following commands at the dot prompt:

```
USE BADFILE
COPY TO GOODFILE
COPY REST TO TEMP
USE GOODFILE
APPEND FROM TEMP
```

GOODFILE.DBF is the same as BADFILE.DBF except that the record with the end-of-file marker is missing. Besides the absolute certainty of losing a record, this procedure has other risks. One is that you may not have enough disk space for the copies. Another is that there may be a second extra end-of-file marker later in the original file. It will prevent a single COPY REST command from actually copying the rest of the file. In such a case, you will need another COPY REST, and you will end up losing two records. Murphy's Law, of course, states that these records will be the most important ones in the file.

 ## Recovery Using DEBUG

A far better solution to the Class 2 damage problem is to remove the extra marker(s) by converting them to spaces. No record data is then lost. As explained earlier, an extra end-of-file marker is just a Ctrl-Z (1A hex) character in the delete status byte of a valid record. If the character were anywhere else in a record, it would get no special treatment. But when it appears in the delete status byte, dBASE regards it as an end-of-file marker. All you must do to repair Class 2 damage, therefore, is to locate any Ctrl-Z characters in the records and change them to spaces (20 hex). If the file is small, you can do this easily with DEBUG.

For example, consider the simple datafile CC2.DBF with the following structure:

```
Structure for database: cc2.dbf
Number of data records:      18
Date of last update   : 09/01/88
Field  Field Name  Type       Width    Dec
    1  SURNAME     Character     15
    2  FNAME       Character     15
    3  LASTTRAN    Date           8
    4  TEL         Character      8
** Total **                      47
```

Although the structure indicates 18 records, a LISTing displays only 9, indicating the probable presence of an extra end-of-file marker.

```
Record#  SURNAME        FNAME          LASTTRAN TEL
      1  Zuckerman      Addison B.     07/10/86 882-8264
      2  Wood           Anthony G.     06/01/86 827-3741
      3  Tomlinson      Blake          06/02/86 733-8729
      4  Werner         Bradley A.     06/02/86 929-2873
      5  Vavrick        Charles E.     06/03/86 684-3838
      6  Swartwout      David B.       06/01/86 828-7371
      7  Smith          Donald S.      07/10/86 929-4188
      8  Sherman        Edward L.      06/28/86 237-2724
      9  Schaeffer      Evan J.        06/30/86 929-2473
    .
```

Continuing the LISTing with the **LIST REST** command, we see:

```
. list rest
Record#  SURNAME        FNAME          LASTTRAN TEL
     10                                  /  /
     11  Reilly         Gerard J.      07/07/86 882-7874
     12  Peek           Jack           06/01/86 292-9494
     13  Orcutt         James G.       07/08/86 526-1587
     14  Mench          John J.        07/12/86 834-8269
     15  Mayberry       John P.        07/06/86 923-9199
     16  Mancini        Joseph A.      06/01/86 482-8342
     17  Liva           Kerney         06/18/86 499-1873
     18  Learmouth      Louis D.       06/19/86 919-2838
    .
```

Note that record 10 (the one immediately before Gerard Reilly's) seems to be blank. Let's try moving the file pointer to it with the GOTO command:

```
. GOTO 10
Record is out of range.
        ?
GOTO 10
    .
```

dBASE's "Record is out of range" message provides further evidence that there is a Ctrl-Z (1A hex) in the first byte of record 10.

Since CC2.DBF is a small file that fits in memory, we use DEBUG to repair it. We start by examining the CPU registers with the R (Register) command.

```
C:\DEBUG CC2.DBF
-R
AX=0000  BX=0000  CX=0400  DX=0000  SP=FFEE  BP=0000  SI=0000  DI=0000
DS=34AF  ES=34AF  SS=34AF  CS=34AF  IP=0100   NV UP EI PL NZ NA PO NC
```

The BX/CX registers indicate that the file is 400 hex (1024 decimal) bytes long. Its memory image therefore occupies addresses 0100 through 04FF. We do not need to examine it for extra end-of-file markers. We need only search for 1A hex in its memory image. Specifically, we give the command

```
-S 100 4FF 1A
```

DEBUG responds with the following addresses:

```
34AF:0348
34AF:04EF
```

Incidentally, you can easily determine if either address contains the true end-of-file marker. Merely add the header length to the length of the record area, and add 100 hex (DEBUG's load address offset) as follows:

header length	$= (4 \times 32) + 33$	$=$	161 decimal	$=$	00A1 hex
record area	$= 18 \times 47$	$=$	846 decimal	$=$	034E hex
load offset		$=$	256 decimal	$=$	0100 hex
Total		$=$	**1263 decimal**	$=$	**04EF hex**

Hence, you conclude correctly that the true EOF is at address 04EF. The other one is probably the extra marker that caused the problem. You should confirm this by examining the area around address 0348 to see whether the 1A is in the delete status byte of the record immediately preceding the Reilly record. Dumping memory from 0330 on shows the following:

```
-D 330 3AF
34AF:0330  20 20 20 20 20 20 20 20-31 39 38 36 30 36 33 30         19860630
34AF:0340  39 32 39 2D 32 34 37 33-1A 52 6F 6F 66 20 20 20   929-2473.Roof
34AF:0350  20 20 20 20 20 20 20 20-46 72 65 64 65 72 69 63          Frederic
34AF:0360  6B 20 45 2E 20 20 20 31-39 38 36 30 38 31 32 32   k E.  198608122
34AF:0370  35 34 2D 39 39 39 32 20-52 65 69 6C 6C 79 20 20   54-9992 Reilly
34AF:0380  20 20 20 20 20 20 20 20-47 65 72 61 72 64 20 4A 2E        Gerard J.
34AF:0390  20 20 20 20 20 20 31 39-38 36 30 37 30 37 38 38       1986070788
34AF:03A0  32 2D 37 38 37 34 20 50-65 65 6B 20 20 20 20 20   2-7874 Peek
```

Sure enough, 0348 is the address of the delete status byte. It is therefore the extra end-of-file marker that we are trying to find. The only thing left to do is to change it to a space, which we can do with DEBUG's Enter command:

```
-E 348 20
```

Now write the modified file back to disk and exit from DEBUG.

Finally, we confirm the repair by opening the file in dBASE and LISTing it. The result is:

```
Record#  SURNAME      FNAME         LASTTRAN  TEL
      1  Zuckerman    Addison B.    07/10/86  882-8264
      2  Wood         Anthony G.    06/01/86  827-3741
      3  Tomlinson    Blake         06/02/86  733-8729
      4  Werner       Bradley A.    06/02/86  929-2873
      5  Vavrick      Charles E.    06/03/86  684-3838
      6  Swartwout    David B.      06/01/86  828-7371
      7  Smith        Donald S.     07/10/86  929-4188
      8  Sherman      Edward L.     06/28/86  237-2724
      9  Schaeffer    Evan J.       06/30/86  929-2473
     10  Roof         Frederick E.  08/12/86  254-9992
     11  Reilly       Gerard J.     07/07/86  882-7874
     12  Peek         Jack          06/01/86  292-9494
     13  Orcutt       James G.      07/08/86  526-1587
     14  Mench        John J.       07/12/86  834-8269
     15  Mayberry     John P.       07/06/86  923-9199
     16  Mancini      Joseph A.     06/01/86  482-8342
     17  Liva         Kerney        06/18/86  499-1873
     18  Learmouth    Louis D.      06/19/86  919-2838
```

The job is done. The file is intact, and the data in record 10 has not been lost.

Recovery Using Norton Utilities

The Norton Utilities (Advanced Edition) let you search for text in a target file. Once you find it, you can overwrite it manually. In our example, we will search for the end-of-file marker (1A hex). Norton's search screen appears as follows:

```
Menu 1.4.2
                              Text to Search For


              Search data, in character format:
              *


              Tab switches between the character and hex windows


              Search data, in hexadecimal format:
              1A



                    1 character in search string

 Text to Search For                          Where to search
   →                                         cc2.dbf
```

Note: A right arrow in the above and subsequent screens depicts an end-of-file marker Ctrl-Z (1A hex).

The following screen indicates a successful find:

```
Menu 1.4.3
                        Searching for data




                   Searching the file cc2.dbf


                             Found!


                   Press any key to continue...



 ┌──────────────────────────────────┬─────────────────────────┐
 │ Text to Search For               │ Where to search         │
 │  →                               │ cc2.dbf                 │
 └──────────────────────────────────┴─────────────────────────┘
```

When you press a key, the following screen appears in text format. The sought-for marker is in boldface. Here, the correct marker was found immediately, but this is not always the case. Remember that Norton's search always starts at the beginning of the file, and 1A's can appear legitimately in the file header. So repetitive search may be necessary to reach the troublesome one.

```
┌─ cc2.dbf ──────────────────────────────────── Text format ─┐
│  Cluster 322, Sectors 652-653          File offset 512, hex 200 │
│  more...                                                    │
│     L.      19860628237-2724 Schaeffer    Evan J.     19860630929-2473 │
│     end-file-markerRoof         Frederick E.   19860812254-9992 Reilly │
│         Gerard J.      19860707882-7874 Peek        Jack          198606 │
│  01292-9494 Orcutt        James G.     19860708526-1587 Mench  │
│  John J.        19860712834-8269 Mayberry      John P.        19860706923 │
│  -9199 Mancini        Joseph A.     19860601482-8342 Liva          Kerne │
│  y         19860618499-1873 Learmouth      Louis D.      19860619919-2838 │
│    arker                                                    │
│                                                             │
│                                                             │
│                                                             │
│                                                             │
│                                                             │
│                                                             │
│                    Press Enter to continue                  │
│  1Help   2Hex    3Text   4Dir    5FAT    6Partn  7     8      9Undo   10QuitNU │
└─────────────────────────────────────────────────────────────┘
```

Upon switching to the hex display, the following screen appears (marker shown in boldface):

```
┌─ cc2.dbf ──────────────────────────────────── Hex format ─┐
│ Cluster 322, Sectors 652-653              File offset 512, hex 200│
│204C2E20 20202020 20313938 36303632 38323337 2D323732  L.     19860628237-272│
│34205363 68616566 66657220 20202020 20457661 6E204A2E  4 Schaeffer      Evan J.│
│20202020 20202020 31393836 30363330 3932392D 32343733          19860630929-2473│
│1A526F6F 66202020 20202020 20202020 46726564 65726963  →Roof            Frederic│
│6B20452E 20202031 39383630 38313232 35342D39 39393220  k E.     19860812254-9992│
│5265696C 6C792020 20202020 20202047 65726172 64204A2E  Reilly           Gerard J.│
│20202020 20203139 38363037 30373838 322D3738 37342050          19860707882-7874 P│
│65656B20 20202020 20202020 20204A61 636B2020 20202020  eek              Jack│
│20202020 20313938 36303630 31323932 2D393439 34204F72           19860601292-9494 Or│
│63757474 20202020 20202020 204A616D 65732047 2E202020  cutt             James G.│
│20202020 31393836 30373038 3532362D 31353837 204D656E           19860708526-1587 Men│
│63682020 20202020 20202020 4A6F686E 204A2E20 20202020  ch               John J.│
│20202031 39383630 37313238 33342D38 32363920 4D617962          19860712834-8269 Mayb│
│65727279 20202020 2020204A 6F686E20 502E2020 20202020  erry         John P.│
│20203139 38363037 30363932 332D3931 3939204D 616E6369   19860706923-9199 Manci│
│6E692020 20202020 20204A6F 73657068 20412E20 20202020  ni           Joseph A.│
│20313938 36303630 31343832 2D383334 32204C69 76612020  19860601482-8342 Liva│
│20202020 20202020 204B6572 6E657920 20202020 20202020           Kerney│
│31393836 30363138 3439392D 31383733 204C6561 726D6F75  19860618499-1873 Learmou│
│74682020 20202020 4C6F7569 7320442E 20202020 20202031  th       Louis D.        1│
│39383630 36313939 31392D32 3833381A 4C697661 20202020  9860619919-2838│
└───────────────────────────────────────────────────────┘
```

It is now easy to move the cursor to the 1A and overwrite it with 20 (an ASCII space) or switch to the right-hand display and overwrite the Ctrl-Z symbol by pressing the space bar.

If the datafile has more extra end-of-file markers, you would repeat the process for each one. Be careful, of course, not to change the marker at the true end of the file. Also remember that the file header may contain legitimate Ctrl-Z characters that you should not change.

 # Recovery Using DiskMinder

DiskMinder has a "search and replace" feature that makes it superior to the Norton Utilities for detecting and removing extra end-of-file markers. Since an end-of-file marker can appear legitimately in the file header, there is no point in searching for it there. We will, instead, move to the first character beyond the header (i.e., the first character of the first record) before initiating the search and replace.

After selecting the CC2.DBF file in DiskMinder and moving to the File Editing Mode screen, we can easily find the last byte of the header. We then move the cursor to the first byte beyond it (shown in boldface below):

```
File Editing Mode                                            DiskMinder
[Esc] Displays Main Menu

          +0 +1 +2 +3 +4 +5 +6 +7 +8 +9 +A +B +C +D +E +F    0    4    8    C
   0000   03 58 09 1D 12 00 00 00 A1 00 2F 00 00 00 00 00    ♥X....i./.....
   0010   00 00 00 00 00 00 00 00 00 00 00 00 00 00 00 00    ................
   0020   53 55 52 4E 41 4D 45 00 00 00 00 43 03 00 47 7F    SURNAME....C♥.G
   0030   0F 00 00 00 01 00 00 00 00 00 00 00 00 00 00 00    ..............
   0040   46 4E 41 4D 45 00 00 00 00 00 00 43 12 00 47 7F    FNAME......C.G
   0050   0F 00 00 00 01 00 00 00 00 00 00 00 00 00 00 00    ..............
   0060   4C 41 53 54 54 52 41 4E 00 00 00 44 21 00 47 7F    LASTTRAN...D!.G
   0070   08 00 00 00 01 00 00 00 00 00 00 00 00 00 00 00    ..............
   0080   54 45 4C 00 00 00 00 00 00 00 00 43 29 00 47 7F    TEL........C).G
   0090   08 00 00 00 01 00 00 00 00 00 00 00 00 00 00 00    ..............
   00A0   0D 20 5A 75 63 6B 65 72 6D 61 6E 20 20 20 20 20    . Zuckerman
   00B0   20 41 64 64 69 73 6F 6E 20 42 2E 20 20 20 20 20     Addison B.
   00C0   31 39 38 36 30 37 31 30 38 38 32 2D 38 32 36 34    19860710882-8264
   00D0   20 57 6F 6F 64 20 20 20 20 20 20 20 20 20 20 20     Wood
   00E0   41 6E 74 68 6F 6E 79 20 47 2E 20 20 20 20 20 31    Anthony G.      1
   00F0   39 38 36 30 36 30 31 38 32 37 2D 33 37 34 31 20    9860601827-3741

Editing File CC2.DBF
Offset          161 of 1,023                  Cluster 000FH  Sector      38
```

DiskMinder -- Copyright 1988 Westlake Data Corporation

Now we invoke the search and replace feature. DM produces the following display near the center of the screen. In it, we specify Ctrl-Z (1A hex) as the "Data to find" and "space" (hex 20) as the replacement.

```
Data to find:
1A 00 00 00 00 00 00 00    →.......
00 00 00 00 00 00 00 00    ........
00 00 00 00 00 00 00 00    ........
00 00 00 00 00 00 00 00    ........


Replace with:
20 00 00 00 00 00 00 00    .......
00 00 00 00 00 00 00 00    ........
00 00 00 00 00 00 00 00    ........
00 00 00 00 00 00 00 00    ........
```

DiskMinder then finds each end-of-file marker and replaces it with a space when authorized. The first such replacement is shown on the following screen. The boldface 20 hex has replaced the 1A hex that was originally there.

```
Continue   Update   Move                                    Confirmation
Continue with editing

            +0 +1 +2 +3 +4 +5 +6 +7 +8 +9 +A +B +C +D +E +F    0   4   8   C
    0000    20 4C 2E 20 20 20 20 20 20 31 39 38 36 30 36 32    L.      1986062
    0010    38 32 33 37 2D 32 37 32 34 20 53 63 68 61 65 66    8237-2724 Schaef
    0020    66 65 72 20 20 20 20 20 20 45 76 61 6E 20 4A 2E    fer       Evan J.
    0030    20 20 20 20 20 20 20 20 31 39 38 36 30 36 33 30        19860630
    0040    39 32 39 2D 32 34 37 33 20 52 6F 6F 66 20 20 20    929-2473 Roof
    0050    20 20 20 20 20 20 20 20 46 72 65 64 65 72 69 63            Frederic
    0060    6B 20 45 2E 20 20 20 31 39 38 36 30 38 31 32 32    k E.    198608122
    0070    35 34 2D 39 39 39 32 20 52 65 69 6C 6C 79 20 20    54-9992 Reilly
    0080    20 20 20 20 20 20 20 47 65 72 61 72 64 20 4A 2E            Gerard J.
    0090    20 20 20 20 20 20 31 39 38 36 30 37 30 37 38 38          1986070788
    00A0    32 2D 37 38 37 34 20 50 65 65 6B 20 20 20 20 20    2-7874 Peek
    00B0    20 20 20 20 20 20 4A 61 63 6B 20 20 20 20 20 20          Jack
    00C0    20 20 20 20 20 31 39 38 36 30 36 30 31 32 39 32          19860601292
    00D0    2D 39 34 39 34 20 4F 72 63 75 74 74 20 20 20 20    -9494 Orcutt
    00E0    20 20 20 20 20 4A 61 6D 65 73 20 47 2E 20 20 20          James G.
    00F0    20 20 20 20 31 39 38 36 30 37 30 38 35 32 36 2D          19860708526-

Editing File CC2.DBF
Offset        584 of 1,023                     Cluster 000FH  Sector      39
```

DiskMinder -- Copyright 1988 Westlake Data Corporation

When using DM to remove end-of-file markers, remember not to remove the
legitimate one at the true end of the file.

 # Recovery Using Mace's dBFix

Mace's dBFix removes extra end-of-file markers as it makes its single pass
through the datafile. For a large datafile, given dBFix's need to write to a different
output file, the recovery may require a great deal of both time and disk space.

 # Recovery Using dSALVAGE Professional

We will illustrate recovery using dSALVAGE Professional in detail by showing
all screens and messages that you will encounter. The entire process (including
file selection, diagnosis, and repair) requires just 11 keystrokes, each of which is
a simple response to a menu or a message. The repair itself is fully automatic and
is done in-place without a separate output file. dSALVAGE removes all extra
end-of-file markers in a single operation, leaving the legitimate marker intact.
When you invoke dSALVAGE Professional, the main menu (Figure 15-1)
appears.

```
┌──────────────────────────────────────────────────────────────────┐
│ Version 2.10              * dSALVAGE PROFESSIONAL *                 │
├──────────────────────────────────────────────────────────────────┤
│                                                                    │
│             (C) Copyright 1989 Comtech Publishing Ltd.             │
├──────────────────────────────────────────────────────────────────┤
│                        M A I N   M E N U                           │
│                                                                    │
│          F2   File Operations                                      │
│               ♦  Select Input/Output Files                         │
│               ♦  Change defaults                                   │
│          F3   Diagnosis and Repair                                 │
│               ♦  Internal damage                                   │
│               ♦  External (DOS level) damage                       │
│          F4   Invoke Editor                                        │
│               ♦  Header Editor                                     │
│               ♦  Record Editor                                     │
│               ♦  Byte Stream Editor                               │
│               ♦  Hex Editor                                        │
│          F5   Unzap Selected File                                  │
│               ♦  Automatic Unzap                                   │
│               ♦  Manually Assisted Unzap                           │
│                                                                    │
├──────────────────────────────────────────────────────────────────┤
│    F1 = Help                               Press ESC to Quit       │
└──────────────────────────────────────────────────────────────────┘
```

Figure 15-1. dSALVAGE Professional's Main Menu

We press the F2 function key to obtain the screen in Figure 15-2.

```
┌──────────────── Setup and File Selection Menu ────────────────┐
│   F1  Help                      F5   Change Directory          │
│   F2  Select Input File         F6   Change Selection Filter   │
│   F3  Type Name of Input File   F7   Delete File               │
│   F4  Type Name of Output File  F10  Hide/Show Menu            │
└───────────────────────────────────────────────────────────────┘

┌───────────────────────────────────────────────────────────┐
│    CC2.DBF      1024   09-01-88  18:05:16                  │
│    SFILE1.DBF  13106   05-06-88  17:55:10                  │
│                                                           │
│                                                           │
│                                                           │
│                                                           │
│                                                           │
└───────────────────────────────────────────────────────────┘
```

Press ESC to return to Main Menu after completing operations on this screen

Figure 15-2. dSALVAGE Professional's Setup and File Selection Menu

We press F2 again, highlighting the file CC2.DBF. We press Enter to select it and Esc to return to the main menu and enter the Diagnosis and Repair module. Figure 15-3 shows its menu.

```
INPUT FILE........ CC2.DBF          dBASE VERSION..... DBASE-III+ / IV
HEADER SIZE....... 161              LAST UPDATED...... 9-1-88
FIELDS PER RECORD. 4                TOTAL RECORDS..... 18
FILE SIZE......... 1024             RECORD SIZE....... 47
                                    CLUSTER SIZE...... 512
CURRENT DIRECTORY. C:\
OUTPUT WRITTEN TO. C:\CC2.DBF
DIRECTORY FILTER.. *.DBF            RECOMMENDED REPAIR: none

┌───────────────────── Diagnosis & Repair Menu ─────────────────────┐
│                                                                    │
│      F1  Help                        F3  Internal Damage Repair    │
│      F2  Check file for damage       F4  External Damage Repair    │
│                                      F5  Execute Recommended Repair │
│                                                                    │
└───────────────────── Press ESC to return to Main Menu ────────────┘
```

Figure 15-3. dSALVAGE Professional's Diagnosis and Repair Menu

We press F2 to check the file for damage. The diagnostic message shown in Figure 15-4 appears.

```
INPUT FILE........ CC2.DBF          dBASE VERSION..... DBASE-III+ / IV
HEADER SIZE....... 161              LAST UPDATED...... 9-1-88
FIELDS PER RECORD. 4                TOTAL RECORDS..... 18
FILE SIZE......... 1024             RECORD SIZE....... 47
                                    CLUSTER SIZE...... 512
CURRENT DIRECTORY. C:\
OUTPUT WRITTEN TO. C:\CC2.DBF
DIRECTORY FILTER.. *.DBF            RECOMMENDED REPAIR: none

┌───────────────────── Diagnosis & Repair Menu ─────────────────────┐
│                                                                    │
│      F1  Help                        F3  Internal Damage Repair    │
├────────────────────────────────────────────────────────────────────┤
│ File contains extraneous end of file markers (Class 2).            │
│ CLASS 2 repair is recommended:  Press Enter, then F3, then F3      │
│   or Press Enter then F5 to Execute Recommended Repair             │
│ No dBASE header errors detected.                                   │
│                                                                    │
│                                                                    │
└───────────────────── Press Enter to Continue ─────────────────────┘
```

Figure 15-4. dSALVAGE Professional's Diagnosis of Class 2 Damage

We thus have confirmation of Class 2 damage and no other forms. We now press Enter, then F5 to execute the recommended recovery process. The message shown in Figure 15-5 appears at the bottom of the screen.

```
INPUT FILE........ CC2.DBF          dBASE VERSION..... DBASE-III+ / IV
HEADER SIZE....... 161              LAST UPDATED...... 9-1-88
FIELDS PER RECORD. 4                TOTAL RECORDS..... 18
FILE SIZE......... 1024             RECORD SIZE....... 47
                                    CLUSTER SIZE...... 512

CURRENT DIRECTORY. C:\
OUTPUT WRITTEN TO. C:\CC2.DBF
DIRECTORY FILTER.. *.DBF            RECOMMENDED REPAIR: CLASS 2
```

```
You have entered the Class 2 repair state.  One or more end-of-file markers
exist in the record area of the file.  If the header is OK, this can be
repaired automatically.

If you answer NO to the automatic option, you should do the following BEFORE
performing Class 2 recovery:  position the data file (using the Record
Editor) to where you wish removal of unwanted EOF's to begin.  Then answer
YES when asked about blanking EOF's from the current file position.

──────────────── Press Enter to Continue ────────────────
```

Figure 15-5.   dSALVAGE Professional Performing Class 2 Repair

As directed, we press Enter, and the following message appears in a window near the center of the screen:

```
header valid, ok to automatically start blanking of EOF's ? Y/N
```

We press "Y" for Yes and, after a few seconds, we see:

```
INPUT FILE........ CC2.DBF          dBASE VERSION..... DBASE-III+ / IV
HEADER SIZE....... 161              LAST UPDATED...... 9-1-88
FIELDS PER RECORD. 4                TOTAL RECORDS..... 18
FILE SIZE......... 1024             RECORD SIZE....... 47
                                    CLUSTER SIZE...... 512
CURRENT DIRECTORY. C:\
OUTPUT WRITTEN TO. C:\CC2.DBF
DIRECTORY FILTER.. *.DBF            RECOMMENDED REPAIR: CLASS 2


        ┌─────────────────────────────────────────────────────┐
        │            1 EOF's eliminated from file              │
        │                                                     │
        └──────── Press any Key to Continue ──────────────────┘
```

The job is done.

We can now open the file in dBASE and LIST it to confirm the repair.

```
Record#  SURNAME       FNAME          LASTTRAN  TEL
      1  Zuckerman     Addison B.     07/10/86  882-8264
      2  Wood          Anthony G.     06/01/86  827-3741
      3  Tomlinson     Blake          06/02/86  733-8729
      4  Werner        Bradley A.     06/02/86  929-2873
      5  Vavrick       Charles E.     06/03/86  684-3838
      6  Swartwout     David B.       06/01/86  828-7371
      7  Smith         Donald S.      07/10/86  929-4188
      8  Sherman       Edward L.      06/28/86  237-2724
      9  Schaeffer     Evan J.        06/30/86  929-2473
     10  Roof          Frederick E.   08/12/86  254-9992
     11  Reilly        Gerard J.      07/07/86  882-7874
     12  Peek          Jack           06/01/86  292-9494
     13  Orcutt        James G.       07/08/86  526-1587
     14  Mench         John J.        07/12/86  834-8269
     15  Mayberry      John P.        07/06/86  923-9199
     16  Mancini       Joseph A.      06/01/86  482-8342
     17  Liva          Kerney         06/18/86  499-1873
     18  Learmouth     Louis D.       06/19/86  919-2838
```

The file is once more intact, and the data in record 10 has been recovered.

The Hex Editor in dSALVAGE Professional is another convenient tool for removing extra end-of-file markers. After you select the file and invoke the Editor Menu, the screen shown in Figure 15-6 appears.

```
INPUT FILE........ CC2.DBF         dBASE VERSION..... DBASE-III+ / IV
HEADER SIZE....... 161             LAST UPDATED...... 9-1-88
FIELDS PER RECORD. 4               TOTAL RECORDS..... 18
FILE SIZE......... 1024            RECORD SIZE....... 47
                                   CLUSTER SIZE...... 512
CURRENT DIRECTORY. C:\
OUTPUT WRITTEN TO. C:\CC2.DBF
DIRECTORY FILTER.. *.DBF           RECOMMENDED REPAIR: none

─────────────────────── Editor Menu ───────────────────────

  F1   Help            F3   Record Editor        F5   Hex Editor
  F2   Header Editor   F4   Byte-Stream Editor

──────────── Press ESC to return to Main Menu ────────────


```

Figure 15-6.   dSALVAGE Professional's Editor Menu

When you press the F5 function key to select the Hex Editor, the following screen appears:

```
─────────────── Hex Editor Commands ───────────────
  F1       Help           PgUp  Prev Screen         HOME  Beginning of File
  F10      Hide/Show Menu PgDn  Next Screen         END   End of File
  ALT-S    Search         Arrow keys to move cursor TAB   Hex  ASCII Display
  ALT-A    Repeat Search
──────────── Press ESC to Return to Editor Menu ────────────

03 58 09 1D 12 00 00 00 A1 00 2F 00 00 00 00 00  ♥X.   ì /
00 00 00 00 00 00 00 00 00 00 00 00 00 00 00 00
53 55 52 4E 41 4D 45 00 00 00 00 43 03 00 47 7F  SURNAME    C♥ G
0F 00 00 00 01 00 00 00 00 00 00 00 00 00 00 00
46 4E 41 4D 45 00 00 00 00 00 43 12 00 47 7F     FNAME      C G
0F 00 00 00 01 00 00 00 00 00 00 00 00 00 00
4C 41 53 54 54 52 41 4E 00 00 00 44 21 00 47 7F  LASTTRAN   D! G
08 00 00 00 01 00 00 00 00 00 00 00 00 00 00
54 45 4C 00 00 00 00 00 00 00 43 29 00 47 7F     TEL        C) G
08 00 00 00 01 00 00 00 00 00 00 00 00 00 00
0D 20 5A 75 63 6B 65 72 6D 61 6E 20 20 20 20 20  . Zuckerman
20 41 64 64 69 73 6F 6E 20 42 2E 20 20 20 20 20   Addison B.
31 39 38 36 30 37 31 30 38 38 32 2D 38 32 36 34  19860710882-8264
20 57 6F 6F 64 20 20 20 20 20 20 20 20 20 20 20   Wood
41 6E 74 68 6F 6E 79 20 47 2E 20 20 20 20 20 31  Anthony G.      1
39 38 36 30 36 30 31 38 32 37 2D 33 37 34 31 20  9860601827-3741
```

Record 1   file position 162

Although the header is displayed and is available for editing, the cursor (not shown above) is initially at the first byte of the first record, as you can see from the Record and File Position counters at the bottom of the screen. From this position, you can look for end-of-file markers in the records with the editor's Search feature. Afterward, the following screen appears:

```
────────────────────── Hex Editor Commands ──────────────────────
│ F1     Help           PgUp  Prev Screen          HOME  Beginning of File │
│ F10    Hide/Show Menu  PgDn  Next Screen          END   End of File        │
│ ALT-S  Search          Arrow keys to move cursor  TAB   Hex  ASCII Display  │
│ ALT-A  Repeat Search                                                        │
────────────────── Press ESC to Return to Editor Menu ──────────────────
```

```
20 4C 2E 20 20 20 20 20 20 31 39 38 36 30 36 32   L.        1986062
38 32 33 37 2D 32 37 32 34 20 53 63 68 61 65 66   8237-2724 Schaef
66 65 72 20 20 20 20 20 20 45 76 61 6E 20 4A 2E   fer       Evan J.
20 20 20 20 20 20 20 20 31 39 38 36 30 36 33 30            19860630
39 32 39 2D 32 34 37 33 1A 52 6F 6F 66 20 20 20   929-2473→Roof
20 20 20 20 20 20 20 20 46 72 65 64 65 72 69 63            Frederic
6B 20 45 2E 20 20 20 31 39 38 36 30 38 31 32 32   k E.     198608122
35 34 2D 39 39 39 32 20 52 65 69 6C 79 20 20 20   54-9992 Reilly
20 20 20 20 20 20 20 47 65 72 61 72 64 20 4A 2E          Gerard J.
20 20 20 20 20 20 31 39 38 36 30 37 30 37 38 38          1986070788
32 2D 37 38 37 34 20 50 65 65 6B 20 20 20 20 20   2-7874 Peek
20 20 20 20 20 20 4A 61 63 6B 20 20 20 20 20 20          Jack
20 20 20 20 20 31 39 38 36 30 36 30 31 32 39 32          19860601292
2D 39 34 39 34 20 4F 72 63 75 74 74 20 20 20 20   -9494 Orcutt
20 20 20 20 20 4A 61 6D 65 73 20 47 2E 20 20 20          James G.
20 20 20 20 31 39 38 36 30 37 30 38 35 32 36 2D          19860708526-
```

The cursor (not shown above) moves automatically to the first end-of-file marker in the record area of the file. In our sample case, it lies at the beginning of record 10 (shown in boldface). You can change the marker to a space by simply typing 20 (the ASCII space character) over the 1A. Alternatively, you can press the Tab key to move the cursor to the ASCII display at the right and press the space bar once to change the EOF marker to a space. The Repeat Search feature of dSALVAGE Professional lets you find and replace all additional extra end-of-file markers.

 Summary

Extra end-of-file markers are the most common form of datafile damage. A typical symptom is a LISTing that shows fewer records than indicated in the file's structure. Repair involves finding the markers and changing them to spaces. You can do this with DEBUG if the file is small. For large files, the DiskMinder sector editor's search and replace feature is useful since you can start the search at the end of the header. You must be careful, however, not to remove the legitimate marker at the end of the file. dSALVAGE Professional diagnoses the damage before doing the repair. It does not remove the legitimate marker.

16

Repair of Class 3 Damage: Partially Overwritten Header

Class 3 damage involves a partially overwritten header with the space originally allocated to it still intact. The intact space distinguishes Class 3 damage from Class 5 damage. In some cases, dBASE will open a file having Class 3 damage, but in other cases it will report "not a dBASE database". Whether dBASE will open the file depends on the exact nature of the damage. dBASE checks some areas of the header but not all. If the header is healthy enough to pass the checks but has damage in other areas, dBASE will open the file, but you may see strange things when you list its structure or records.

Consider the following examples.

Example 1—Invalid Field Type

The SURNAME field is type "A", an invalid type. DEBUG displays the header as follows. Note the invalid field type in boldface.

```
C:\DEBUG HTEST.DBF
-D
2F90:0100  03 58 09 05 50 00 00 00-A1 00 2F 00 00 00 00 00   .X..P...../.....
2F90:0110  00 00 00 00 00 00 00 00-00 00 00 00 00 00 00 00   ................
2F90:0120  53 55 52 4E 41 4D 45 00-00 00 00 00 41 05 00 27 64   SURNAME....A..'d
2F90:0130  0F 00 00 00 01 00 00 00-00 00 00 00 00 00 00 00   ................
2F90:0140  46 4E 41 4D 45 00 00 00-00 00 00 43 14 00 27 64   FNAME......C..'d
2F90:0150  0F 00 00 00 01 00 00 00-00 00 00 00 00 00 00 00   ................
2F90:0160  4C 41 53 54 54 52 41 4E-00 00 00 44 6B 00 27 64   LASTTRAN...Dk.'d
2F90:0170  08 00 00 00 01 00 00 00-00 00 00 00 00 00 00 00   ................
```

dBASE will open the file, but when you list the structure, you see:

```
Structure for database: C:htest.dbf
Number of data records:      80
Date of last update  : 09/05/88
Field  Field Name  Type       Width    Dec
    1  SURNAME     ED     15
    2  FNAME       Character    15
    3  LASTTRAN    Date          8
    4  TEL         Character     8
** Total **                     47
```

Observe that dBASE shows the SURNAME field to be of type "ED" (an invalid type). If you try to list the data in the SURNAME and FNAME fields, you get the following error message:

```
. list surname,fname
Syntax error.
              ?
list surname,fname
.
```

Example 2—Field Name Containing
Control and Graphics Characters

There are control and graphics characters in the first field name. DEBUG displays the header as follows. Note the part of the field name shown in boldface.

```
C:\DEBUG HTEST2.DBF
-D
1887:0100  03 58 09 05 50 00 00 00-A1 00 2F 00 00 00 00 00   .X..P...../.....
1887:0110  00 00 00 00 00 00 00 00-00 00 00 00 00 00 00 00   ................
1887:0120  53 14 E9 19 14 C3 45 00-00 00 00 43 05 00 27 64   S.....E....C..'d
1887:0130  0F 00 00 00 01 00 00 00-00 00 00 00 00 00 00 00   ................
1887:0140  46 4E 41 4D 45 00 00 00-00 00 00 43 14 00 27 64   FNAME......C..'d
1887:0150  0F 00 00 00 01 00 00 00-00 00 00 00 00 00 00 00   ................
1887:0160  4C 41 53 54 54 52 41 4E-00 00 00 44 6B 00 27 64   LASTTRAN...Dk.'d
1887:0170  08 00 00 00 01 00 00 00-00 00 00 00 00 00 00 00   ................
```

dBASE will open the file, but when you list its structure, you see:

```
        Structure for database: C:htest2.dbf
        Number of data records:      80
        Date of last update   : 09/05/88
        Field  Field Name  Type        Width     Dec
            1  S¶☉↓¶E      Character     15
            2  FNAME       Character     15
            3  LASTTRAN    Date           8
            4  TEL         Character      8
        ** Total **                      47
```

Example 3.—Arbitrary Text in Header

There is arbitrary text in the field definition part of the header. DEBUG displays the header as follows. Note the text in boldface.

```
C:\DEBUG HTEST3.DBF
-D
1887:0100  03 58 09 05 50 00 00 00-A1 00 2F 00 00 00 00 00   .X..P...../.....
1887:0110  00 00 00 00 00 00 00 00-00 00 00 00 00 00 00 00   ................
1887:0120  4E 6F 77 20 69 73 20 74-68 65 20 74 69 6D 65 20   Now is the time
1887:0130  66 6F 72 20 61 6C 6C 20-67 6F 6F 64 20 6D 65 6E   for all good men
1887:0140  20 74 6F 20 63 6F 6D 65-20 74 6F 20 74 68 65 20   to come to the
1887:0150  61 69 64 20 6F 66 20 74-68 65 20 70 61 72 74 79   aid of the party
1887:0160  2E 41 53 54 54 52 41 4E-00 00 00 44 6B 00 27 64   .ASTTRAN...Dk.'d
1887:0170  08 00 00 00 01 00 00 00-00 00 00 00 00 00 00 00   ................
```

dBASE will open the file, but when you list its structure, you see:

```
        Structure for database: C:htest3.dbf
        Number of data records:      80
        Date of last update   : 09/05/88
        Field  Field Name  Type        Width     Dec
            1  Now is the            102
            2   to come to            97
            3  .ASTTRAN    Date           8
            4  TEL         Character      8
        ** Total **                     216
```

When you try to display the records, you see:

```
. disp all
Record#  Now is the t♣
                               to come to k
                                              .ASTTRAN TEL
        1
                                               /  /   les E.
        2
                                              12/14/77 Schaeffe
        3  r
                                               /  /     198606
        4  0
                                              01/.)/00       Ke
        5  r
                                               /  /   5827-641
```

These are typical examples of minor Class 3 damage in which dBASE can still open the file. With more severe damage, dBASE simply reports "not a dBASE database" when you try to open the file.

Although many techniques are available for repairing a datafile having Class 3 damage, selecting the correct one depends on whether you can determine that the header damage is Class 3 rather than Class 5. Unfortunately dBASE does not provide enough information to make this determination. Proper damage diagnosis is a critical element in file recovery, but it is not always easy with general-purpose utilities.

Let's first assume that you have established the existence of Class 3 damage. We will examine several recovery options.

◈ Recovery from Minor Class 3 Header Damage Using DEBUG

We can use DEBUG to change the offending characters if the file is small and the header damage is minor.

To illustrate this option, we will use HTEST2.DBF as an example. DEBUG displays the header as follows. The binary and graphics characters appear in boldface.

```
C:\DEBUG HTEST2.DBF
-D
1887:0100  03 58 09 05 50 00 00 00-A1 00 2F 00 00 00 00 00   .X..P...../.....
1887:0110  00 00 00 00 00 00 00 00-00 00 00 00 00 00 00 00   ................
1887:0120  53 14 E9 19 14 C3 45 00-00 00 00 43 05 00 27 64   S.....E....C..'d
1887:0130  0F 00 00 00 01 00 00 00-00 00 00 00 00 00 00 00   ................
1887:0140  46 4E 41 4D 45 00 00 00-00 00 00 43 14 00 27 64   FNAME......C..'d
1887:0150  0F 00 00 00 01 00 00 00-00 00 00 00 00 00 00 00   ................
1887:0160  4C 41 53 54 54 52 41 4E-00 00 00 44 6B 00 27 64   LASTTRAN...Dk.'d
1887:0170  08 00 00 00 01 00 00 00-00 00 00 00 00 00 00 00   ................
```

The only thing you must do is replace the offending characters with ones acceptable to dBASE. They need not necessarily be the characters that were originally in the header. For example, you could replace the five offending characters starting at memory address 0121 with "ABCDE" if you wished. The field name would then be "SABCDEE", which sounds weird but is fine as far as dBASE is concerned. On the other hand, if you know the original name of the field, you can replace the five characters accordingly.

To replace the bad characters starting at address 0121, use DEBUG's Enter command by typing the following at the prompt:

```
E 121 "URNAM"
```

or

```
E 121 55 52 4E 41 4D
```

That is, you can enter the characters directly or their ASCII hex values. Appendix C contains an ASCII table for your convenience.

To confirm the replacement, use DEBUG's Dump command again:

```
-D 100
1887:0100  03 58 09 05 50 00 00 00-A1 00 2F 00 00 00 00 00   .X..P...../.....
1887:0110  00 00 00 00 00 00 00 00-00 00 00 00 00 00 00 00   ................
1887:0120  53 55 52 4E 41 4D 45 00-00 00 00 43 05 00 27 64   SURNAME....C..'d
1887:0130  0F 00 00 00 01 00 00 00-00 00 00 00 00 00 00 00   ................
1887:0140  46 4E 41 4D 45 00 00 00-00 00 00 43 14 00 27 64   FNAME......C..'d
1887:0150  0F 00 00 00 01 00 00 00-00 00 00 00 00 00 00 00   ................
1887:0160  4C 41 53 54 54 52 41 4E-00 00 00 44 6B 00 27 64   LASTTRAN...Dk.'d
1887:0170  08 00 00 00 01 00 00 00-00 00 00 00 00 00 00 00   ................
```

The memory image of the file has been repaired, but you must still write it back to disk before exiting from DEBUG.

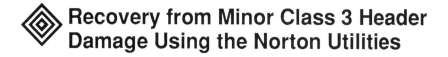

Recovery from Minor Class 3 Header Damage Using the Norton Utilities

We can also use the Norton Utilities to change the offending characters if the header damage is minor. Once again, we assume that you have determined that the damage is Class 3.

Upon invoking the Norton Utilities, we move to Menu 1 to choose an item on the following screen:

```
Menu 1
                         Explore disk


                 Choose item

                 Information on item

                 Edit/display item

                 Search item/disk for data

                 Write item to disk

                 Return to main menu


             Select new item, drive, or directory

Item type  | Drive | Directory name            | File name
Directory  | A:    | \                         | Root dir
```

After we select "Choose item," the following screen appears:

```
Menu 1.1
                          Choose item


                   Change drive

                   change Directory

                   File

                   cLuster

                   Sector

                   Return to Explore disk


                 Select a file


Item type  | Drive | Directory name            | File name
Directory  | A:    | \                         | Root dir
```

After we select "File," the following screen appears:

```
Menu 1.1.3
                        Select file or sub-directory

                             Boot area
                             FAT area
                             Root dir
                             sample.doc
                             htest.dbf
                             newfile.dbf
                             foobar.dbf




                        7 entries to choose from
                        Speed search:
```

Item type File	Drive A:	Directory name \	File name

After we move the cursor down to highlight "htest.dbf," the following screen appears:

```
Menu 1
                        Explore disk



                        Choose item

                        Information on item

                        Edit/display item

                        Search item/disk for data

                        Write item to disk

                        Return to main menu


                   Examine or modify the selected item
```

Item type File	Drive A:	Directory name \	File name htest.dbf

After we select "Edit/display item," the following screen appears:

```
 ┌─ htest.dbf ─────────────────────────────────── Text format ─┐
 │   Cluster 11  Sectors 30-31                 File offset 0, hex 00 │
 │                                                             │
 │   .X .P./S.....EC.FNAMEC.LASTTRANDTELC                      │
 │                                                             │
 │   Zuckerman     Addison B.    19860710882-8264 Wood         Anthony G. │
 │        19860601827-3741 Tomlinson      Blake       19860602733-8729 Wern │
 │   er       Bradley A.    19860602929-2873 Vavrick      Charles E. │
 │   19860603684-3838 Swartwout     David B.      19860601828-7371 Steenburg │
 │        Denise R.    19860611119-8282 Smith      Donald S.      19860 │
 │   710929-4188 Sherman      Edward L.     19860628237-2724 Schaeffer │
 │    Evan J.     19860630929-2473 Roof         Frederick E.  1986081225 │
 │   4-9992 Reilly      Gerard J.    19860707882-7874 Porravecchio   Harv │
 │   ey D.    19860614249-1592 Peek       Jack        19860601292-949 │
 │   4 Orcutt      James G.     19860708526-1587 Mench      John J. │
 │        19860712834-8269 Mayberry    John P.       19860706923-9199 Man │
 │   cini       Joseph A.    19860601482-8342 Liva        K │
 │                                                             │
 │                                                             │
 │                                                             │
 │                                                             │
 │                     Press Enter to continue                 │
 │ 1Help   2Hex   3Text  4Dir   5     6     7     8      9Undo  10QuitNU │
 └─────────────────────────────────────────────────────────────┘
```

After we press the F2 key to select the Hex display format, the following screen appears. The troublesome area is in boldface:

```
 ┌─ htest.dbf ──────────────────────────────────── Hex format ─┐
 │  Cluster 11  Sectors 30-31                  File offset 0, hex 00 │
 │ 03580905 50000000 A1002F00 00000000 00000000 00000000 ♥X.♣P...í./............ │
 │ 00000000 00000000 5314E919 14C34500 00000043 00000000 ........S¶⊖↓ƒ¶E....C.... │
 │ 0F000000 00000000 00000000 00000000 464E414D 45000000 ..............FNAME... │
 │ 00000043 00000000 0F000000 00000000 00000000 00000000 ...C.................. │
 │ 4C415354 5452414E 00000044 00000000 08000000 00000000 LASTTRAN...D........... │
 │ 00000000 00000000 54454C00 00000000 00000000 00000043 ........TEL........C.... │
 │ 08000000 00000000 00000000 00000000 0D205A75 636B6572 ............... Zucker │
 │ 6D616E20 20202020 20416464 69736F6E 20422E20 20202020 man      Addison B. │
 │ 31393836 30373130 3838322D 38323634 20576F6F 64202020 19860710882-8264 Wood │
 │ 20202020 20202020 416E7468 6F6E7920 472E2020 20202031 Anthony G.      1 │
 │ 39383630 36303138 32372D33 37343120 546F6D6C 696E736F 9860601827-3741 Tomlinso │
 │ 6E202020 20202042 6C616B65 20202020 20202020 20203139 n       Blake       19 │
 │ 38363036 30323733 332D3837 32392057 65726E65 72202020 860602733-8729 Werner │
 │ 20202020 20204272 61646C65 7920412E 20202020 20313938 Bradley A.      198 │
 │ 36303630 32393239 2D323837 33205661 76726963 6B202020 60602929-2873 Vavrick │
 │ 20202020 20436861 726C6573 20452E20 20202020 31393836 Charles E.      1986 │
 │ 30363033 3638342D 33383338 20537761 7274776F 75742020 0603684-3838 Swartwout │
 │ 20202020 44617669 6420422E 20202020 20202031 39383630 David B.      19860 │
 │ 36303138 32382D37 33373120 53746565 6E627572 67202020 601828-7371 Steenburg │
 │ 20202044 656E6973 6520522E 20202020 20203139 38363036 Denise R.      198606 │
 │ 31313131 392D3832 38322053 6D697468 20202020 20202020 11119-8282 Smith │
 │ 2020446F 6E616C64          Press Enter to continue      Donald │
 │ 1Help   2Hex   3Text  4Dir   5     6     7     8      9Undo  10QuitNU │
 └─────────────────────────────────────────────────────────────┘
```

We now move the cursor to the first boldface "¶" character. We then type "URNAM" after which the screen appears as follows (corrected characters in boldface):

```
┌─ htest.dbf ──────────────────────────────── Hex format ─┐
  Cluster 11  Sectors 30-31                    File offset 38, hex 26
 03580905 50000000 A1002F00 00000000 00000000 00000000 ♥X.♣P...i./............
 00000000 00000000 5355524E 414D4500 00000043 00000000 ........SURNAME....C....
 0F000000 00000000 00000000 00000000 464E414D 45000000 ..............FNAME...
 00000043 00000000 0F000000 00000000 00000000 00000000 ...C..................
 4C415354 5452414E 00000044 00000000 08000000 00000000 LASTTRAN...D...........
 00000000 00000000 54454C00 00000000 00000043 00000000 ........TEL........C....
 08000000 00000000 00000000 00000000 0D205A75 636B6572 ............... Zucker
 6D616E20 20202020 20416464 69736F6E 20422E20 20202020 man       Addison B.
 31393836 30373130 3838322D 38323634 20576F6F 64202020 19860710882-8264 Wood
 20202020 20202020 416E7468 6F6E7920 472E2020 20202031       Anthony G.       1
 39383630 36303138 32372D33 37343120 546F6D6C 696E736F 9860601827-3741 Tomlinso
 6E202020 20202042 6C616B65 20202020 20202020 20203139 n      Blake           19
 38363036 30323733 332D3837 32392057 65726E65 72202020 860602733-8729 Werner
 20202020 20204272 61646C65 7920412E 20202020 20313938       Bradley A.       198
 36303630 32393239 2D323837 33205661 76726963 6B202020 60602929-2873 Vavrick
 20202020 20436861 726C6573 20452E20 20202020 31393836       Charles E.       1986
 30363033 3638342D 33383338 20537761 7274776F 75742020 0603684-3838 Swartwout
 20202020 44617669 6420422E 20202020 20202020 39383630       David B.         19860
 36303138 32382D37 33373120 53746565 6E627572 67202020 601828-7371 Steenburg
 20202044 656E6973 6520522E 20202020 20203139 38363036       Denise R.        198606
 31313131 392D3832 38322053 6D697468 20202020 20202020 11119-8282 Smith
 2020446F 6E616C64            Press Enter to continue    Donald
 1Help   2Hex    3Text   4Dir    5       6       7       8       9Undo   10QuitNU
```

After making the above changes and exiting from this screen, we see:

```
┌─────────────────────────────────────────────────────────────┐
│ Menu 1.3                                                      │
│                  Save or discard changes made to data         │
│                                                               │
│                                                               │
│                                                               │
│          You have made changes to the cluster in memory       │
│                                                               │
│            (Changes are made and shown highlighted when       │
│            data is displayed in the hexadecimal format)       │
│                                                               │
│                                                               │
│                                                               │
│                   Write the changed data                      │
│                                                               │
│                   Review the changed data                     │
│                                                               │
│                   Discard the changes                         │
│                                                               │
│                 Write the changes to disk                     │
│                                                               │
└─────────────────────────────────────────────────────────────┘
```

After we select "Write the changed data", the message "Writing changed data..." appears, confirming the changes in the disk file.

We can now exit from the program. The repair is complete.

Recovery from Minor Class 3 Header Damage Using DiskMinder

We will now perform the same repair using DiskMinder.

After selecting the file HTEST.DBF and entering the File Editing Mode, we see the beginning of the file in both hex and ASCII form as follows. The offending bytes in the first field definition block appear in boldface:

```
File Editing Mode                                               DiskMinder
[Esc] Displays Main Menu

        +0 +1 +2 +3 +4 +5 +6 +7 +8 +9 +A +B +C +D +E +F   0   4   8   C
0000    03 58 09 05 50 00 00 00 A1 00 2F 00 00 00 00 00   ♥X.♣P...i./.....
0010    00 00 00 00 00 00 00 00 00 00 00 00 00 00 00 00   ................
0020    53 14 E9 19 14 C3 45 00 00 00 00 43 00 00 00 00   S¶Θ↑↓¶E....C....
0030    0F 00 00 00 00 00 00 00 00 00 00 00 00 00 00 00   ................
0040    46 4E 41 4D 45 00 00 00 00 00 00 43 00 00 00 00   FNAME......C....
0050    0F 00 00 00 00 00 00 00 00 00 00 00 00 00 00 00   ................
0060    4C 41 53 54 54 52 41 4E 00 00 00 44 00 00 00 00   LASTTRAN...D....
0070    08 00 00 00 00 00 00 00 00 00 00 00 00 00 00 00   ................
0080    54 45 4C 00 00 00 00 00 00 00 00 43 00 00 00 00   TEL........C....
0090    08 00 00 00 00 00 00 00 00 00 00 00 00 00 00 00   ................
00A0    0D 20 5A 75 63 6B 65 72 6D 61 6E 20 20 20 20 20   . Zuckerman
00B0    20 41 64 64 69 73 6F 6E 20 42 2E 20 20 20 20 20    Addison B.
00C0    31 39 38 36 30 37 31 30 38 38 32 2D 38 32 36 34   19860710882-8264
00D0    20 57 6F 6F 64 20 20 20 20 20 20 20 20 20 20 20    Wood
00E0    41 6E 74 68 6F 6E 79 20 47 2E 20 20 20 20 20 31   Anthony G.     1
00F0    39 38 36 30 36 30 31 38 32 37 2D 33 37 34 31 20   9860601827-3741

Editing File A:\HTEST.DBF
Offset       0 of 3,921                    Cluster 000BH  Sector     30
```

DiskMinder -- Copyright 1988 Westlake Data Corporation

To repair the file, we simply move the cursor to the offending characters and overwrite them with acceptable characters (shown in boldface below). In this case, we type the characters "URNAM".

```
File Editing Mode                                         DiskMinder
[Esc] Displays Main Menu                       File Changed but not written

       +0 +1 +2 +3 +4 +5 +6 +7 +8 +9 +A +B +C +D +E +F   0   4   8   C
  0000 03 58 09 05 50 00 00 00 A1 00 2F 00 00 00 00 00   ♥X.♣P...í./.....
  0010 00 00 00 00 00 00 00 00 00 00 00 00 00 00 00 00   ................
  0020 53 55 52 4E 41 4D 45 00 00 00 00 00 43 00 00 00   SURNAME....C....
  0030 0F 00 00 00 00 00 00 00 00 00 00 00 00 00 00 00   ................
  0040 46 4E 41 4D 45 00 00 00 00 00 00 00 43 00 00 00   FNAME.......C....
  0050 0F 00 00 00 00 00 00 00 00 00 00 00 00 00 00 00   ................
  0060 4C 41 53 54 54 52 41 4E 00 00 00 00 44 00 00 00   LASTTRAN...D....
  0070 08 00 00 00 00 00 00 00 00 00 00 00 00 00 00 00   ................
  0080 54 45 4C 00 00 00 00 00 00 00 00 00 43 00 00 00   TEL.........C....
  0090 08 00 00 00 00 00 00 00 00 00 00 00 00 00 00 00   ................
  00A0 0D 20 5A 75 63 6B 65 72 6D 61 6E 20 20 20 20 20   . Zuckerman
  00B0 20 41 64 64 69 73 6F 6E 20 42 2E 20 20 20 20 20    Addison B.
  00C0 31 39 38 36 30 37 31 30 38 38 32 2D 38 32 36 34   19860710882-8264
  00D0 20 57 6F 6F 64 20 20 20 20 20 20 20 20 20 20 20    Wood
  00E0 41 6E 74 68 6F 6E 79 20 47 2E 20 20 20 20 20 31   Anthony G.      1
  00F0 39 38 36 30 36 30 31 38 32 37 2D 33 37 34 31 20   9860601827-3741

Editing File A:\HTEST.DBF
Offset        38 of 3,921              Cluster 000BH  Sector        30
```

DiskMinder -- Copyright 1988 Westlake Data Corporation

After making the change, we write it to disk and the job is done. DiskMinder requires fewer keystrokes than the Norton Utilities to do the repair.

 Recovery from Minor Class 3 Header Damage Using Disk Repair

Let's now perform the same repair using Disk Repair.

When we invoke it, the disk directory appears on the first screen as follows:

```
                    Disk Repair -- Directory Mode

   Filename.Ext Filesize  Date      Time     Attr Clust Reserved bytes

   SAMPLE  .DOC    5040   08/30/88  17:35:52  20  0002  00000000000000000000
   HTEST   .DBF    3922   09/05/88  16:44:34  20  0007  00000000000000000000
   NEWFILE .DBF    1536   09/03/88  18:51:12  20  000B  00000000000000000000
   FOOBAR  .DBF    3922   09/05/88  17:24:34  20  000F  00000000000000000000
      .       .       .       .         .      .    .          .
      .       .       .       .         .      .    .          .
      .       .       .       .         .      .    .          .

        Drive Cylinder Head Sector Cluster      Directory Mode
         00     000     0     06     FFFE
   Command:
     F1 Help F2 Explain F3/F4 Sector F5 File F6 Mem F7 Dir F8 FAT F9 Param F10 INT
```

After positioning the cursor on the HTEST.DBF directory line and pressing the
F3 key for sector-mode display and editing, we see:

```
                    Disk Repair -- BIOS Sector Mode

 Addr   +0        +4        +8        +C          ASCII

00000   03580905  50000000  A1002F00  00000000    ".X..P...í./....."
00010   00000000  00000000  00000000  00000000    "................"
00020   5314E919  14C34500  00000043  00000000    "S.Θ...E....C...."
00030   0F000000  00000000  00000000  00000000    "................"
00040   464E414D  45000000  00000043  00000000    "FNAME......C...."
00050   0F000000  00000000  00000000  00000000    "................"
00060   4C415354  5452414E  00000044  00000000    "LASTTRAN...D...."
00070   08000000  00000000  00000000  00000000    "................"
00080   54454C00  00000000  00000043  00000000    "TEL........C...."
00090   08000000  00000000  00000000  00000000    "................"
000A0   0D205A75  636B6572  6D616E20  20202020    ". Zuckerman     "
000B0   20416464  69736F6E  20422E20  20202020    " Addison B.     "
000C0   31393836  30373130  3838322D  38323634    "19860710882-8264"
000D0   20576F6F  64202020  20202020  20202020    " Wood           "
000E0   416E7468  6F6E7920  472E2020  20202031    "Anthony G.     1"
000F0   39383630  36303138  32372D33  37343120    "9860601827-3741 "


        Drive Cylinder Head Sector Cluster         BIOS Sector Mode
        00    001      0    05     0007
```

The offending characters appear in boldface in the above display. We will now
move the cursor to the character immediately following the "S" on the third line.
At this point, we type "URNAM" and press the Enter key to return the cursor to
the bottom of the screen. It now appears as follows:

```
                    Disk Repair -- BIOS Sector Mode

 Addr   +0        +4        +8        +C          ASCII

00000   03580905  50000000  A1002F00  00000000    ".X..P...í./....."
00010   00000000  00000000  00000000  00000000    "................"
00020   5355524E  414D4500  00000043  00000000    "SURNAME....C...."
00030   0F000000  00000000  00000000  00000000    "................"
00040   464E414D  45000000  00000043  00000000    "FNAME......C...."
00050   0F000000  00000000  00000000  00000000    "................"
00060   4C415354  5452414E  00000044  00000000    "LASTTRAN...D...."
00070   08000000  00000000  00000000  00000000    "................"
00080   54454C00  00000000  00000043  00000000    "TEL........C...."
00090   08000000  00000000  00000000  00000000    "................"
000A0   0D205A75  636B6572  6D616E20  20202020    ". Zuckerman     "
000B0   20416464  69736F6E  20422E20  20202020    " Addison B.     "
000C0   31393836  30373130  3838322D  38323634    "19860710882-8264"
000D0   20576F6F  64202020  20202020  20202020    " Wood           "
000E0   416E7468  6F6E7920  472E2020  20202031    "Anthony G.     1"
000F0   39383630  36303138  32372D33  37343120    "9860601827-3741 "


        Drive Cylinder Head Sector Cluster         BIOS Sector Mode
        00    001      0    05     0007             (buffer modified)
Command:
  (The data in the buffer has been modified.)
```

Note the message indicating that a change has been made. We now need only press W to write the change to disk and Q to exit from Disk Repair. The repair is complete. Disk Repair requires fewer keystrokes than the Norton Utilities to do the job.

Extensive Class 3 Header Damage

The previous example is a simple recovery problem since the header damage is slight and easy to repair. If the header damage is massive (as is often the case with Class 3 damage), the foregoing recovery process is impractical. For example, imagine trying to repair the following header (in OLDFILE.DBF) character-by-character (the area of damage appears in boldface):

```
oldfile.dbf  Hex format
Cluster 11  Sectors 30-31                        File offset 0, hex 00
03580905 50000000 A1002F00 00000000 000000D5 02A8B4C7 ♥X.♣P...í./........¿...
EFFABAB9 C3D4FAEF 5314E919 14C3EFFF C9D20345 99ABA8EA ⌒s¶☺↓¶∩.♥EöⁱΩ.......
BFF934C3 100808E7 F43BCAA9 9BDEE4C3 C9F8B4A5 D5E7C2D9 4τ;¢Σ'Ñτ..............
E9B5C7C3 DEEAA8E2 A1C3AFAE BEFBDE00 3966D6B8 C3A98B8D ΘΩ¿í»«.9fìì..........
C4A2F12F 3AC3414E BAB3BEEF F5C3C8B3 A7482F78 D4C3E9B8 6/:AN∩ºH/xΘ..........
ABFEC3C9 FEAF7F6E DE45F9DE C3FFEAAB CEC70043 00000000 »nE.Ω.C..............
08000000 00000000 00000000 00000000 0D205A75 636B6572 .............. Zucker
6D616E20 20202020 20416464 69736F6E 20422E20 20202020 man     Addison B.
```

Incidentally, dBASE will open this file but will display nothing but rubbish if you ask for a structure listing. The only reasonable solution to such extensive damage is header replacement.

 Header Replacement

Recovery from Major Class 3 Header Damage Using DEBUG

Here we use dBASE and DEBUG to construct a replacement header and attach the records to it. The file must be small enough to fit into low memory.

Although this procedure is cumbersome, it is instructive in that it shows how to modify a DBF file and combine it with a header using DEBUG and DOS' COPY command. The required steps are:

1. Build a new header in dBASE. It must match the pattern of the data in the damaged file.

2. Use DOS' COPY to combine the new header and the damaged file.

3. Remove the damaged header by moving the records forward to the address immediately following the new header.

4. Correct the record count in the header.

As an example, we will use our previously described file OLDFILE.DBF. Examining it with DEBUG reveals:

```
C:\DEBUG OLDFILE.DBF
-D 100 1FF
1887:0100  03 58 09 05 50 00 00 00-A1 00 2F 00 00 00 00 00   .X..P...../.....
1887:0110  00 00 00 D5 02 A8 B4 C7-EF FA BA B9 C3 D4 FA EF   ................
1887:0120  53 14 E9 19 14 C3 EF FF-C9 D2 03 45 99 AB A8 EA   S..........E....
1887:0130  BF F9 34 C3 10 08 08 E7-F4 3B CA A9 9B DE E4 C3   ..4......;......
1887:0140  C9 F8 B4 A5 D5 E7 C2 D9-E9 B5 C7 C3 DE EA A8 E2   ................
1887:0150  A1 C3 AF AE BE FB DE 00-39 66 D6 B8 C3 A9 8B 8D   ........9f......
1887:0160  C4 A2 F1 2F 3A C3 41 4E-BA B3 BE EF F5 C3 C8 B3   .../:.AN........
1887:0170  A7 48 2F 78 D4 C3 E9 B8-AB FE C3 C9 FE AF 7F 6E   .H/x...........n
1887:0180  DE 45 F9 DE C3 FF EA AB-CE C7 00 43 00 00 00 00   .E.........C....
1887:0190  08 00 00 00 00 00 00 00-00 00 00 00 00 00 00 00   ................
1887:01A0  0D 20 5A 75 63 6B 65 72-6D 61 6E 20 20 20 20 20   . Zuckerman
1887:01B0  20 41 64 64 69 73 6F 6E-20 42 2E 20 20 20 20 20    Addison B.
1887:01C0  31 39 38 36 30 37 31 30-38 38 32 2D 38 32 36 34   19860710882-8264
1887:01D0  20 57 6F 6F 64 20 20 20-20 20 20 20 20 20 20 20    Wood
1887:01E0  41 6E 74 68 6F 6E 79 20-47 2E 20 20 20 20 20 31   Anthony G.     1
1887:01F0  39 38 36 30 36 30 31 38-32 37 2D 33 37 34 31 20   9860601827-3741
```

As you can see, the header is badly damaged (the damage is shown in boldface above).

Based on recollection of the original header or by deducing the number of fields and their sizes by examining the data with DEBUG (often a difficult and tedious process), you can build a new header by constructing the following file in dBASE:

```
Structure for database: C:newhead.dbf
Number of data records:       0
Date of last update   : 09/05/88
Field  Field Name  Type      Width    Dec
    1  SURNAME     Character     15
    2  FNAME       Character     15
    3  LASTTRAN    Date           8
    4  TEL         Character      8
** Total **                      47
```

It is not necessary to have correct field names or types when building this new header. You can name the fields anything you want and call them all character fields if in doubt. The only essential factor is correct field widths. When viewed in DEBUG, the header appears as follows:

```
1887:0100  03 58 09 05 00 00 00 00-A1 00 2F 00 00 00 00 00   .X......../.....
1887:0110  00 00 00 00 00 00 00 00-00 00 00 00 00 00 00 00   ................
1887:0120  53 55 52 4E 41 4D 45 00-00 00 00 43 00 00 00 00   SURNAME....C....
1887:0130  0F 00 00 00 00 00 00 00-00 00 00 00 00 00 00 00   ................
1887:0140  46 4E 41 4D 45 00 00 00-00 00 00 43 00 00 00 00   FNAME......C....
1887:0150  0F 00 00 00 00 00 00 00-00 00 00 00 00 00 00 00   ................
1887:0160  4C 41 53 54 54 52 41 4E-00 00 00 44 00 00 00 00   LASTTRAN...D....
1887:0170  08 00 00 00 00 00 00 00-00 00 00 00 00 00 00 00   ................
1887:0180  54 45 4C 00 00 00 00 00-00 00 00 43 00 00 00 00   TEL........C....
1887:0190  08 00 00 00 00 00 00 00-00 00 00 00 00 00 00 00   ................
1887:01A0  0D 1A EE 86 8C 1E C4 86-9A CE 01 46 1C 89 46 E2   ..........F..F.
```

Note the garbage after the end-of-file marker at address 01A1. We can ignore it since the ensuing COPY operation will not carry it along anyway.

We now build a new file (NEWFILE.DBF) composed of NEWHEAD.DBF and OLDFILE.DBF with DOS' COPY command.

```
C:\COPY NEWHEAD.DBF+OLDFILE.DBF NEWFILE.DBF
NEWHEAD.DBF
OLDFILE.DBF
        1 File(s) copied
```

Now we examine the result with DEBUG:

```
C:\DEBUG NEWFILE.DBF
-R
AX=0000  BX=0000  CX=0FF3  DX=0000  SP=298E  BP=0000  SI=0000  DI=0000
DS=1887  ES=1887  SS=1887  CS=1887  IP=0100   NV UP EI PL NZ NA PO NC
```

The BX/CX registers indicate a file size of FF3. Since the file starts at address 0100, it cannot extend beyond address 10F2. We should expect to find the end-of-file marker, therefore, at address 10F2. To confirm this, we search the file from the end of the new header (at address 01A1) to address 10FF:

```
-S1A0 10FF 1A
1887:10F2
```

Sure enough, there is an end-of-file marker at address 10F2. If we now display the entire file from addresses 0100 through 10F2, we see:

```
-D 0100 10F2
1887:0100  03 58 09 05 00 00 00 00-A1 00 2F 00 00 00 00 00   .X......../.....
1887:0110  00 00 00 00 00 00 00 00-00 00 00 00 00 00 00 00   ................
1887:0120  53 55 52 4E 41 4D 45 00-00 00 00 43 00 00 00 00   SURNAME....C....
1887:0130  0F 00 00 00 00 00 00 00-00 00 00 00 00 00 00 00   ................
1887:0140  46 4E 41 4D 45 00 00 00-00 00 00 43 00 00 00 00   FNAME......C....
1887:0150  0F 00 00 00 00 00 00 00-00 00 00 00 00 00 00 00   ................
```

```
1887:0160  4C 41 53 54 54 52 41 4E-00 00 00 44 00 00 00 00   LASTTRAN...D....
1887:0170  08 00 00 00 00 00 00 00-00 00 00 00 00 00 00 00   ................
1887:0180  54 45 4C 00 00 00 00 00-00 00 00 43 00 00 00 00   TEL........C....
1887:0190  08 00 00 00 00 00 00 00-00 00 00 00 00 00 00 00   ................
1887:01A0  0D 03 58 09 05 50 00 00-00 A1 00 2F 00 00 00 00   ..X..P...../....
1887:01B0  00 00 00 00 D5 02 A8 B4-C7 EF FA BA B9 C3 D4 FA   ................
1887:01C0  EF 53 14 E9 19 14 C3 EF-FF C9 D2 03 45 99 AB A8   .S..........E...
1887:01D0  EA BF F9 34 C3 10 08 08-E7 F4 3B CA A9 9B DE E4   ...4......;.....
1887:01E0  C3 C9 F8 B4 A5 D5 E7 C2-D9 E9 B5 C7 C3 DE EA A8   ................
1887:01F0  E2 A1 C3 AF AE BE FB DE-00 39 66 D6 B8 C3 A9 8B   .........9f.....
1887:0200  8D C4 A2 F1 2F 3A C3 41-4E BA B3 BE EF F5 C3 C8   ..../:.AN.......
1887:0210  B3 A7 48 2F 78 D4 C3 E9-B8 AB FE C3 C9 FE AF 7F   ..H/x...........
1887:0220  6E DE 45 F9 DE C3 FF EA-AB CE C7 00 43 00 00 00   n.E.........C...
1887:0230  00 08 00 00 00 00 00 00-00 00 00 00 00 00 00 00   ................
1887:0240  00 0D 20 5A 75 63 6B 65-72 6D 61 6E 20 20 20 20   .. Zuckerman
1887:0250  20 20 41 64 64 69 73 6F-6E 20 42 2E 20 20 20 20     Addison B.
1887:0260  20 31 39 38 36 30 37 31-30 38 38 32 2D 38 32 36    19860710882-826
1887:0270  34 20 57 6F 6F 64 20 20-20 20 20 20 20 20 20 20   4 Wood
1887:0280  20 41 6E 74 68 6F 6E 79-20 47 2E 20 20 20 20 20    Anthony G.
1887:0290  31 39 38 36 30 36 30 31-38 32 37 2D 33 37 34 31   19860601827-3741
1887:02A0  20 54 6F 6D 6C 69 6E 73-6F 6E 20 20 20 20 20 20    Tomlinson
```

```
           .   .   .   .   .   .   .   .   .   .   .   .   .   .   .   .   .   .
           .   .   .   .   .   .   .   .   .   .   .   .   .   .   .   .   .   .
           .   .   .   .   .   .   .   .   .   .   .   .   .   .   .   .   .   .
```

```
1887:1090  31 32 38 34 20 4C 61 76-65 6C 6C 6F 72 20 20 20   1284 Lavellor
1887:10A0  20 20 20 20 4C 6F 75 69-73 20 50 2E 20 20 20 20       Louis P.
1887:10B0  20 20 20 31 39 38 36 30-37 30 32 32 38 33 2D 39      19860702283-9
1887:10C0  34 35 32 20 4A 6F 6E 65-73 20 20 20 20 20 20 20   452 Jones
1887:10D0  20 20 20 50 61 74 72 69-63 6B 20 4A 2E 20 20 20      Patrick J.
1887:10E0  20 20 31 39 38 36 30 36-31 30 38 32 38 2D 35 34     19860610828-54
1887:10F0  35 38 1A                                          58.
```

The display shows that, if we remove the boldface region from the file, the first good record would start immediately after the last byte of the new header. This is what we now do.

Although DEBUG has no command for removing part of a file, it does allow us to move a block of data. Therefore, we will move a block (starting at address 0242 and extending to the end-of-file at address 10F2) forward in the file. The first byte of the first good record should end up immediately after the end of the new header (that is, at address 01A1). The result is to overwrite and thus remove the boldface section.

The following Move command does the job:

```
-M 242 10F2 1A1
```

After the move, the file appears as follows:

```
1887:0100  03 58 09 05 00 00 00 00-A1 00 2F 00 00 00 00 00   .X......./.....
1887:0110  00 00 00 00 00 00 00 00-00 00 00 00 00 00 00 00   ...............
1887:0120  53 55 52 4E 41 4D 45 00-00 00 00 43 00 00 00 00   SURNAME....C....
1887:0130  0F 00 00 00 00 00 00 00-00 00 00 00 00 00 00 00   ...............
1887:0140  46 4E 41 4D 45 00 00 00-00 00 00 43 00 00 00 00   FNAME......C....
1887:0150  0F 00 00 00 00 00 00 00-00 00 00 00 00 00 00 00   ...............
1887:0160  4C 41 53 54 54 52 41 4E-00 00 00 44 00 00 00 00   LASTTRAN...D....
1887:0170  08 00 00 00 00 00 00 00-00 00 00 00 00 00 00 00   ...............
1887:0180  54 45 4C 00 00 00 00 00-00 00 00 43 00 00 00 00   TEL........C....
1887:0190  08 00 00 00 00 00 00 00-00 00 00 00 00 00 00 00   ...............
1887:01A0  0D 20 5A 75 63 6B 65 72-6D 61 6E 20 20 20 20 20   . Zuckerman
1887:01B0  20 41 64 64 69 73 6F 6E-20 42 2E 20 20 20 20 20    Addison B.
1887:01C0  31 39 38 36 30 37 31 30-38 38 32 2D 38 32 36 34   19860710882-8264
1887:01D0  20 57 6F 6F 64 20 20 20-20 20 20 20 20 20 20 20    Wood
1887:01E0  41 6E 74 68 6F 6E 79 20-47 2E 20 20 20 20 20 31   Anthony G.     1
1887:01F0  39 38 36 30 36 30 31 38-32 37 2D 33 37 34 31 20   9860601827-3741
     .    .   .   .   .   .   .   .   .   .   .   .   .   .   .   .   .
     .    .   .   .   .   .   .   .   .   .   .   .   .   .   .   .   .
     .    .   .   .   .   .   .   .   .   .   .   .   .   .   .   .   .
```

We must do one more thing to complete the repair. We must determine the number of records in the file so that we can update the header. As it stands now, the record count in the header is zero. To determine the number of records, all we do is measure the size of the record area and divide by the record width (known to be 47).

The Move command moved the end-of-file marker forward along with the records. In fact, there are now two markers, one at the original location and a second at the new location. You can use the search command to find them:

```
-S 1A0 10FF 1A
1887:1051
1887:10F2
```

The first address shown (1051) is the location of the moved EOF marker.

Now, since the records start at address 1A1 and the EOF marker is at address 1051, you can use DEBUG's H (hexadecimal arithmetic) command as follows to determine the size of the record area:

```
-H 1051 01A1
```

The results are the sum and difference:

```
11F2   0EB0
```

The difference, EB0 hex (3760 decimal), is the size of the file's record area. Dividing 3760 by 47 (the record size) yields 80 decimal (50 hex). This is the record count. You can write it into the proper byte of the header with the command

```
-E 104 50
```

The repair is complete. You can now write the corrected file to disk and exit from DEBUG.

 Recovery from Major Class 3 Header Damage Using dSALVAGE Professional

dSALVAGE Professional has the advantage that it both diagnoses the damage and does the repair. Furthermore, it can transplant a new header onto the damaged file without using a separate output file. The program can handle files of any size.

For illustration, we use the same files here as in the DEBUG example. OLDF-ILE.DBF is a datafile having extensive header damage. dBASE will open it, but will display rubbish if you request a structure listing. NEWHEAD.DBF is an empty file with a healthy structure that matches the data in OLDFILE.

After we invoke dSALVAGE Professional, select OLDFILE.DBF, and enter the diagnostic module, the following screen appears. Note that the FIELDS PER RECORD display is correct even though the field definitions in the header have been overwritten. dSALVAGE uses the valid header information to compute the number of fields per record.

```
INPUT FILE........ OLDFILE.DBF      dBASE VERSION..... DBASE-III+ / IV
HEADER SIZE....... 161              LAST UPDATED...... 9-5-88
FIELDS PER RECORD. 4                TOTAL RECORDS..... 80
FILE SIZE......... 3922             RECORD SIZE....... 47
                                    CLUSTER SIZE...... 512
CURRENT DIRECTORY. C:\
OUTPUT WRITTEN TO. C:\OLDFILE.DBF
DIRECTORY FILTER.. *.DBF            RECOMMENDED REPAIR: none

 ───────────────────────Diagnosis & Repair Menu───────────────────
 ┌──────────────────────────────────────────────────────────────┐
   F1  Help                        F3  Internal Damage Repair
   F2  Check file for damage       F4  External Damage Repair
                                   F5  Execute Recommended Repair

 ────────────────────Press ESC to return to Main Menu──────────────
 └──────────────────────────────────────────────────────────────┘
```

When we press the F2 key, dSALVAGE diagnoses the damage and reports as follows at the bottom of the screen:

```
INPUT FILE........ OLDFILE.DBF      dBASE VERSION..... DBASE-III+ / IV
HEADER SIZE....... 161              LAST UPDATED...... 9-5-88
FIELDS PER RECORD. 4                TOTAL RECORDS..... 80
FILE SIZE......... 3922             RECORD SIZE....... 47
                                    CLUSTER SIZE...... 512
CURRENT DIRECTORY. C:\
OUTPUT WRITTEN TO. C:\OLDFILE.DBF
DIRECTORY FILTER.. *.DBF            RECOMMENDED REPAIR: none

──────────────────── Diagnosis & Repair Menu────────────────────

   F1  Help                         F3  Internal Damage Repair

File contains header damage (Class 3 or Class 5).
One or more field names in header are invalid.
CLASS 3 repair is recommended:  Press Enter then F3 then F4
  or Press Enter then F5 to Execute Recommended Repair




──────────────────── Press Enter to Continue ────────────────────
```

We press Enter to acknowledge the diagnostic message and F5 to execute the recommended repair. A message window appears near the center of the screen as follows:

```
INPUT FILE........ OLDFILE.DBF      dBASE VERSION..... DBASE-III+ / IV
HEADER SIZE....... 161              LAST UPDATED...... 9-5-88
FIELDS PER RECORD. 4                TOTAL RECORDS..... 80
FILE SIZE......... 3922             RECORD SIZE....... 47
                                    CLUSTER SIZE...... 512
CURRENT DIRECTORY. C:\
OUTPUT WRITTEN TO. C:\OLDFILE.DBF
DIRECTORY FILTER.. *.DBF            RECOMMENDED REPAIR: CLASS 3


    ┌────────────────────────────────────────────────────────┐
    │ Do you want to read in a new header from another file ? Y/N │
    └────────────────────────────────────────────────────────┘


   If you have a data file containing a healthy header that matches the
   data in this damaged file, the header can be copied from that file.
   Just answer Y to above question and you will be asked for the name of
   the donor file.  If you do not have such a file, answer N to the above
   question and you will be given the opportunity to construct a new
   header based upon the data in the damaged file.
```

In our example, we will specify a donor file. If we did not have one, we would use dSALVAGE Professional's header builder.

After we press "Y" for Yes, the following window appears, asking for a file with a valid header that matches the data pattern. We type NEWHEAD.DBF:

```
                           enter file to read header from
    NEWHEAD.DBF
```

dSALVAGE locates the specified file and reads the header into memory if it passes validity tests. The following message then appears:

```
              header file read, header contains no errors

                     ____ Press any Key to Continue ____
```

dSALVAGE next scans the file until it finds a proper end-of-file marker or until it can find no more data that matches the field pattern defined in the header. Note that the record count on the following screen is zero, indicating that the donor file was empty.

```
    INPUT FILE........ OLDFILE.DBF      dBASE VERSION..... DBASE-III+ / IV
    HEADER SIZE....... 161              LAST UPDATED...... 9-12-88
    FIELDS PER RECORD. 4                TOTAL RECORDS..... 0
    FILE SIZE......... 3922             RECORD SIZE....... 47
                                        CLUSTER SIZE...... 512
    CURRENT DIRECTORY. C:\
    OUTPUT WRITTEN TO. C:\OLDFILE.DBF
    DIRECTORY FILTER.. *.DBF            RECOMMENDED REPAIR: CLASS 3


        _____
              Pattern match stopped at dBASE file EOF

                    ____ Press any Key to Continue ____




    scanning, (ESC to abort)        Record 80        file position 3875
```

dSALVAGE next asks for approval to transfer the record count to the header by displaying the following window:

```
  transfer record count of 80 to header (N leaves it alone) ? Y/N
```

We answer by pressing the Y key. This completes the recovery process, but you can, of course, ask dSALVAGE to run another diagnostic check to look for secondary damage. In this case, there is no other damage, and the diagnostic message reflects a clean bill-of-health for the file as follows:

```
INPUT FILE........ OLDFILE.DBF      dBASE VERSION..... DBASE-III+ / IV
HEADER SIZE....... 161              LAST UPDATED...... 9-12-88
FIELDS PER RECORD. 4                TOTAL RECORDS..... 80
FILE SIZE......... 3922             RECORD SIZE....... 47
                                    CLUSTER SIZE...... 512
CURRENT DIRECTORY. C:\
OUTPUT WRITTEN TO. C:\OLDFILE.DBF
DIRECTORY FILTER.. *.DBF            RECOMMENDED REPAIR: none

                    ───────── Diagnosis & Repair Menu ─────────

    F1  Help                       F3   Internal Damage Repair

No dBASE header errors detected.
No record errors detected.
No unwanted EOF's detected in file.




                    ───── Press Enter to Continue ─────
```

The file has been completely recovered. dSALVAGE, having determined that the original space allocated to the header was still intact, simply wrote a new valid header over the old damaged one (as a kind of transplant).

dSALVAGE Professional also lets you construct a new file header and assign whatever names you want to the fields. This is particularly important in situations where your dBASE programs expect fields to have specific names.

Recovery from Major Class 3 Header Damage Using Mace's dBFix

dBFix lets you construct a new file header based on the information in the file's records, but it does not allow you to transplant a header from another file. Constructing a new header is often a tedious iterative process, since it can be difficult to determine the correct starting and ending points of fields by examining the data. dBFix assigns its own arbitrary names to the fields in the new header.

 ## Summary

Class 3 damage is uncommon in a DBF datafile. A more frequent occurrence is a completely overwritten or missing header. We will discuss that case in Chapter 18 as Class 5 damage. The ability to distinguish between Class 3 and Class 5 damage is important for the following reasons:

- Class 5 recovery takes more disk space since it requires a separate output file.

- Class 3 recovery is easier and faster since the file is repaired in place.

You can use various software tools to repair minor header damage. Severe damage calls for a specialized tool such as dSALVAGE Professional.

Header damage often is the result of re-booting a computer while a datafile is open.

Repair of Class 4 Damage: Data Offset

Class 4 damage involves an offset or displacement of field data from its normal position in the records. As you saw in Chapter 13, such an offset might appear as follows when viewed with the BROWSE command:

```
SURNAME-------- FNAME---------- STREET-----------------------------
Koehler         Michael A.      77 Woodsmeadow
Kennett         Mohan S.        21 Barons St.
Jankowski       Paul D.         196 Kenwood
Holmes          Philip O.       157 Barberry Terrace
Hatch           Richard A.      257 Clay Ave.
Gruber          Richard J.      5093 S. Lima Rd.
Gielberg        Robert          198 Avenue Road
Friday          Robert E.       4511 Whitehall Drive
```

189

```
Finein          Robert 460 3612 9248Tomlinson     Earle F.
1   228F   21.711 5 860608 260 3 741 2971Werner      Germaine M.
1   171T    0.001 4 860602 760 3 470 2874Wensley     James G.
1   114F   14.381 7 860612 160 3 723 8728Wendler     Robert H.
1    57T    0.001 2 860602 560 3 743 6283Wendel      Kenneth N.
1     7T    0.001 1 860602 060 3 102 3535Wells       Robert C.
3   832T    0.001 9 860603 380 2 982 7264Wells       William R.
3   806T    0.001 5 860621 080 2 382 8289Webster     Ronald B.
3   754T    0.001 6 860622 580 2 482 3764Pestka      Richard M.
```

BROWSE		<C:>	XFILE		Rec: 29/807	

View and edit fields.

The cause could be erroneous links in the file's allocation chain. The symptom can also appear in a copy of a file with erroneous links. The former case involves external damage, and we will treat it elsewhere. In the original file, the missing data is generally intact. Not only can it be recovered from the data area of the disk, but it can also be reinserted at the correct location in the file. In the copy, however, the damage is internal. The missing data was not transferred since neither dBASE nor DOS recognized it as part of the original file. The best that we can do in such a case is remove the offset. When confronted with offset in a copied file, you should repair the original if it is still available.

To understand the reason for data offset, we must discuss the structural relationship between record boundaries and cluster boundaries in the data area of a disk. The following diagram shows part of a stored datafile. We assume the clusters are contiguous to simplify the diagram, although contiguity is not necessary.

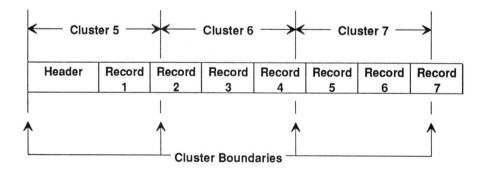

The file starts in cluster 5 and extends through cluster after cluster. The diagram shows only part of it. Its end is somewhere off to the right, occupying the last cluster specified in the allocation chain. Each cluster has a fixed length (number of bytes) on a given disk. Each record in the datafile also has a fixed length. The length of the header is not usually equal to the length of a record, although it could be.

As you can see, record boundaries do not normally coincide with cluster boundaries. In fact, there is theoretically only a single case in which the two could coincide throughout the length of the file: when the file header is exactly the same length as a record and the cluster length is an exact multiple of the record length. But the header always contains an odd number of bytes in a dBASE III PLUS or dBASE IV datafile. Since the number of bytes in a cluster is always even (a multiple of 512), the cluster size cannot be an integer multiple of the header size. In a dBASE III file, on the other hand, the header size is always even. But the cluster size is still never an integer multiple of the header size for values ranging from 512 bytes to 8192 bytes.

Now suppose that the link to cluster 6 had been skipped in the file's allocation chain (that is, cell 5 in the FAT points to cell 7 instead of to cell 6). Neither DOS nor dBASE would consider cluster 6 to be part of the file. Hence, when you examine the file with the dBASE LIST or BROWSE command, you would see the data in cluster 5, followed immediately by the data in cluster 7.

Now examine the cluster boundaries carefully. The beginning of record 2 lies near the end of cluster 5, and the end of record 4 lies at the beginning of cluster 7. When dBASE displays the file, it decides where fields (and records) start and end from information contained in the header, **not from the data itself**. Hence, when dBASE displays the records, it formats the data according to the field pattern defined in the header and the cluster sequence defined in the File Allocation Table. That is, dBASE merely takes the next character on the disk and puts it in the next predefined record position of the display, regardless of whether it makes any sense there. This is why you may see alphabetic characters in numeric fields, for example, when viewing a file having offset. In dBASE's view, record 2 may consist of the beginning of record 2, the end of record 4, and maybe a small part of record 5. The result is that the display will show data in the wrong fields or split between fields as in our illustration.

The file under consideration has external damage in that links in its allocation chain have been skipped. Recall that CHKDSK refers to such links as "lost clusters." Skipped links are a special form of lost clusters. The links that originally joined them at both ends are part of the same file's allocation chain. See the discussion of lost clusters in Chapter 7.

The data in the skipped clusters is still on the disk and can be recovered. That is the subject of Chapter 19. But here we are discussing Class 4 internal damage, so we must consider what happens when we copy the file. DOS, and therefore dBASE, thinks the file resides in clusters 5, 7, 8, and so on. They do not recognize cluster 6 as part of it. If you copy the file, the copy consists of the data in clusters 5, 7, 8, and so on. The data in cluster 6 is not transferred. The resulting file appears as follows on a disk having the same cluster size:

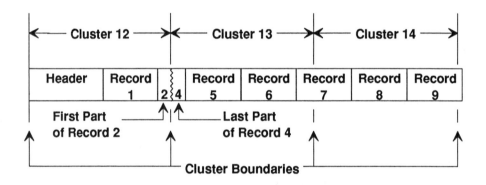

The new cluster numbers here are arbitrary. The copied file could be anywhere on the target disk. As you can see, the copy is corrupted at the boundary between clusters 12 and 13. One record is shorter than normal and consists of part of record 2 and part of record 4. dBASE sees record 2 as consisting of the two pieces plus the first part of record 5. This discontinuity at the cluster boundary produces the offset in a display of the records.

On the target disk, the file allocation chain is normal. There are no lost or skipped clusters. As data in the skipped clusters on the original disk was not copied, it cannot be recovered if you are working with the target disk. The only repair that you can do on the copy is to remove the offset by eliminating the short "record". Since we need to move data rather than replace it, general purpose utilities and sector editors are useless here.

Repairing Data Offset With DEBUG

If the damaged file is small, we can use DEBUG to repair it. All we must do is "squeeze" the "short" record out of the file. Its loss is insignificant in comparison with the cluster(s) full of data already lost when the copy was made. Figure 17-1 illustrates the process. The damaged file appears on top, and the final repaired file underneath. The illustration does not imply two different files, since the repair can be done in place.

The process involves moving up the good records that lie beyond the "short" record. The result is to overwrite the "short" record and literally squeeze it out of the file.

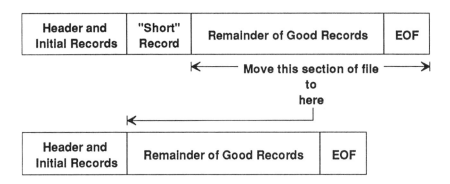

Figure 17-1. Squeezing a Short Record out of a Datafile

We will use the file TEST4.DBF to illustrate the recovery. Its directory listing is:

```
C:\DIR A:

 Volume in drive A has no label
 Directory of  A:\

TEST4     DBF      3072    9-12-88    9:29p
         1 File(s)     359424 bytes free
```

Since Class 4 damage does not involve the header, dBASE can open the file, and a structure listing is normal.

```
Structure for database: A:test4.dbf
Number of data records:      80
Date of last update   : 09/05/88
Field  Field Name  Type      Width    Dec
    1  SURNAME     Character    15
    2  FNAME       Character    15
    3  LASTTRAN    Date          8
    4  TEL         Character     8
** Total **                     47
```

When viewed in the BROWSE mode, however, the file appears as follows:

```
SURNAME-------- FNAME---------- LASTTRAN TEL-----
Cook            Terrance        06/01/86 828-2436
Burkey          Thomas J.       06/26/86 187-3618
Balsamo         William C.      06/02/86 427-2324
Azar            William G.      06/01/86 957-3576
Warden          Carol K.        06/21/86 247-7738
Singer          Eddie           07/03/86 882-7337
Phipps          Howard M.       07/02/86 191-9154
McNulty         John J.         06/13/86 746-4919
Klocke254 Adolf         Willi   /  /     198606
6541-4355 Power s        Harry  /  /.    198607
2919-1820 Hoell rich     Jack   /  /     198606
8364-8282 Parsn ip       James  /  /.    198606
6919-9293 McCli ntock    John   /  /     198606
5192-8283 Eddy           Ronal  /  /     198606
7817-4888 Burke tt       Thoma  /  /K.   198606
1473-8287 Bedna r        Wayne  /  /.    198606
1477-6254 Austi n        Willi . /  / J  198606
```

```
   BROWSE        |<A:>|TEST4            |Rec: 33/80
```

View and edit fields.

A word of caution is appropriate here. If you move to the last record of this file while in BROWSE and press the down arrow key, your computer may lock up. You will then have no alternative other than to re-boot. Re-booting the computer while a datafile is open often causes header damage.

When you see a display like the one shown above, you cannot tell whether the damage is Class 4 or external (involving skipped clusters). If you are dealing with an original file (rather than a copy), you should exit from dBASE and run CHKDSK. It will tell you if the allocation chain has lost clusters. If so, the damage is external and you should deal with it as such (see Chapter 7). If your file is a copy and CHKDSK does not report lost clusters, you can proceed with Class 4 repair. This case shows clearly why accurate diagnosis is important before attempting recovery.

In the BROWSE display, the characters in boldface (together with the space following the "4" in the sequence "**Klocke254**") form the "short" record. Although you cannot tell from the display, "Klocke" is actually the last six characters of the cluster immediately prior to the lost cluster(s) and "254" is the first three characters of the first cluster following them.

If we move the entire tail of the file forward so that the "A" of "Adolf" occupies the position now occupied by the "K" of "Klocke," we can correct the offset. Let's now see how to do this.

First start DEBUG and load the file into memory with

```
DEBUG TEST4.DBF
```

At the prompt, give the R (Register) command to determine the exact size of the file:

```
-R
AX=0000  BX=0000  CX=0C00  DX=0000  SP=470E  BP=0000  SI=0000  DI=0000
DS=34AF  ES=34AF  SS=34AF  CS=34AF  IP=0100   NV UP EI PL NZ NA PO NC
```

The BX/CX registers indicate that the file size is 0C00 hex. Since the file starts at address 0100, it therefore cannot extend beyond address 0CFF. Now search for the character sequence "Klocke254" in it with the S (Search) command:

```
-S 100 CFF "Klocke254"
34AF:08FA
```

DEBUG indicates that the target string starts at memory address 08FA.

Dumping memory from address 08B0 on shows:

```
-D 8B0
34AF:08B0  64 20 4D 2E 20 20 20 20-20 20 31 39 38 36 30 37   d M.      198607
34AF:08C0  30 32 31 39 31 2D 39 31-35 34 20 4D 63 4E 75 6C   02191-9154 McNul
34AF:08D0  74 79 20 20 20 20 20 20-20 20 4A 6F 68 6E 20 4A   ty        John J
34AF:08E0  2E 20 20 20 20 20 20 20-20 31 39 38 36 30 36 31   .        1986061
34AF:08F0  33 37 34 36 2D 34 39 31-39 20 4B 6C 6F 63 6B 65   3746-4919 Klocke
34AF:0900  32 35 34 20 41 64 6F 6C-66 20 20 20 20 20 20 20   254 Adolf
34AF:0910  20 20 20 57 69 6C 6C 69-73 20 20 20 20 20 20 20      Willis
34AF:0920  20 20 31 39 38 36 30 36-31 36 35 34 31 2D 34 33     19860616541-43
```

We indeed see "Klocke254" starting at address 08FA. We also see the character sequence "Adolf" starting at address 0904. Hence, we can squeeze the "short" record out of the file by moving its tail (extending from the "A" of "Adolf" at address 0904 to the end of the file at address 0CFF) forward to address 08FA, thereby overwriting "Klocke254" and removing the offset. Merely give the M (Move) command:

```
-M 904 CFF 8FA
```

Now we reexamine the file:

```
-D 8B0
34AF:08B0  64 20 4D 2E 20 20 20 20-20 20 31 39 38 36 30 37   d M.      198607
34AF:08C0  30 32 31 39 31 2D 39 31-35 34 20 4D 63 4E 75 6C   02191-9154 McNul
34AF:08D0  74 79 20 20 20 20 20 20-20 20 4A 6F 68 6E 20 4A   ty        John J
34AF:08E0  2E 20 20 20 20 20 20 20-20 31 39 38 36 30 36 31   .        1986061
34AF:08F0  33 37 34 36 2D 34 39 31-39 20 41 64 6F 6C 66 20   3746-4919 Adolf
34AF:0900  20 20 20 20 20 20 20 20-20 57 69 6C 6C 69 73 20            Willis
34AF:0910  20 20 20 20 20 20 20 20-31 39 38 36 30 36 31 36           19860616
34AF:0920  35 34 31 2D 34 33 35 35-20 50 6F 77 65 72 73 20   541-4355 Powers
```

After we write the repaired file to disk and exit from DEBUG, a BROWSE shows the following, confirming successful repair of the offset:

```
SURNAME--------  FNAME----------  LASTTRAN  TEL-----
Cook             Terrance         06/01/86  828-2436
Burkey           Thomas J.        06/26/86  187-3618
Balsamo          William C.       06/02/86  427-2324
Azar             William G.       06/01/86  957-3576
Warden           Carol K.         06/21/86  247-7738
Singer           Eddie            07/03/86  882-7337
Phipps           Howard M.        07/02/86  191-9154
McNulty          John J.          06/13/86  746-4919
Adolf            Willis           06/16/86  541-4355
Powers           Harry S.         07/12/86  919-1820
Hoellrich        Jack             06/18/86  364-8282
```

```
Parsnip          James A.        06/26/86 919-9293
McClintock       John N.         06/05/86 192-8283
Eddy             Ronald          06/17/86 817-4888
Burkett          Thomas K.       06/21/86 473-8287
Bednar           Wayne F.        06/01/86 477-6254
Austin           William J.      06/29/86 879-2742
```

```
    BROWSE           |<A:>|TEST4                    |Rec: 33/80
```

View and edit fields.

We have just one more detail to handle. The file structure still indicates 80 records. We know that some were lost in the copying process, but we don't know how many. The simplest way to correct the record count in the header is to copy the file using the dBASE COPY command. dBASE will make the required correction.

```
Structure for database: test4.dbf
Number of data records:      80
Date of last update  : 09/05/88
Field  Field Name  Type      Width    Dec
    1  SURNAME     Character    15
    2  FNAME       Character    15
    3  LASTTRAN    Date          8
    4  TEL         Character      8
** Total **                     47
```

```
. copy to outfile4
     58 records copied
. use outfile4
```

Another LIST STRUCTURE shows the corrected record count.

```
Structure for database: outfile4.dbf
Number of data records:      58
Date of last update  : 09/12/88
Field  Field Name  Type      Width    Dec
    1  SURNAME     Character    15
    2  FNAME       Character    15
    3  LASTTRAN    Date          8
    4  TEL         Character      8
** Total **                     47
```

Recovery is now complete.

Repairing Data Offset with dSALVAGE Professional

Although DEBUG is an effective tool for removing data offset from small files, it has no diagnostic capability and cannot handle large files. dSALVAGE Professional, on the other hand, provides all the capabilities needed for file diagnosis and recovery. We will now examine its use in repairing offset.

After invoking dSALVAGE Professional, selecting the file TEST4.DBF, and running the standard diagnostic check, we see the following screen:

```
INPUT FILE........ TEST4.DBF        dBASE VERSION..... DBASE-III+ / IV
HEADER SIZE....... 161              LAST UPDATED...... 9-5-88
FIELDS PER RECORD. 4                TOTAL RECORDS..... 80
FILE SIZE......... 3072             RECORD SIZE....... 47
                                    CLUSTER SIZE...... 2048
CURRENT DIRECTORY. C:\
OUTPUT WRITTEN TO. C:\TEST4.DBF
DIRECTORY FILTER.. *.DBF            RECOMMENDED REPAIR: none

───────────────── Diagnosis & Repair Menu ─────────────────

    F1  Help                        F3  Internal Damage Repair

File contains record damage (Class 1 or Class 4).
40 records match header pattern out of expected 80
Data stored in record field do not match header definition for field.
Deleted flag in record(s) invalid (not * or space).
Decimal point out of position (or missing) in numeric field.
dBASE Record EOF marker not where expected.
CLASS 4 repair is recommended:  Press Enter, then F3, then F5
  or Press Enter then F5 to Execute Recommended Repair
No dBASE header errors detected.
No unwanted EOF's detected in file.
──────────────── Press Enter to Continue ────────────────
```

The diagnostic message at the bottom itemizes the damage and recommends Class 4 repair.

Remember that Class 4 damage usually indicates lost data clusters (perhaps the result of a copy), thereby limiting recovery to the removal of the offset.

The Class 4 repair module scans the file and stops at the "record" containing the offset. It appears on the next screen as follows:

```
─────────────────────Class 4 Repair Commands ──────
F1 Help                                    ALT-T        Check Record
F2 Count Good Records  F10   Hide/Show Menu HOME/END    First/Last Record
F4 Re-Align File        PgUp  Prev Record   ^PgUp/^PgDn Vert Screen Scroll
F5 Continue From Here   PgDn  Next Record   ^HOME/^END  Horiz Screen Scroll
─────────────── Press ESC to Return to Internal Repair Menu──────
```

```
DELETEFLAG :
   SURNAME : Klocke254 Adolf
     FNAME :          Willi
  LASTTRAN : s
       TEL :    198606
         :
         :
         :
         :
         :
         :
         :
         :
         :
         :

                    error    Record 41      file position 2042
```

Note that dSALVAGE positions the file at record 41, displays it, and reports an "error" at the bottom of the screen. In the menu at the top, you can see the "F4 Re-Align Record" instruction. Pressing the F4 key starts an automatic realignment that does the same job we performed with the DEBUG Move command. That is, dSALVAGE slides the data part of the file (from the point of offset) through the displayed fields until it is aligned with the field and record boundaries. Afterward, the screen appears as follows:

```
─────────────────────Class 4 Repair Commands ──────
F1 Help                                    ALT-T        Check Record
F2 Count Good Records  F10   Hide/Show Menu HOME/END    First/Last Record
F4 Re-Align File        PgUp  Prev Record   ^PgUp/^PgDn Vert Screen Scroll
F5 Continue From Here   PgDn  Next Record   ^HOME/^END  Horiz Screen Scroll
─────────────── Press ESC to Return to Internal Repair Menu──────
```

```
DELETEFLAG :
   SURNAME : Adolf
     FNAME : Willis
  LASTTRAN : 19860616
       TEL : 541-4355
         :
         :
         :
         :
         :
         :
         :
         :
         :
         :

arrow keys to slide, CR to end        Record 41      file position 2052
```

Note that record 41 (and all subsequent ones) have been realigned successfully, and the "error" indicator has disappeared. All you must do now is press the Enter key to accept the re-alignment.

Before proceeding, we should note that dSALVAGE displays data without the formatting dBASE assigns to it. See, for example, the date in the LASTTRAN field. dBASE would display it as 06/16/86, but the stored characters have the form 19860616 (year, month, day). dSALVAGE displays the characters without rearranging them.

After you press the Enter key, dSALVAGE produces the following message in a window near the center of the screen:

```
ok to re-align past 9 characters of file? Y/N
```

This message indicates that dSALVAGE will remove the 9 characters passed over during re-alignment if you so authorize. After you press "Y" and the Esc key, dSALVAGE displays the following message near the center of the screen:

```
OK to write change to output? Y/N
```

You can now authorize dSALVAGE to write the file changes back to disk. It then tallies the number of good records left in the file. It does this with a pattern-matching process that stops as soon as it encounters either the legitimate dBASE end-of-file marker or data that does not match the pattern described in the file header. Afterward, the following window appears near the center of the screen:

```
Pattern match stopped at dBASE file EOF
────────────────── Press any Key to Continue ──────────────────
```

After you press a key, dSALVAGE displays the following message in a window near the center of the screen.

```
transfer record count of 58 to header (N leaves it alone) ? Y/N
```

A few words are in order here. dSALVAGE has found 58 consecutive records it judged to be valid. The fact that the tally stopped at an end-of-file marker indicates strongly that there are no more recoverable records. Sometimes, however, a datafile may have secondary damage that cannot be detected until the primary damage has been repaired. Suppose, for example, the tally process stopped because of a pattern-match failure. If you believed there might be more recoverable records, you could simply respond negatively to the transfer question. Then set the header's record count to a slightly higher number with dSALVAGE's Header Editor, and rerun the diagnostic to search for secondary damage.

For our current example, a positive response to the question allows dSALVAGE to write the new record count into the file header. The job is now done. The following screen appears, showing the corrected record count:

```
INPUT FILE........ TEST4.DBF       dBASE VERSION..... DBASE-III+ / IV
HEADER SIZE....... 161             LAST UPDATED...... 9-5-88
FIELDS PER RECORD. 4               TOTAL RECORDS..... 58
FILE SIZE......... 3072            RECORD SIZE....... 47
                                   CLUSTER SIZE...... 2048
CURRENT DIRECTORY. C:\
OUTPUT WRITTEN TO. C:\TEST4.DBF
DIRECTORY FILTER.. *.DBF           RECOMMENDED REPAIR: none

───────────────── Diagnosis & Repair Menu ─────────────────

    F1  Help                       F3  Internal Damage Repair
    F2  Check file for damage      F4  External Damage Repair
                                   F5  Execute Recommended Repair

───────────── Press ESC to return to Main Menu ─────────────
```

After recovery and before exiting from dSALVAGE Professional, you should always check the file for residual damage via the Diagnosis and Repair Menu. Doing that here makes the following diagnostic message appear, confirming that the file is completely healthy once more.

```
 INPUT FILE........ TEST4.DBF        dBASE VERSION..... DBASE-III+ / IV
 HEADER SIZE....... 161              LAST UPDATED...... 9-5-88
 FIELDS PER RECORD. 4                TOTAL RECORDS..... 58
 FILE SIZE......... 3072             RECORD SIZE....... 47
                                     CLUSTER SIZE...... 2048
 CURRENT DIRECTORY. C:\
 OUTPUT WRITTEN TO. C:\TEST4.DBF
 DIRECTORY FILTER.. *.DBF            RECOMMENDED REPAIR: none

 ─────────────── Diagnosis & Repair Menu ───────────────

     F1  Help                         F3  Internal Damage Repair

 No dBASE header errors detected.
 No record errors detected.
 No unwanted EOF's detected in file.




 ─────────────── Press Enter to Continue ───────────────
```

You can now exit from dSALVAGE confident that the recovery is complete.

 # Summary

When you view a file in the dBASE BROWSE mode and see offset, you cannot tell whether it is due to lost clusters. If not, the proper repair procedure is removal of the offset. But if it is, such repair will fail to recover file data that still exists on the disk. This shows the importance of doing a thorough diagnosis before repair. dSALVAGE Professional diagnoses a file, detects the difference between these two cases, and recommends the appropriate recovery process.

18

Repair of Class 5 Damage: Destroyed or Missing Header

At first glance, Class 3 and Class 5 damage produce the same symptoms. In both cases, for example, dBASE says that the file is "not a dBASE database" when you try to open it. Hence, you cannot examine it with dBASE. But the two classes differ in one key aspect. With Class 3 damage, the space originally allocated to the header is intact, although the information in it may have been overwritten. But with Class 5, the header is partly or totally lost, and the file may start inside a record.

With regard to recovery, the two damage classes are quite different. As Chapter 16 showed, the existence of the original header space in the Class 3 case allows us to transplant a new header without changing the file's size. Hence, we can do the repair "in place" without creating a separate output file. In the Class 5 case, however, the repaired file is larger than the damaged one.

This chapter examines the recovery of datafiles having Class 5 damage. With Class 5, as with most internal damage, the tools designed to work with directories and FATs are useless. The tools we discuss here are DEBUG and dSALVAGE Professional. DEBUG works for small files, whereas dSALVAGE works for files of any size. The advantages of dSALVAGE are that it has diagnostic as well as recovery capability and that its recovery process is largely automatic.

◈ Using DEBUG to Repair Class 5 Damage in a Small File

Conceptually, recovery with DEBUG is simple but tedious. It involves creating a new file structure and merging it with the records from the damaged file. The repair may leave the file with offset. Then complete recovery also requires the Class 4 procedure described in Chapter 17.

Recovery involves the following steps:

1. Load DEBUG and the damaged file into memory. The file must be small.

2. Move the 'tail' (that is, the part containing only the records and the end-of-file marker) to the beginning.

3. Write the modified file back to disk.

4. Enter dBASE and create an empty file with a structure matching the records in the damaged file.

5. Exit from dBASE and use DEBUG to load the empty file into memory at address 0100.

6. Load the modified damaged file into memory immediately after the header of the empty file. The combined file has a valid header and the records from the original file.

7. Make the header reflect the approximate maximum number of records in the new file.

8. Adjust the CPU's BX and CX registers to reflect the new file size.

9. Write the new file to disk.

10. Use the dBASE COPY command to make the header reflect the exact number of records in the file.

You will need two pieces of information during recovery. Both are obtainable directly from the damaged file. They are:

- The number of fields and their widths

- The size of the damaged file

The small file we use in our example is P3D5.DBF.

Start by examining the file's directory listing to determine its size. When we type DIR P3D5.DBF at the DOS prompt, the following display appears:

```
P3D5  DBF     3603   6-12-88   1:47p
```

The only important number here is the file size (3603 bytes). It is the approximate (but not necessarily accurate) size of the file. Approximate is sufficient for now.

Since the file is 3603 decimal (E13 hex) bytes long, and it will be loaded into memory starting at address 0100, it will not extend beyond address 0F12 (since 0E13+FF=0F12).

Next load DEBUG and the damaged file into memory with the command

```
DEBUG P3D5.DBF
```

A dump now shows the following (with non-essential parts of the display removed for brevity):

```
-D 100 F12
34D1:0100  E6 C3 AB D8 E9 C7 B1 06-F7 C3 39 01 15 27 72 CD   ..........9..'r.
34D1:0110  A4 5E 9F B8 D2 E9 C3 FA-C9 D9 EB AE 48 AA BE DC   .^..........H...
34D1:0120  7F F7 D9 CE AB D2 C9 E1-A8 6F 83 F6 99 CA B6 D9   .........o......
34D1:0130  C2 E7 F9 F2 D5 BA CE D7-02 21 97 16 E4 D9 9E 2F   .........!...../
34D1:0140  A4 C7 B9 E2 D6 7E E7 D2-C4 A3 C3 D6 D9 EB CF 8E   .....~..........
34D1:0150  F4 E7 A1 B5 C8 F4 A4 C8-E2 01 06 19 E4 D1 E0 F0   ................
34D1:0160  C7 DD E1 A7 B5 3E 6F 72-65 6C 61 6E 64 20 20 20   .....oreland
34D1:0170  20 56 41 31 32 32 32 32-4C 61 77 79 65 72 20 20    VA12222Lawyer
34D1:0180  44 31 38 31 37 20 41 64-61 6D 73 20 20 20 20 20   D1817 Adams
34D1:0190  20 4A 6F 68 6E 20 51 75-69 6E 63 79 20 20 20 35    John Quincy    5
34D1:01A0  20 48 61 72 76 61 72 64-20 53 74 20 20 20 20 20    Harvard St
34D1:01B0  20 20 20 42 72 61 69 6E-74 72 65 65 20 20 20 20      Braintree
34D1:01C0  20 20 20 4D 41 31 33 33-33 33 4C 61 77 79 65 72      MA13333Lawyer
34D1:01D0  20 20 44 31 38 32 35 20-4A 61 63 6B 73 6F 6E 20    D1825 Jackson
34D1:01E0  20 20 20 41 6E 64 72 65-77 20 20 20 20 20 20 20      Andrew
     .     .     .     .     .     .     .     .     .     .     .
     .     .     .     .     .     .     .     .     .     .     .
```

```
34D1:0BF0  53 74 2E 20 20 20 20 20-20 20 20 4F 78 6E 61 72   St.        Oxnar
34D1:0C00  64 20 20 20 20 20 20 20-20 20 20 4F 48 31 37 35   d          OH175
34D1:0C10  33 32 41 63 74 6F 72 20-20 20 52 31 39 38 31 1A   32Actor    R1981.
     .   .   .   .   .   .   .   .   .   .   .   .   .   .   .
     .   .   .   .   .   .   .   .   .   .   .   .   .   .   .
     .   .   .   .   .   .   .   .   .   .   .   .   .   .   .
```

Although the beginning of the file should contain the header, it actually contains only trash, including standard typewriter characters, control characters, and graphics characters.

From the above display, we can find the starting address of the first healthy record. It is the beginning of the 'tail' mentioned earlier. Recall that dBASE reserves the first byte of each record for the deletion status. It is either a space (20 hex) for an undeleted record or an asterisk (2A hex) for a deleted one. Examining the above display shows that the first healthy record starts at address 0185. It consists of the characters " Adams   John Quincy".

We now move the 'tail' of the file (addresses 0185 through 0F12) down to address 0100 using the Move command:

```
M 185 F12 0100
```

After the move, the file appears as follows:

```
34D1:0100  20 41 64 61 6D 73 20 20-20 20 20 20 4A 6F 68 6E    Adams       John
34D1:0110  20 51 75 69 6E 63 79 20-20 20 35 20 48 61 72 76    Quincy    5 Harv
34D1:0120  61 72 64 20 53 74 20 20-20 20 20 20 20 42 72       ard St         Br
34D1:0130  61 69 6E 74 72 65 65 20-20 20 20 20 20 4D 41       aintree        MA
34D1:0140  31 33 33 33 33 4C 61 77-79 65 72 20 20 44 31 38    13333Lawyer  D18
34D1:0150  32 35 20 4A 61 63 6B 73-6F 6E 20 20 20 20 41 6E    25 Jackson     An
34D1:0160  64 72 65 77 20 20 20 20-20 20 20 31 20 4E 6F       drew         1 No
34D1:0170  6E 65 20 53 74 20 20 20-20 20 20 20 20 20 20 20    ne St
34D1:0180  57 61 78 68 61 77 20 20-20 20 20 20 20 20 20 20    Waxhaw
34D1:0190  53 43 31 35 35 35 35 4C-61 77 79 65 72 20 20 44    SC15555Lawyer  D
34D1:01A0  31 38 32 39 20 56 61 6E-20 42 75 72 65 6E 20 20    1829 Van Buren
34D1:01B0  4D 61 72 74 69 6E 20 20-20 20 20 20 20 20 33 20    Martin          3
34D1:01C0  46 69 72 73 74 20 53 74-20 20 20 20 20 20 20 20    First St
34D1:01D0  20 20 4B 69 6E 64 65 72-68 6F 6F 6B 20 20 20 20      Kinderhook
34D1:01E0  20 20 4E 59 31 36 36 36-36 4C 61 77 79 65 72 20      NY16666Lawyer
34D1:01F0  20 44 31 38 33 37 20 48-61 72 72 69 73 6F 6E 20     D1837 Harrison
34D1:0200  20 20 57 69 6C 6C 69 61-6D 20 48 2E 20 20 20 20      William H.
     .   .   .   .   .   .   .   .   .   .   .   .   .   .   .
     .   .   .   .   .   .   .   .   .   .   .   .   .   .   .
     .   .   .   .   .   .   .   .   .   .   .   .   .   .   .
34D1:0B70  20 20 20 20 20 20 4F 78-6E 61 72 64 20 20 20 20          Oxnard
34D1:0B80  20 20 20 20 20 20 4F 48-31 37 35 33 32 41 63 74          OH17532Act
34D1:0B90  6F 72 20 20 20 52 31 39-38 31 1A 20 41 63 74 6F    or   R1981. Acto
     .   .   .   .   .   .   .   .   .   .   .   .   .   .   .
     .   .   .   .   .   .   .   .   .   .   .   .   .   .   .
     .   .   .   .   .   .   .   .   .   .   .   .   .   .   .
```

The file now contains the records without a header. Note that the first byte of the first record lies at address 0100 as we intended.

The next steps in the process are to save the modified file, exit from DEBUG, and create a new file structure. But what should the structure be? Perhaps you have saved a copy of the original on paper or in a disk file. If so, you can use it to build the new structure.

If you have no copy or are not sure it is up to date, you can use DEBUG's Dump to get the information from the current file. Simply use the D command a few times (starting with D 100). It will display some records. From their contents, you should be able to identify the fields, their widths, and usually their types. Write down this information before exiting from DEBUG.

The field types need not be correct. When in doubt, assume a character field. If you are wrong, you can change types later with dBASE's MODIFY STRUC-TURE command. Incidentally, it is easy to identify memo fields since they contain strings of 10 ASCII digits (left-filled with the space character 20 hex or, in dBASE IV, with the zero character 30 hex).

What **is** important is that you identify ALL fields and determine their widths accurately. Mistakes in the widths will cause progressive offset from record to record, and you may have to perform the whole process over. You will not lose data, but the repetition takes time.

Now write the file back to disk and exit from DEBUG.

The next step is to invoke dBASE and CREATE an empty file TEMP.DBF. Make its structure consistent with the information you just assembled. It does not matter what you call the fields. They can all be of character type. When you finish creating the structure, respond negatively to dBASE's question about whether you want to add records now. Then QUIT dBASE.

At this point you have a valid file structure in TEMP.DBF and all the records (without a structure) in P3D5.DBF. The time has come to merge the two files with DEBUG.

First, load TEMP.DBF into memory at address 0100 with the command

```
DEBUG TEMP.DBF
```

TEMP.DBF contains nine fields in our example. Therefore, its header is 321 decimal or 141 hex bytes long (since $9 \times 32 + 33 = 321$). The file contains no records, but it has an end-of-file marker immediately following the header. As DEBUG loaded it at address 0100, the file cannot extend beyond address 0241.

The TEMP file, as viewed with the DEBUG Dump command, appears as follows:

```
-D 100 24F
287A:0100  03 55 0A 09 00 00 00 00-42 01 52 00 00 00 00 00   .U......B.R.....
287A:0110  00 00 00 00 00 00 00 00-00 00 00 00 00 00 00 00   ................
287A:0120  53 55 52 4E 41 4D 45 00-00 00 00 43 00 00 00 00   SURNAME....C....
287A:0130  0B 00 00 00 00 00 00 00-00 00 00 00 00 00 00 00   ................
287A:0140  46 4E 41 4D 45 00 00 00-00 00 00 43 00 00 00 00   FNAME......C....
287A:0150  0E 00 00 00 00 00 00 00-00 00 00 00 00 00 00 00   ................
287A:0160  53 54 52 45 45 54 00 00-00 00 00 43 00 00 00 00   STREET.....C....
287A:0170  14 00 00 00 00 00 00 00-00 00 00 00 00 00 00 00   ................
287A:0180  43 49 54 59 00 00 00 00-00 00 00 43 00 00 00 00   CITY.......C....
287A:0190  10 00 00 00 00 00 00 00-00 00 00 00 00 00 00 00   ................
287A:01A0  53 54 41 54 45 00 00 00-00 00 00 43 00 00 00 00   STATE......C....
287A:01B0  02 00 00 00 00 00 00 00-00 00 00 00 00 00 00 00   ................
287A:01C0  5A 49 50 00 00 00 00 00-00 00 00 43 00 00 00 00   ZIP........C....
287A:01D0  05 00 00 00 00 00 00 00-00 00 00 00 00 00 00 00   ................
287A:01E0  4F 43 43 55 50 41 54 49-4F 4E 00 43 00 00 00 00   OCCUPATION.C....
287A:01F0  08 00 00 00 00 00 00 00-00 00 00 00 00 00 00 00   ................
287A:0200  50 41 52 54 59 00 00 00-00 00 00 43 00 00 00 00   PARTY......C....
287A:0210  01 00 00 00 00 00 00 00-00 00 00 00 00 00 00 00   ................
287A:0220  59 45 41 52 00 00 00 00-00 00 00 4E 00 00 00 00   YEAR.......N....
287A:0230  04 00 00 00 00 00 00 00-00 00 00 00 00 00 00 00   ................
287A:0240  0D 1A 00 00 00 00 00 00-00 00 00 00 00 00 00 00   ................
```

Note the end-of-file marker (1A hex) at address 0241. This is exactly where it should be in a dBASE III PLUS or dBASE IV file having 9 fields and no records, since it is the first address beyond the end of the header.

The next step is to load the records from P3D5.DBF into memory **at address 0241** to merge them with the new header. You must first identify the file to be loaded using DEBUG's Name command as follows:

```
N P3D5.DBF
```

Now load the file with the Load command

```
L 241
```

It tells DEBUG to load P3D5.DBF into memory, starting at address 0241.

We have merged the two files, but we must handle some details. The bytes in addresses 0104 through 0107 are all zero, indicating no records in the file. We must correct them to reflect the actual count. However, we are not sure how many records there are since some were lost when the file was damaged.

It would be convenient if dBASE would let you LIST the records at this point, since it would count them. But dBASE will not LIST a file if the structure indicates that it has no records. The simplest solution to this quandary is to fool dBASE by putting a dummy number in addresses 0104 through 0107. The number need not be correct. It must only be **at least as large** as the actual number of records now in the file.

Before performing the repair, we checked the damaged file and found it to be 3603 bytes long. Now that we have reconstructed the header, we know that the record width is 82 bytes. Dividing 3603 by 82 gives a little less than 44. Hence the damaged file could not have contained more than 44 records. Nor can the repaired file. Since 44 decimal is 2C hex, we should replace the 00 at address 0104 with 2C. Use the DEBUG Enter command.

```
E 104 2C
```

Before writing the file to disk, we must do one more thing. We must ensure that the new file size (expressed in hex bytes) is in registers BX and CX (high order bytes in BX). The size of the merged file cannot exceed 321 bytes (for the header) plus the 3603 bytes observed earlier. Hence, we should make the total file size 3924 bytes (decimal) or F54 hex.

To place the size in the registers, give the command

```
R CX
```

DEBUG will display

```
CX hhhh
:_
```

where 'hhhh' is the current contents of the CX register. Simply type F54 and press the Enter key to change it to 0F54. Similarly, set BX to zero by giving the command

```
R BX
```

and entering 0 at the colon prompt. The file size is set.

We can now write the salvaged P3D5 file to disk and exit from DEBUG.

The only task yet to be done is to correct the record count in the file header. We can do this in dBASE by opening the repaired file and copying it with the COPY command. dBASE will automatically put the correct count in the header of the new file.

The job is done, and the file has been recovered.

Before feeling completely confident that you have salvaged your file, LIST or BROWSE it in dBASE. If you see no problems, you are finished. If you still see problems, you can complete the repair with one of the procedures in this book.

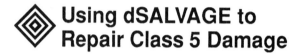

Using dSALVAGE to Repair Class 5 Damage

We will use the same P3D5.DBF datafile here as in the last section. As before, we need a valid header to do the repair.

In the standard version of dSALVAGE, we can use the Byte Stream Editor to get the structure information from the existing file. We then use the information to construct a new header with dBASE. dSALVAGE Professional has a header builder with which you can construct a new header without using dBASE. We will use the standard version here, however, since the problem serves as a good example of using the Byte Stream Editor.

Simply invoke dSALVAGE, select the file P3D5.DBF, and call up the editor. The screen shown next will appear. The file position indicator in the lower right corner always shows where the cursor is. By moving it to a character, marking down the position count, moving the cursor again, and subtracting the old position count from the new one, you can determine the number of intervening characters. In this way, you can determine field and record lengths.

As in the DEBUG example earlier, the field types need not be correct. When in doubt, assume a character field. It is important, however, that you identify ALL fields and determine their widths accurately.

Since the header is invalid, the record number on the status line (at the bottom of the screen) is meaningless. But the "file position" counter is always valid. If you move the cursor to the space just before the name "Adams" (shown as the " ▮ " character near the beginning of the third line of the display), the position counter indicates that it is byte 134 in the file.

```
┌──────────────────── Byte Stream Editor Commands ────────────────────┐
│ F1    Help          ALT-B Mark Block    ALT-W Write Block PgUp Prev Screen │
│ F10   Hide/Show menu ALT-M Move Block    ALT-G Goto Byte   PgDn Next Screen │
│ ALT-S Search        ALT-C Copy Block    ALT-U Undelete     HOME Top of File │
│ ALT-A Repeat Search ALT-D Delete Block  Arrow Keys         END  End of File │
└──────────────── Press ESC to Return to Editor Menu ──────────────┘
```

```
┌──────────────────────────────────────────────────────────────────┐
│ ν|ķ╪ө▓╫◄═╎ᖯᕋ5′г─ᐢˆƒ┐ᔈ╎·╦╷ᕘ◄Ͱ┙┙▄◢╤┘╟╓╎㎖╻ᒪᐃᵒ&╪ᐁ⁴‖┘╥╥·≥ᒥ╫╫╫◙ℸᶘᵃ˟∑┘Ռ⁄
│ ᖆᖫ╟╻⌐⊤╥─ɑ┃╻┘ᶞ˟ᔈ┌гᵞ┤‖ᖙ╙ᵞ▓◙╪↓∑ᖙᵞɑ≡‖┃ᴘᶴ⌐│>oreland     Vᗅ12222Lawyer       │
│ D1817█Adams      John Quincy    5 Harvard St          Braintree             │
│    MA13333Lawyer  D1825 Jackson     Andrew        1 None St                 │
│      Waxhaw           SC15555Lawyer  D1829 Van Buren  Martin                │
│    3 First St        Kinderhook      NY16666Lawyer  D1837 Harr              │
│ ison    William H.   5 Hampden Ave      Berkeley          VA12222           │
│ Soldier W1841 Tyler     John        33 William and Mary Green               │
│ way        VA12222Lawyer  W1841 Polk      James         4 Unive             │
│ rsity       Pineville      ND14444Lawyer  D1845 Taylor      Zac             │
│ hary     13 Maple Lane     Orange          VA12222Soldier W1                │
│ 849 Fillmore   Millard     3 Folley St.       Locke                        │
│  NY15555Lawyer  W1850 Johnson     Andrew      1 None St.                    │
│    Raleigh        NC14444Tailor  N1865 Grant      Ulysses S.                │
│  3 West Point      Point Pleasant  OH12345Soldier R1869 Hayes               │
│       Rutherford B.  7 Kenyon Dr.      Delaware       OH13344La             │
└──────────────────────────────────────────────────────────────────┘
                        Record 1          file position 134
```

When we move the cursor to the space immediately preceding the name "Jackson" (which obviously marks the beginning of the next record), the position indicator displays 216. Subtracting 134 from 216 gives the record size: 82. By moving the cursor similarly from field to field and noting the file position at the first character of each, we can determine individual field widths.

We can now use the information just acquired to create a new file NEWHEAD.DBF using the dBASE CREATE command.

Now that NEWHEAD contains a valid header, recovery can proceed. After we again invoke dSALVAGE, select P3D5.DBF, and enter the Diagnosis and Repair module, the following screen appears:

```
┌──────────────────────────────────────────────────────────────────┐
│ INPUT FILE........ P3D5.DBF        dBASE VERSION.....                  │
│ HEADER SIZE....... -15369          LAST UPDATED...... 9-13-88          │
│ FIELDS PER RECORD. -481            TOTAL RECORDS..... 112314345        │
│ FILE SIZE......... 2847            RECORD SIZE....... 313              │
│                                    CLUSTER SIZE...... 512              │
│ CURRENT DIRECTORY. C:\                                                 │
│ OUTPUT WRITTEN TO. C:\P3D5.DBF                                         │
│ DIRECTORY FILTER.. *.DBF                                               │
│                                                                       │
│ ┌──────────────── Diagnosis & Repair Menu ────────────────┐          │
│ │                                                          │          │
│ │     F1  Help                F3  Internal Damage Repair   │          │
│ │     F2  Check file for damage   F4  External Damage Repair│         │
│ │                                                          │          │
│ └──────────── Press ESC to return to Main Menu ───────────┘          │
│ ┌──────────────────────────────────────────────────────────┐        │
│ │                                                            │        │
│ │                                                            │        │
│ │                                                            │        │
│ │                                                            │        │
│ └────────────────────────────────────────────────────────────┘      │
│ Your Choice[ ]                                                        │
└──────────────────────────────────────────────────────────────────┘
```

Pay particular attention to the information at the top. Note that some values (HEADER SIZE and FIELDS PER RECORD) are negative. Since dSALVAGE gets them from the header, this is a further indication of damage. Pressing the F2 key to check the file for damage produces the diagnostic message below, confirming the existence of header damage.

```
INPUT FILE........ P3D5.DBF      dBASE VERSION.....
HEADER SIZE....... -15369        LAST UPDATED...... 9-13-88
FIELDS PER RECORD. -481          TOTAL RECORDS..... 112314345
FILE SIZE......... 2847          RECORD SIZE....... 313
                                 CLUSTER SIZE...... 512
CURRENT DIRECTORY. C:\
OUTPUT WRITTEN TO. C:\P3D5.DBF
DIRECTORY FILTER.. *.DBF

────────────────── Diagnosis & Repair Menu──────────────

      F1  Help                   F3  Internal Damage Repair

File contains header damage (Class 3 or Class 5).
dBASE version number is incorrect and further header damage may exist.
You MUST either import a valid header OR repair the header before
  recovery operations can continue.
CLASS 5 repair is recommended:  Press Enter then F3 then F6




─────────────────── Press Enter to Continue──────────────
```

dSALVAGE recommends Class 5 repair. After pressing the Enter key, the F3 key, and the F6 key as it recommends (or, in dSALVAGE Professional, after simply authorizing execution of its recovery recommendation), we see the following message in a window near the center of the screen. It requests a name for the output file that the recovery process will produce:

```
      enter  [device:path]<filename> to write output file to
   T5FIX.DBF
```

We call the output file T5FIX.DBF as indicated above. dSALVAGE now requests the name of a file containing a healthy matching header. We need only specify NEWHEAD.DBF as follows:

```
                         enter file to read header from
     NEWHEAD.DBF
```

dSALVAGE automatically obtains the header from NEWHEAD and displays the following message in a window near the center of the screen:

```
           header file read, header contains no errors

                 ──── Press any Key to Continue ────
```

Next, dSALVAGE automatically moves the data portion of the damaged file until it is correctly positioned and aligned at the end of the new header. The following screen appears. dSALVAGE has done the equivalent of the DEBUG Move command automatically without requiring specific addresses.

```
 INPUT FILE........ P3D5.DBF      dBASE VERSION..... DBASE-III+
 HEADER SIZE....... 321           LAST UPDATED...... 9-13-88
 FIELDS PER RECORD. 9             TOTAL RECORDS..... 0
 FILE SIZE......... 2847          RECORD SIZE....... 82
                                  CLUSTER SIZE...... 512

 DELETEFLAG :
    SURNAME : Adams
      FNAME : John Quincy
     STREET : 5 Harvard St
       CITY : Braintree
      STATE : MA
        ZIP : 13333
 OCCUPATION : Lawyer
      PARTY : D
       YEAR : 1825
            :
            :
            :
            :
            :
            :

 arrow keys to slide, CR to end        Header position 134
```

When the automatic alignment is complete, pressing the Enter key produces the following message in a window near the center of the screen:

```
┌────────────────────────────────────────────────────────────┐
│        ok to re-align past 132 characters of file? Y/N      │
└────────────────────────────────────────────────────────────┘
```

dSALVAGE is now ready to "squeeze" 132 bytes out of the file. They are remnants of the damaged header and the partial record. After we answer affirmatively, dSALVAGE runs a pattern match in the record area of the file. It stops when it finds either an end-of-file marker or an invalid record. In this case, it finds an EOF and displays the following message:

```
┌────────────────────────────────────────────────────────────┐
│            Pattern match stopped at dBASE file EOF          │
└─────────────── Press any Key to Continue ──────────────────┘
```

dSALVAGE next displays a message indicating how many valid records it found and asks for your authorization to write the record count into the header:

```
┌────────────────────────────────────────────────────────────┐
│         transfer count of 33 records to header ? Y/N        │
└────────────────────────────────────────────────────────────┘
```

Answering affirmatively completes the recovery and the following screen appears. Note that the TOTAL RECORDS count in the header is now 33.

```
┌─────────────────────────────────────────────────────────────────────┐
│  INPUT FILE........ T5FIX.DBF      dBASE VERSION..... DBASE-III+      │
│  HEADER SIZE....... 321            LAST UPDATED...... 9-13-88         │
│  FIELDS PER RECORD. 9              TOTAL RECORDS..... 33              │
│  FILE SIZE......... 3035           RECORD SIZE....... 82              │
│                                    CLUSTER SIZE...... 512             │
│  CURRENT DIRECTORY. C:\                                              │
│  OUTPUT WRITTEN TO. C:\T5FIX.DBF                                     │
│  DIRECTORY FILTER.. *.DBF                                            │
│                                                                      │
│    ┌──────────────────────────────────────────────────────────────┐ │
│    │ class 5 repair complete, input file closed, operating now on output file │
│    └───────────────────Press any Key to Continue ──────────────┘ │
│                                                                      │
│                                                                      │
│                                                                      │
│                                                                      │
│                Record 33        file position 2946                   │
└─────────────────────────────────────────────────────────────────────┘
```

Before exiting from dSALVAGE, we run a final check of the file using the diagnostic module to look for secondary damage. If there is any, dSALVAGE will advise you how to continue the recovery. In our example, there is no further damage, so dSALVAGE gives the file a clean bill of health as follows:

```
INPUT FILE........ T5FIX.DBF      dBASE VERSION..... DBASE-III+
HEADER SIZE....... 321            LAST UPDATED...... 9-13-88
FIELDS PER RECORD. 9              TOTAL RECORDS..... 33
FILE SIZE......... 3035           RECORD SIZE....... 82
                                  CLUSTER SIZE...... 512

CURRENT DIRECTORY. C:\
OUTPUT WRITTEN TO. C:\T5FIX.DBF
DIRECTORY FILTER.. *.DBF

─────────────── Diagnosis & Repair Menu ───────────────

       F1  Help                  F3  Internal Damage Repair

No dBASE header errors detected.
No record errors detected.
No unwanted EOF's detected in file.




─────────────── Press Enter to Continue ───────────────
```

The task is done.

 # Summary

If you reboot your computer or an electrical disturbance occurs while a datafile is open, the probability of severe header damage is high. Repair of such damage requires both file merging and data repositioning. You can do this manually with DEBUG for small files, but large files require a specialized tool such as dSALVAGE. Severe header damage is often accompanied by secondary damage (usually offset). With dSALVAGE, you can detect and repair it easily.

19

Recovery from Lost Cluster Damage

◈ Skipped Clusters in the Allocation Chain

As discussed in Chapter 7, a datafile with skipped clusters in its allocation chain will usually appear to have its data offset or displaced relative to the field boundaries when LISTed or BROWSEd in dBASE. A typical FAT appears as follows:

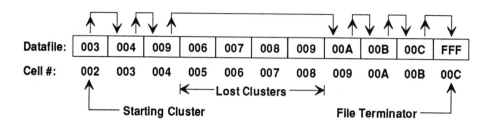

A displacement usually appears at the point where the last record (or partial record) in cluster 4 is followed immediately by the first one (or partial) in cluster 9. I say "usually" instead of "always" since the records could line up perfectly, just as an answer to a crossword puzzle could miraculously fit into the wrong squares going in the wrong direction. Of course, this occurs only when you are trying to demonstrate the problem to an unhappy client. In any case, however, the record area of the file will appear smaller than either the record count (in the header) or the file size (in the directory) indicates.

The number of records displayed in a dBASE LISTing of the file will be less than the count shown in a listing of its structure. In the typical case, offset coupled with a reduced record area indicates skipped-cluster damage. In the rare case of no apparent offset, however, you could misinterpret skipped-cluster damage as Class 2 (extra end-of-file marker) damage unless you run CHKDSK. The reason is that in both situations the STRUCTURE LISTing and the content of the RECCOUNT() function are identical, but the record count returned by the COUNT command is smaller.

Although CHKDSK can recognize skipped clusters, reinserting them properly in the file is very difficult, especially on a typical hard disk where many files are both fragmented and interleaved. If the record and cluster boundaries coincide, it is a simple matter to run CHKDSK, convert the lost clusters to a file, and APPEND it to the damaged file. The appended records would be out of order, of course, but the data would have been recovered intact. Unfortunately, such coincidence is rare.

The general purpose tools discussed in Chapter 8 are unsatisfactory for restoring a file with skipped cluster damage. To recover such a file, the tool must be able to do the following:

- Recognize a disparity betweem the size of the record area and other file parameters.

- Detect a discontinuity in the data pattern.

- Distinguish among Class 2 (extra end-of-file marker) damage, Class 4 (data offset) damage, and lost cluster damage.

- Re-insert the lost clusters at the proper location in the damaged file.

The only tool we have discussed that has all these capabilities is dSALVAGE. Hence, we will use it to illustrate recovery. First, let's examine the directory and FAT of a sample floppy disk containing the file LC1.DBF that has skipped cluster damage.

```
C:DIR A:

 Volume in drive A has no label
 Directory of  A:\

BLANKRES DBF     1409    5-31-88   10:55a
COM      DBF    64306    5-22-88   12:55p
CLCODE   DBF     5935    5-31-88    6:05p
OPENFILS PRG     1195    9-18-88    5:36p
IACT     PRG     3983    9-27-86    7:39p
APPLOG   DBF     6514    9-19-88   11:54a
MAILLIST DBF     1922    9-19-88   11:54a
APPFILE  DBF     1306    9-19-88   11:54a
LC1      DBF    47475   10-17-88   12:04p
SNTABLE  DBF      884    1-05-88    7:31p
PURGE    PRG     1071    1-09-88    1:20p
CUSTLIST PRG     3952    9-12-86    5:40p
LABELS   PRG     2802    4-19-88   11:45p
SJOUR    DBF    16574    9-27-86    1:32a
INVOICE  PRG    31349    1-04-87   10:23p
SCOM     PRG     5939    9-27-86   11:46p
LAYAWAY  DBF     1976    9-27-86   12:43a
LAYAWAY  PRG     1850    9-12-86    5:48p
        18 File(s)    154624 bytes free
```

When viewed with DiskMinder, the disk's directory appears as follows:

```
Directory Editing Mode                                      DiskMinder
[Esc] Displays Main Menu

Filename.Ext      Size     Date      Time    Attr  Clu  Reserved
BLANKRES.DBF      1409   05/31/88  10:55:20   20  0002  00000000000000000000
COM     .DBF     64306   05/22/88  12:55:08   20  0004  00000000000000000000
CLCODE  .DBF      5935   05/31/88  18:05:04   20  0043  00000000000000000000
OPENFILS.PRG      1195   09/18/88  17:36:04   20  0049  00000000000000000000
IACT    .PRG      3983   09/27/86  19:39:11   20  004B  00000000000000000000
APPLOG  .DBF      6514   09/19/88  11:54:14   20  006F  00000000000000000000
MAILLIST.DBF      1922   09/19/88  11:54:14   20  0076  00000000000000000000
APPFILE .DBF      1306   09/19/88  11:54:15   20  0078  00000000000000000000
LC1     .DBF     47475   10/17/88  12:04:25   20  004F  00000000000000000000
SNTABLE .DBF       884   01/05/88  19:31:29   20  007C  00000000000000000000
PURGE   .PRG      1071   01/09/88  13:20:12   20  007D  00000000000000000000
CUSTLIST.PRG      3952   09/12/86  17:40:03   20  0083  00000000000000000000
LABELS  .PRG      2802   04/19/88  23:45:12   20  0087  00000000000000000000
SJOUR   .DBF     16574   09/27/86  01:32:19   20  008A  00000000000000000000
INVOICE .PRG     31349   01/04/87  22:23:19   20  009B  00000000000000000000
SCOM    .PRG      5939   09/27/86  23:46:28   20  00BE  00000000000000000000
LAYAWAY .DBF      1976   09/27/86  00:43:08   20  00C4  00000000000000000000
LAYAWAY .PRG      1850   09/12/86  17:48:04   20  00C6  00000000000000000000

Editing Directory A:\
         Entry    1 of 112                 Cluster  n/aH  Sector       5
```

The File Allocation Table appears as follows (with the chain for LC1.DBF shown in boldface):

```
Fat Editing Mode                                            DiskMinder
[Esc] Displays Main Menu

Clu    +0  +1  +2  +3    +4  +5  +6  +7    +8  +9  +A  +B    +C  +D  +E  +F
0000  FFD FFF 003 FFF   005 006 007 008   009 00A 00B 00C   00D 00E 00F 010
0010  011 012 013 014   015 016 017 018   019 01A 01B 01C   01D 01E 01F 020
0020  021 022 023 024   025 026 027 028   029 02A 02B 02C   02D 02E 02F 030
0030  031 032 033 034   035 036 037 038   039 03A 03B 03C   03D 03E 03F 040
0040  041 042 FFF 044   045 046 047 048   FFF 04A FFF 04C   04D 04E FFF 050
0050  051 052 053 054   055 056 057 058   059 05A 05B 05C   05D 05E 05F 060
0060  061 062 063 064   065 066 067 068   069 06A 06B 06C   06D 06E 07A 070
0070  071 072 073 074   075 FFF 077 FFF   079 FFF 07B 0BC   FFF 07E FFF 080
0080  081 082 0BA 084   085 086 FFF 088   089 FFF 08B 08C   08D 08E 08F 090
0090  091 092 093 094   095 096 097 098   099 09A FFF 09C   09D 09E 09F 0A0
00A0  0A1 0A2 0A3 0A4   0A5 0A6 0A7 0A8   0A9 0AA 0AB 0AC   0AD 0AE 0AF 0B0
00B0  0B1 0B2 0B3 0B4   0B5 0B6 0B7 0B8   0B9 FFF 0BB 0BC   0BD 0C8 0BF 0C0
00C0  0C1 0C2 0C3 FFF   0C5 FFF 0C7 FFF   0C9 0CA 0CB 0CC   FFF 000 000 000
00D0  000 000 000 000   000 000 000 000   000 000 000 000   000 000 000 000
00E0  000 000 000 000   000 000 000 000   000 000 000 000   000 000 000 000
00F0  000 000 000 000   000 000 000 000   000 000 000 000   000 000 000 000

Editing FAT entry for cluster     04FH             FAT1 Sector        1
                        sector     166             FAT2 Sector        3
```

On examining the FAT display carefully, you can see that LC1.DBF has 41 clusters allocated to it. But its directory entry indicates a size of 47475. The file should therefore occupy 47 clusters on a floppy disk having 1024-byte clusters. The difficulty, of course, lies in finding the six missing clusters. To do this, you could either examine all clusters not allocated to LC1.DBF or compare the FAT against the directory to determine which clusters are not accounted for. But even this information may not suffice to rebuild an allocation chain (although it would here in our simplified example).

You also usually need to examine the data on both sides of each cluster boundary to reassemble the missing clusters **in the correct order**. The process is tedious, even for a floppy disk. Doing it on a large hard disk would be prohibitively time-consuming. Also, rebuilding a file allocation chain manually is risky and could cause worse damage. Only very knowledgeable users should attempt it.

For reference, the unaccounted-for clusters in our example are 7F, 80, 81, 82, BA, and BB, as you will see later.

Before starting the recovery, let's examine part of the file as it appears in the dBASE BROWSE mode:

```
SURNAME-------- FNAME--------- STREET----------------------
Morris          Jerome A.      1253 LaBaron Circle
Meyers          John G.        48 Trafalgar
Maszle          John R.        2301 Westside
Lyons           Joseph W.      78 Bunker Hill Circle
Looter          Leslie A.      5838 Rightway Lane
Perkins         Michael        3453 Hulberton Rd.
Knox            Michael D.     744 University Pk.
Kalvitis        Phil           Ri chard      268 Bohic       Vin
 4601764-8724Qu igley          Ha rold F.    269 Zornow      Aji
85614188-2499Qu art            Wi lliam M.   270 Trabold     Cla
76614563-5453Pu rcell          Ke nneth      271 Sirkus      Ear
68614919-1919Pu gliese         Do uglas H.   272 Nazzaro     Jam
51614728-1919Pr ystal          Er ik M.      273 Marshall    Joh
42614246-4483Pr est            Wa yne A.     274 Knight      Mic
34614929-3847Pr iesmeyer       Ja mes H.     275 Hauenstein  Ric
25614197-7979Po wers           Jo hn         276 Fletcher    Rob
17614918-6240Po st             Ro bert G.    277 Clapp       Tho
```

```
BROWSE          |<A:>|LC1                |Rec: 221/311      |
```

View and edit fields.

You can clearly see the offset, but you cannot distinguish between Class 4 and skipped cluster damage. We now invoke dSALVAGE, choose the file operations option from the main menu, and change the directory to drive A. Although we are using dSALVAGE here, the process is basically the same as with dSALVAGE Professional. The following screen appears:

```
─────────────── Setup and File Selection Menu ───────────────
 F1    Help                              F5    Change Directory
 F2    Select Input File                 F6    Change Selection Filter
 F3    Type in Name of Input File        F7    Delete File
 F4    Type in Name of Output File       F10   Hide/Show Menu
────────────────── Press ESC to Continue ──────────────────

    BLANKRES.DBF    1409   05-31-88   10:55:40
         COM.DBF   64306   05-22-88   12:55:16
      CLCODE.DBF    5935   05-31-88   18:05:08
      APPLOG.DBF    6514   09-19-88   11:54:28
    MAILLIST.DBF    1922   09-19-88   11:54:28
     APPFILE.DBF    1306   09-19-88   11:54:30
         LC1.DBF   47475   10-17-88   12:04:50
     SNTABLE.DBF     884   01-05-88   19:31:58
       SJOUR.DBF   16574   09-27-86   01:32:38
     LAYAWAY.DBF    1976   09-27-86   00:43:16



Your Choice[ ]
```

We select LC1.DBF, return to the main menu, and select the Diagnosis and Repair option. The following screen appears:

```
INPUT FILE........ LC1.DBF        dBASE VERSION..... DBASE-III+
HEADER SIZE....... 513            LAST UPDATED...... 10-17-88
FIELDS PER RECORD. 15             TOTAL RECORDS..... 311
FILE SIZE......... 47475          RECORD SIZE....... 151
                                  CLUSTER SIZE...... 1024
CURRENT DIRECTORY. A:\
OUTPUT WRITTEN TO. A:\LC1.DBF
DIRECTORY FILTER.. *.DBF

──────────────── Diagnosis & Repair Menu ────────────────

        F1   Help                    F3   Internal Damage Repair
        F2   Check file for damage   F4   External Damage Repair
──────────── Press ESC to return to Main Menu ────────────




Your Choice[ ]
```

When we press the F2 key to check the file for damage, dSALVAGE runs its diagnostics and reports as follows:

```
INPUT FILE........ LC1.DBF          dBASE VERSION..... DBASE-III+
HEADER SIZE....... 513              LAST UPDATED...... 10-17-88
FIELDS PER RECORD. 15               TOTAL RECORDS..... 311
FILE SIZE......... 47475            RECORD SIZE....... 151
                                    CLUSTER SIZE...... 1024
CURRENT DIRECTORY. A:\
OUTPUT WRITTEN TO. A:\LC1.DBF
DIRECTORY FILTER.. *.DBF

─────────────── Diagnosis & Repair Menu ───────────────

      F1  Help                    F3  Internal Damage Repair

File contains record damage (Class 1 or Class 4).
227 records match header pattern out of expected 311
Record(s) contain binary (less than hex 20) data.
Deleted flag in record(s) invalid (not * or space).
dBASE Record EOF marker not where expected.
Data area in file smaller than expected. File could have external
 damage with missing clusters. Exit dSALVAGE now and run CHKDSK.
 IF CHKDSK REPORTS ALLOCATION ERRORS with this file or lost clusters
 run External Repair in dSALVAGE. Press Enter, then F4.
 IF NO ERRORS ARE REPORTED BY CHKDSK then
 CLASS 4 repair is recommended:  Press Enter, then F3, then F5
No dBASE header errors detected:
No unwanted EOF's detected in file.
──────── Pg-Up,Pg-Dn,↑↓, for rest of message, press Enter to Continue ────────
```

dSALVAGE detects a discontinuity in the data, ascertains that lost cluster damage is likely, and recommends that we run CHKDSK. We now exit from dSALVAGE and run CHKDSK without the /F option initially to avoid premature decisions on corrective measures. It produces the following report:

```
C:\CHKDSK A:

Errors found, F parameter not specified.
Corrections will not be written to disk.

A:\LC1.DBF
   Allocation error, size adjusted.

6 lost clusters found in 1 chains.
Convert lost chains to files  (Y/N)? n
    6144 bytes disk space
         would be freed.
```

CHKDSK does not uncover cross-linking or other unusual problems, so we run it again (this time with the /F option) and tell it to convert the lost chains to files.

Following conversion, a directory listing of drive A shows the new file:

```
FILE0000 CHK    6144  10-17-88   1:44p
```

We digress here briefly to observe the consequences of CHKDSK's actions. A display of the disk directory by DiskMinder reveals the new file starting in cluster 7F (shown in boldface below).

```
Directory Editing Mode                                      DiskMinder
[Esc] Displays Main Menu

Filename.Ext    Size    Date      Time    Attr Clu  Reserved
BLANKRES.DBF    1409    05/31/88  10:55:20  20  0002  00000000000000000000
COM     .DBF   64306    05/22/88  12:55:08  20  0004  00000000000000000000
CLCODE  .PRG    5935    05/31/88  18:05:04  20  0043  00000000000000000000
OPENFILS.PRG    1195    09/18/88  17:36:04  20  0049  00000000000000000000
IACT    .PRG    3983    09/27/86  19:39:11  20  004B  00000000000000000000
APPLOG  .DBF    6514    09/19/88  11:54:14  20  006F  00000000000000000000
MAILLIST.DBF    1922    09/19/88  11:54:14  20  0076  00000000000000000000
APPFILE .DBF    1306    09/19/88  11:54:15  20  0078  00000000000000000000
LC1     .DBF   41984    10/17/88  12:04:25  20  004F  00000000000000000000
SNTABLE .DBF     884    01/05/88  19:31:29  20  007C  00000000000000000000
PURGE   .PRG    1071    01/09/88  13:20:12  20  007D  00000000000000000000
CUSTLIST.PRG    3952    09/12/86  17:40:03  20  0083  00000000000000000000
LABELS  .PRG    2802    04/19/88  23:45:12  20  0087  00000000000000000000
SJOUR   .DBF   16574    09/27/86  01:32:19  20  008A  00000000000000000000
INVOICE .PRG   31349    01/04/87  22:23:19  20  009B  00000000000000000000
FILE0000.CHK    6144    10/17/88  13:44:17  00  007F  00000000000000000000
SCOM    .PRG    5939    09/27/86  23:46:28  20  00BE  00000000000000000000
LAYAWAY .DBF    1976    09/27/86  00:43:08  20  00C4  00000000000000000000
LAYAWAY .PRG    1850    09/12/86  17:48:04  20  00C6  00000000000000000000
        .          0    00/00/80  00:00:00  00  0000  00000000000000000000
        .          0    00/00/80  00:00:00  00  0000  00000000000000000000
        .          0    00/00/80  00:00:00  00  0000  00000000000000000000
        .          0    00/00/80  00:00:00  00  0000  00000000000000000000

Editing Directory A:\
         Entry  16 of 112                    Cluster  n/aH  Sector      5
```

Upon selecting FILE0000.CHK and moving to the FAT Editing Mode of Disk-Minder, we see that the file occupies the following six clusters (shown in boldface below): 07F, 080, 081, 082, 0BA, and 0BB. They are exactly the unaccounted-for clusters we identified earlier.

```
Fat Editing Mode                                           DiskMinder
[Esc] Displays Main Menu

Clu  +0  +1  +2  +3    +4  +5  +6  +7    +8  +9  +A  +B    +C  +D  +E  +F
0000 FFD FFF 003 FFF   005 006 007 008   009 00A 00B 00C   00D 00E 00F 010
0010 011 012 013 014   015 016 017 018   019 01A 01B 01C   01D 01E 01F 020
0020 021 022 023 024   025 026 027 028   029 02A 02B 02C   02D 02E 02F 030
0030 031 032 033 034   035 036 037 038   039 03A 03B 03C   03D 03E 03F 040
0040 041 042 FFF 044   045 046 047 048   FFF 04A FFF 04C   04D 04E FFF 050
0050 051 052 053 054   055 056 057 058   059 05A 05B 05C   05D 05E 05F 060
0060 061 062 063 064   065 066 067 068   069 06A 06B 06C   06D 06E 07A 070
0070 071 072 073 074   075 FFF 077 FFF   079 FFF 07B 0BC   FFF 07E FFF 080
0080 081 082 0BA 084   085 086 FFF 088   089 FFF 08B 08C   08D 08E 08F 090
0090 091 092 093 094   095 096 097 098   099 09A FFF 09C   09D 09E 09F 0A0
00A0 0A1 0A2 0A3 0A4   0A5 0A6 0A7 0A8   0A9 0AA 0AB 0AC   0AD 0AE 0AF 0B0
00B0 0B1 0B2 0B3 0B4   0B5 0B6 0B7 0B8   0B9 FFF 0BB FFF   0BD 0C8 0BF 0C0
00C0 0C1 0C2 0C3 FFF   0C5 FFF 0C7 FFF   0C9 0CA 0CB 0CC   FFF 0CE 0CF 0D0
00D0 0D1 FFF 000 000   000 000 000 000   000 000 000 000   000 000 000 000
00E0 000 000 000 000   000 000 000 000   000 000 000 000   000 000 000 000
00F0 000 000 000 000   000 000 000 000   000 000 000 000   000 000 000 000

Editing FAT entry for cluster      07FH              FAT1 Sector        1
                    sector          262              FAT2 Sector        3
```

Now that CHKDSK has created the CHK file, we can resume recovery. This time we do not need to run the diagnostics, so we can move directly to External Damage Repair. It begins by displaying the following screen:

```
INPUT FILE........ LC1.DBF        dBASE VERSION..... DBASE-III+
HEADER SIZE....... 513            LAST UPDATED...... 10-17-88
FIELDS PER RECORD. 15             TOTAL RECORDS..... 311
FILE SIZE......... 41984          RECORD SIZE....... 151
                                  CLUSTER SIZE...... 1024
CURRENT DIRECTORY. A:\
OUTPUT WRITTEN TO. A:\LC1.DBF
DIRECTORY FILTER.. *.DBF

───────────────── Diagnosis & Repair Menu ─────────────────

        F1  Help                    F3  Internal Damage Repair

You have entered the External Damage repair mode.  You will be asked to
specify an Output File if you have not already done so.  You will then be
asked if CHKDSK has recovered any lost clusters and placed them into one
or more CHK files.  If you have not run CHKDSK, exit from dSALVAGE now and
do so.  (The dSALVAGE manual contains instructions on using CHKDSK).  Then
re-enter dSALVAGE which will examine these files and verify that they match
the pattern of your file header.  If so, the good data in your damaged
file, together with the lost data in the CHK file(s), will be written to
a new output file.

───────────────── Press Enter to Continue ─────────────────
```

The following message next appears in a window near the center of the screen:

```
        enter  [device:path]<filename> to write output file to
```

External Repair always requires a separate output file. As you will see shortly, dSALVAGE writes clusters from the damaged file and from the CHK files produced by CHKDSK to the output file in the proper sequence. We should mention that dSALVAGE allows a separate output file in any form of damage repair, even if it is not required.

In our example, we call the output file LC1FIX.DBF and ask that it be written to drive C by entering

```
C:LC1FIX.DBF
```

dSALVAGE then asks the following question in a window near the center of the screen:

```
 ┌─────────────────────────────────────────────────────────────┐
 │  has CHKDSK /F detected and restored any lost clusters? Y/N  │
 └─────────────────────────────────────────────────────────────┘
```

When we respond affirmatively, dSALVAGE proceeds as follows:

1. It searches drive A for CHK files.

2. It examines them to see if they contain data corresponding to the file's structure.

3. It examines their contents at the cluster boundaries to determine where they should be inserted into the output file.

4. It inserts the contents appropriately.

5. It closes the damaged file and opens the output file to allow further user analysis if desired.

6. It displays the following screen, indicating that all actions are done.

```
 ┌────────────────────────────────────────────────────────────────┐
 │  INPUT FILE........ LC1FIX.DBF      dBASE VERSION..... DBASE-III+ │
 │  HEADER SIZE....... 513             LAST UPDATED...... 10-17-88   │
 │  FIELDS PER RECORD. 15              TOTAL RECORDS..... 311        │
 │  FILE SIZE......... 48128           RECORD SIZE....... 151        │
 │                                     CLUSTER SIZE...... 512        │
 │  CURRENT DIRECTORY. C:\                                           │
 │  OUTPUT WRITTEN TO. C:\LC1FIX.DBF                                 │
 │  DIRECTORY FILTER.. *.DBF                                         │
 │                                                                  │
 │   ┌────────────────────────────────────────────────────────┐    │
 │   │ external repair ok, input file closed, operating now on output file │
 │   └──────────────── Press any Key to Continue ─────────────┘    │
 │  └──────────────────── Press ESC to return to Main Menu ──────── │
 │                                                                  │
 │                                                                  │
 │                                                                  │
 │                                                                  │
 └────────────────────────────────────────────────────────────────┘
```

Although recovery is complete, we run a diagnostic check on the output file to look for residual damage. dSALVAGE displays the following screen, indicating no further problems:

```
INPUT FILE........ LC1FIX.DBF      dBASE VERSION..... DBASE-III+
HEADER SIZE....... 513             LAST UPDATED...... 10-17-88
FIELDS PER RECORD. 15              TOTAL RECORDS..... 311
FILE SIZE......... 48128           RECORD SIZE....... 151
                                   CLUSTER SIZE...... 512
CURRENT DIRECTORY. C:\
OUTPUT WRITTEN TO. C:\LC1FIX.DBF
DIRECTORY FILTER.. *.DBF

─────────────── Diagnosis & Repair Menu ───────────────

       F1  Help                    F3  Internal Damage Repair

No dBASE header errors detected.
No record errors detected.
No unwanted EOF's detected in file.




─────────────── Press Enter to Continue ───────────────
```

As a final verification of repair, we examine the recovered file in the BROWSE mode of dBASE. The region containing the original damage now appears as follows:

```
SURNAME-------- FNAME--------- STREET----------------------------
Morris         Jerome A.      1253 LaBaron Circle
Meyers         John G.        48 Trafalgar
Maszle         John R.        2301 Westside
Lyons          Joseph W.      78 Bunker Hill Circle
Looter         Leslie A.      5838 Rightway Lane
Perkins        Michael        3453 Hulberton Rd.
Knox           Michael D.     744 University Pk.
Kalvitis       Phil           4267 Buffalo Road
Hope           Philip A.      148 Mt. Morency Dr.
Harris         Richard A.     18 Log Cabin Circle
Gonzales       Richard T.     172 Surrey Hill Way
Fries          Robert E.      167 Averill Avenue
Federico       Robert N.      466 Morgan St.
Drake          Samuel M.      4595 East Road
Cornell        Ted L.         66 Villa St.
Brown          Thomas P.      64 Pulaski Ave.
Bebb           Wilbur I.      7512 Norton Road

BROWSE          |<C:>|LC1FIX              |Rec: 221/311
```

View and edit fields.

The recovery is complete. There is no longer any evidence of offset, and all the records have been salvaged.

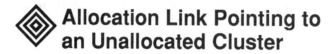

Allocation Link Pointing to an Unallocated Cluster

In Chapter 7, we saw a file that had a link in its allocation chain pointing to an unallocated cell. Figure 19-1 illustrates the case. File A originally started in cluster 2 and ended in cluster C. But cell 4, which originally pointed to cell 5 in File A's chain, was corrupted and now points to cell 37A, an unused cluster. Since there is no pointer to cell 5, cells 5 through C form a chain not identified with any file. CHKDSK defines this situation as "8 lost clusters in 1 chain" and also complains about an invalid cluster.

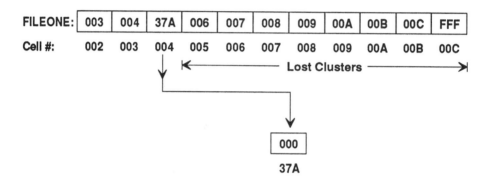

Figure 19-1.   *Allocation Chain Linked to an Unallocated Cluster*

Let's now consider a real case and explore recovery of a file XFILE.DBF on drive A. The directory listing shows:

```
C:\DIR A:

Volume in drive A has no label
Directory of  A:\

XFILE    DBF    11839   1-11-89   1:25p
    1 File(s)    350208 bytes free
```

Part of XFILE, beginning at record 33, appears as follows when viewed in the BROWSE mode:

```
SURNAME-------- FNAME---------- STREET----------------------------
Cook            Terrance        19 Tandoi Drive
Burkey          Thomas J.       8467 Peachy Rd.
Balsamo         William C.      902 Monroe Ave.
Azar            William G.      2010 New St.
Warden          Carol K.        189 Vollmer Pkwy.
Singer          Eddie           73 Fillingham++++++++++++++++++++++
++++++++++++++++ ++++++++++++++++ +++++++++++++++++++++++++++++++++++
++++++++++++++++ ++++++++++++++++ +++++++++++++++++++++++++++++++++++
++++++++++++++++ ++++++++++++++++ +++++++++++++++++++++++++++++++++++
++++++++++++++++ ++++++++++++++++ +++++++++++++++++++++++++++++++++++
++++++++++++++++ ++++++++++++++++ +++++++++++++++++++++++++++++++++++
++++++++++++++++ ++++++++++++++++ +++++++++++++++++++++++++++++++++++
++++++++++++                                     ?
                                                 ?
                                                 ?
   _____
    BROWSE          |<A:>|XFILE                |Rec: 33/75
```

View and edit fields.

Let's examine the directory and FAT of the disk in drive A before running CHKDSK. The directory shows that XFILE.DBF starts in cluster 2:

```
Directory Editing Mode                                    DiskMinder
[Esc] Displays Main Menu
 _____
| Filename.Ext    Size    Date      Time     Attr Clu  Reserved
| XFILE    .DBF   11839  01/11/89  13:25:06   20  0002  0000000000000000000
|             .       0  00/00/80  00:00:00   00  0000  0000000000000000000
|             .       0  00/00/80  00:00:00   00  0000  0000000000000000000
```

Examining the File Allocation Table shows that cell 4 in XFILE's allocation chain (shown below in boldface) points to cell 37, an unallocated cluster.

```
Fat Editing Mode                                          DiskMinder
[Esc] Displays Main Menu
 _____
| Clu     +0  +1  +2  +3    +4  +5  +6  +7    +8  +9  +A  +B    +C  +D  +E  +F
| 0000   FFD FFF 003 004   037 006 007 008   009 00A 00B 00C   FFF 000 000 000
| 0010   000 000 000 000   000 000 000 000   000 000 000 000   000 000 000 000
| 0020   000 000 000 000   000 000 000 000   000 000 000 000   000 000 000 000
| 0030   000 000 000 000   000 000 000 000   000 000 000 000   000 000 000 000
```

Running CHKDSK on drive A without the /F option produces:

```
C:\CHKDSK A:

Errors found, F parameter not specified.
Corrections will not be written to disk.

A:\XFILE.DBF
    Has invalid cluster, file truncated.
A:\XFILE.DBF
    Allocation error, size adjusted.

8 lost clusters found in 1 chains.
Convert lost chains to files  (Y/N)? n
    8192 bytes disk space
          would be freed.
```

Note the complaint about an "invalid cluster" as well as the fact that no cross-linking is reported. Hence, we now run CHKDSK with the /F option and authorize it to convert the lost chain to a file.

```
C:\CHKDSK A:/F
A:\XFILE.DBF
    Has invalid cluster, file truncated.
A:\XFILE.DBF
    Allocation error, size adjusted.

8 lost clusters found in 1 chains.
Convert lost chains to files  (Y/N)? Y
```

A directory listing now shows the presence of a CHK file:

```
C:\DIR A:

 Volume in drive A has no label
 Directory of  A:\

XFILE     DBF     4096   1-11-89   1:25p
FILE0000 CHK     8192   1-11-89   2:59p
         2 File(s)     349759 bytes free
```

Taking another look at the directory and the FAT, we see:

```
Directory Editing Mode                                    DiskMinder
[Esc] Displays Main Menu
```

Filename.Ext	Size	Date	Time	Attr	Clu	Reserved
XFILE .DBF	4096	01/11/89	13:25:06	20	0002	000000000000000000000
FILE0000.CHK	8192	01/11/89	14:59:23	00	0005	000000000000000000000
.	0	00/00/80	00:00:00	00	0000	000000000000000000000
.	0	00/00/80	00:00:00	00	0000	000000000000000000000

Observe that the CHK file (which contains part of the DBF datafile) starts in cluster 5 as we would expect, since it is the first cluster in the lost chain. Upon examining the FAT, we also see an FFF terminator for the truncated XFILE.DBF file in cell 37. The complete allocation chain for XFILE.DBF appears in boldface below:

```
Fat Editing Mode                                          DiskMinder
[Esc] Displays Main Menu
```

Clu	+0	+1	+2	+3	+4	+5	+6	+7	+8	+9	+A	+B	+C	+D	+E	+F
0000	FFD	FFF	**003**	**004**	**037**	006	007	008	009	00A	00B	00C	FFF	000	000	000
0010	000	000	000	000	000	000	000	000	000	000	000	000	000	000	000	000
0020	000	000	000	000	000	000	000	000	000	000	000	000	000	000	000	000
0030	000	000	000	000	000	000	000	**FFF**	000	000	000	000	000	000	000	000

We are now ready to diagnose the datafile using dSALVAGE. The diagnostic report appears as follows:

```
INPUT FILE........ XFILE.DBF      dBASE VERSION..... DBASE-III+
HEADER SIZE....... 513            LAST UPDATED...... 1-11-89
FIELDS PER RECORD. 15             TOTAL RECORDS..... 75
FILE SIZE......... 4096           RECORD SIZE....... 151
                                  CLUSTER SIZE...... 1024
CURRENT DIRECTORY. A:\
OUTPUT WRITTEN TO. A:\XFILE.DBF
DIRECTORY FILTER.. *.DBF
```
```
───────────────────── Diagnosis & Repair Menu ─────────────────

        F1   Help                    F3   Internal Damage Repair

File contains record damage (Class 1 or Class 4).
37 records match header pattern out of expected 75
Record(s) contain binary (less than hex 20) data.
Deleted flag in record(s) invalid (not * or space).
Data area in file smaller than expected. File could have external
  damage with missing clusters. Exit dSALVAGE now and run CHKDSK.
  IF CHKDSK REPORTS ALLOCATION ERRORS with this file or lost clusters
  run External Repair in dSALVAGE. Press Enter, then F4.
  IF NO ERRORS ARE REPORTED BY CHKDSK then
  CLASS 4 repair is recommended: Press Enter, then F3, then F5
────────── Pg-Up,Pg-Dn,↑↓, for rest of message, press Enter to Continue──
```

Since we already ran CHKDSK and converted the lost chain to a file, we now run External Repair in dSALVAGE and define C:XFIX.DBF as the output file. dSALVAGE then recovers the damaged file by inserting the CHK file contents at the correct location, as it did in the earlier "skipped clusters" example.

Examining the XFIX.DBF output file in the BROWSE mode of dBASE confirms the successful recovery.

```
SURNAME-------- FNAME---------- STREET--------------------------
Cook            Terrance        19 Tandoi Drive
Burkey          Thomas J.       8467 Peachy Rd.
Balsamo         William C.      902 Monroe Ave.
Azar            William G.      2010 New St.
Warden          Carol K.        189 Vollmer Pkwy.
Singer          Eddie           73 Fillingham Dr.
Phipps          Howard M.       36 ManorBlack Dr.
McNulty         John J.         75 Mitchell Road
Klockenbrink    Michael F.      133 McKinley St.
Groanfield      Richard L.      311 East Main St.
Desai           Sidney L.       42 Gilmore
Syversen        David           3900 Culver Rd.
Slack           Douglas W.      21 Barons St.
Rounding        Franz O.        596 List Ave.
Nelson          James R.        769 Garson Ave.
Melrose         John J.         230 Columbia Ave.
Knox            Michael D.      1372 Bay Shore Blvd.

BROWSE          |<C:>|XFIX                  |Rec: 33/75

                        View and edit fields.
```

◈ Summary

A file with lost clusters may look the same as one with Class 4 internal damage when you examine it in dBASE. The lost clusters contain file data that can be recovered. If your diagnosis is wrong, however, you might merely correct an offset and fail to recover the data. dSALVAGE is an ideal tool since it eliminates guesswork by doing a thorough diagnosis of the file before recommending a recovery process. It can also reinsert lost clusters into the file at the proper location.

20

Recovery of a
ZAP'd Datafile

You have already seen in Chapter 9 that the ZAP command primarily affects the file's directory listing (by changing the file size) and allocation chain. All it does to the actual file is change the header slightly, plus insert an end-of-file marker just after the last byte. Immediately following a ZAP, all the file's data is still intact, even though neither DOS nor dBASE can find it since it is no longer associated with any file name.

A ZAP'd datafile must be recovered before anything new is written to the disk. The ZAP command deallocates all clusters except those containing the file header. DOS treats deallocated clusters as "available space" and may use them to store the very next file that it writes to the disk. Since overwritten data is not recoverable, it is very important that you do not write anything to disk between the ZAP'ing and the recovery of the file. This is no time to do your spring disk housekeeping.

You cannot recover a ZAP'd file with an un-erase utility since it has not been erased. It still has a valid entry in the disk directory and an allocation chain in the FAT (although perhaps consisting of just a single link). Nor can you recover a ZAP'd file by simply erasing and then unerasing it. Un-erase software relies on a valid file size in the disk directory, but the size of a ZAP'd file no longer represents the original.

Successful un-ZAP'ing of a file involves finding all data clusters that belong to it, determining their order, and using this information to rebuild the file allocation chain and write the correct file size back into the directory. It is, of course, possible to do this manually with a good sector editor and a lot of skill and patience. You must also correct the record count in the file header and remove the end-of-file marker just beyond the header.

If the original file was unfragmented and its original allocation chain did not contain any backward-pointing pointers, manual recovery might be practical, albeit tedious and risky. (The manual rebuilding of allocation chains is risky and should be attempted only by experts). But on a hard disk, files are usually fragmented. This is especially true of database files that are constantly growing as new entries are added. Fragmentation is difficult to avoid.

Fragmentation by itself is not a serious problem, since the FAT still allows DOS to find a file's clusters in the proper order. The main penalty of excessive fragmentation is slower file accesses due to the extra disk head movement required. There are several useful "unfragmenting" programs on the market that will reassemble your disk files into contiguous allocation chains. However, do not use them on a disk containing a ZAP'd file you want to recover. They will reassign its clusters to other files, thereby making recovery impossible.

dSALVAGE is a reliable tool for recovering ZAP'd datafiles. Its un-ZAP'er is fully automatic and uses sophisticated pattern-matching techniques to recover the deallocated clusters, rebuild the file allocation chain, correct the file size in the directory and the record count in the file header, and remove the end-of-file marker that ZAP puts at the end of the header. dSALVAGE lets you recover a ZAP'd file with a single keystroke.

Despite the apparent simplicity of dSALVAGE's recovery process, it is instructive to examine what happens. We use a file ZSAMPLE.DBF for illustration.

A directory listing of our sample disk shows the following:

```
C:\DIR A:

 Volume in drive A has no label
 Directory of  A:\

HARRISON LTR    39391  10-11-88   2:03p
ZSAMPLE  DBF   129317   2-20-86   1:34p
POOL     QTE    20252  10-17-88   4:40p
FISH     DBF    43801  10-11-88  12:33p
         4 File(s)     128001 bytes free
```

When we use dBASE to display the structure of ZSAMPLE.DBF, we see:

```
Structure for database: A:zsample.dbf
Number of data records:     853
Date of last update   : 02/20/86
Field  Field Name  Type       Width    Dec
    1  SURNAME     Character    15
    2  FNAME       Character    15
    3  STREET      Character    35
    4  CITY        Character    18
    5  STATE       Character     2
    6  ZIP         Character     5
    7  ACCTNO      Numeric       5
    8  PAIDUP      Logical       1
    9  LASTTRAN    Date          8
   10  CATEGORY    Numeric       2
   11  AREACODE    Character     3
   12  TEL         Character     8
   13  SLNAME      Character    15
   14  SFNAME      Character    15
   15  ORDER       Numeric       3
** Total **                    151
```

Note that the file contains 853 records with 15 fields each. From the field count, we know that the header is 513 bytes long:

$$15 \times 32 + 33 = 513$$

Since the file is on a floppy disk with a cluster size of 1024 bytes, we know that the entire header (along with some initial records) lies in a single cluster.

When viewed with the BROWSE command, part of the file appears as follows:

```
SURNAME-------- FNAME--------- STREET---------------------
Zuckerman        Addison B.      416 Garfield Avenue
Wood             Anthony G.      16 Readonna Lane
Tomlinson        Blake           520 Mill Road
Werner           Bradley A.      36 Chamberlain
Vavrick          Charles E.      14 Flamingo Dr.
Swartwout        David B.        189 Conkey Avenue
Steenburg        Denise R.       7418 Redman Rd.
Smith            Donald S.       1040 Genesee Pk. Blvd.
Sherman          Edward L.       35 Brooklyn St.
Schaeffer        Evan J.         10 Vinton Rd.
Roof             Frederick E.    12 River St.
Reilly           Gerard J.       6841 County Rd. 32
Porravecchio     Harvey D.       4062 Standord
Peek             Jack            337 Avery Street
Orcutt           James G.        1612 Hennessey Rd.
Mench            John J.         5839 Chile Ave.
Mayberry         John P.         126 Fulton
```

```
  BROWSE          |<A:>|ZSAMPLE              |Rec: 1/853
```

View and edit fields.

When viewed with the DiskMinder sector editor, the directory appears as follows. Note that ZSAMPLE.DBF (shown in boldface) starts in cluster 29.

```
Directory Editing Mode                              DiskMinder
[Esc] Displays Main Menu
```

Filename.Ext	Size	Date	Time	Attr	Clu	Reserved
HARRISON.LTR	39391	10/11/88	14:03:21	20	0002	00000000000000000000
ZSAMPLE .DBF	**129317**	**02/20/86**	**13:34:01**	**20**	**0029**	**00000000000000000000**
POOL .QTE	20252	10/17/88	16:40:27	20	00D3	00000000000000000000
FISH .DBF	43801	10/11/88	12:33:09	20	0037	00000000000000000000
.	0	00/00/80	00:00:00	00	0000	00000000000000000000
.	0	00/00/80	00:00:00	00	0000	00000000000000000000
.	0	00/00/80	00:00:00	00	0000	00000000000000000000
.	0	00/00/80	00:00:00	00	0000	00000000000000000000
.	0	00/00/80	00:00:00	00	0000	00000000000000000000
.	0	00/00/80	00:00:00	00	0000	00000000000000000000
.	0	00/00/80	00:00:00	00	0000	00000000000000000000
.	0	00/00/80	00:00:00	00	0000	00000000000000000000
.	0	00/00/80	00:00:00	00	0000	00000000000000000000

```
Editing Directory A:\
       Entry    2 of 112                  Cluster   n/aH Sector       5
```

DiskMinder — Copyright 1988 Westlake Data Corporation

The file allocation chain for ZSAMPLE.DBF appears in boldface in the FAT display below. Note that the file is fragmented with one part in clusters 29 through 36 and another in clusters 62 through D2. The file FISH.DBF (starting in cluster 37) lies between the two parts.

```
Fat Editing Mode                                        DiskMinder
[Esc] Displays Main Menu

Clu   +0  +1  +2  +3    +4  +5  +6  +7    +8  +9  +A  +B    +C  +D  +E  +F
0000  FFD FFF 003 004   005 006 007 008   009 00A 00B 00C   00D 00E 00F 010
0010  011 012 013 014   015 016 017 018   019 01A 01B 01C   01D 01E 01F 020
0020  021 022 023 024   025 026 027 028   FFF 02A 02B 02C   02D 02E 02F 030
0030  031 032 033 034   035 036 062 038   039 03A 03B 03C   03D 03E 03F 040
0040  041 042 043 044   045 046 047 048   049 04A 04B 04C   04D 04E 04F 050
0050  051 052 053 054   055 056 057 058   059 05A 05B 05C   05D 05E 05F 060
0060  061 FFF 063 064   065 066 067 068   069 06A 06B 06C   06D 06E 06F 070
0070  071 072 073 074   075 076 077 078   079 07A 07B 07C   07D 07E 07F 080
0080  081 082 083 084   085 086 087 088   089 08A 08B 08C   08D 08E 08F 090
0090  091 092 093 094   095 096 097 098   099 09A 09B 09C   09D 09E 09F 0A0
00A0  0A1 0A2 0A3 0A4   0A5 0A6 0A7 0A8   0A9 0AA 0AB 0AC   0AD 0AE 0AF 0B0
00B0  0B1 0B2 0B3 0B4   0B5 0B6 0B7 0B8   0B9 0BA 0BB 0BC   0BD 0BE 0BF 0C0
00C0  0C1 0C2 0C3 0C4   0C5 0C6 0C7 0C8   0C9 0CA 0CB 0CC   0CD 0CE 0CF 0D0
00D0  0D1 0D2 FFF 0D4   0D5 0D6 0D7 0D8   0D9 0DA 0DB 0DC   0DD 0DE 0DF 0E0
00E0  0E1 0E2 0E3 0E4   0E5 0E6 FFF 000   000 000 000 000   000 000 000 000
00F0  000 000 000 000   000 000 000 000   000 000 000 000   000 000 000 000

Editing FAT entry for cluster       029H              FAT1 Sector      1
                        sector        90              FAT2 Sector      3
```

DiskMinder — Copyright 1988 Westlake Data Corporation

We will now erase FISH.DBF and POOL.QTE using the DOS ERASE (DEL) command to make recovery somewhat more difficult. After we erase the files, the disk directory appears as follows:

```
C:\DIR A:

Volume in drive A has no label
Directory of  A:\

HARRISON LTR     39391   10-11-88    2:03p
ZSAMPLE  DBF    129317    2-20-86    1:34p
         2 File(s)     192513 bytes free
```

When viewed with the sector editor, the directory appears as shown below. Note that the only change caused by the erasure is the replacement of the first character of each erased filename with the Greek letter sigma. The file sizes and starting clusters do not change. The erased files appear in boldface.

```
Directory Editing Mode                                  DiskMinder
[Esc] Displays Main Menu

Filename.Ext      Size    Date      Time    Attr Clu   Reserved
HARRISON.LTR     39391  10/11/88  14:03:21   20  0002  00000000000000000000
ZSAMPLE .DBF    129317  02/20/86  13:34:01   20  0029  00000000000000000000
σOOL    .QTE     20252  10/17/88  16:40:27   20  00D3  00000000000000000000
σISH    .DBF     43801  10/11/88  12:33:09   20  0037  00000000000000000000
        .            0  00/00/80  00:00:00   00  0000  00000000000000000000
        .            0  00/00/80  00:00:00   00  0000  00000000000000000000
```

The FAT reveals the deallocated clusters formerly associated with FISH.DBF and POOL.QTE (shown in boldface below):

```
Fat Editing Mode                                          DiskMinder
[Esc] Displays Main Menu

Clu  +0  +1  +2  +3    +4  +5  +6  +7    +8  +9  +A  +B    +C  +D  +E  +F
0000 FFD FFF 003 004   005 006 007 008   009 00A 00B 00C   00D 00E 00F 010
0010 011 012 013 014   015 016 017 018   019 01A 01B 01C   01D 01E 01F 020
0020 021 022 023 024   025 026 027 028   FFF 02A 02B 02C   02D 02E 02F 030
0030 031 032 033 034   035 036 062 000   000 000 000 000   000 000 000 000
0040 000 000 000 000   000 000 000 000   000 000 000 000   000 000 000 000
0050 000 000 000 000   000 000 000 000   000 000 000 000   000 000 000 000
0060 000 000 063 064   065 066 067 068   069 06A 06B 06C   06D 06E 06F 070
0070 071 072 073 074   075 076 077 078   079 07A 07B 07C   07D 07E 07F 080
0080 081 082 083 084   085 086 087 088   089 08A 08B 08C   08D 08E 08F 090
0090 091 092 093 094   095 096 097 098   099 09A 09B 09C   09D 09E 09F 0A0
00A0 0A1 0A2 0A3 0A4   0A5 0A6 0A7 0A8   0A9 0AA 0AB 0AC   0AD 0AE 0AF 0B0
00B0 0B1 0B2 0B3 0B4   0B5 0B6 0B7 0B8   0B9 0BA 0BB 0BC   0BD 0BE 0BF 0C0
00C0 0C1 0C2 0C3 0C4   0C5 0C6 0C7 0C8   0C9 0CA 0CB 0CC   0CD 0CE 0CF 0D0
00D0 0D1 0D2 FFF 000   000 000 000 000   000 000 000 000   000 000 000 000
00E0 000 000 000 000   000 000 000 000   000 000 000 000   000 000 000 000
00F0 000 000 000 000   000 000 000 000   000 000 000 000   000 000 000 000

Editing FAT entry for cluster     037H          FAT1 Sector      1
                         sector   118           FAT2 Sector      3
```

DiskMinder — Copyright 1988 Westlake Data Corporation

We will now ZAP ZSAMPLE.DBF. Afterward, the disk directory appears as follows:

```
C:\DIR A:

 Volume in drive A has no label
 Directory of  A:\

HARRISON LTR     39391  10-11-88   2:03p
ZSAMPLE  DBF      1024  10-28-88   2:39p
         2 File(s)    321536 bytes free
```

As we predicted, ZSAMPLE now occupies 1024 bytes, a single cluster.

Examining the structure of ZSAMPLE verifies that the record count in its header has been set to zero.

```
Structure for database: A:zsample.dbf
Number of data records:         0
Date of last update    : 10/28/88
Field  Field Name  Type        Width    Dec
    1  SURNAME     Character      15
    2  FNAME       Character      15
    3  STREET      Character      35
    4  CITY        Character      18
    5  STATE       Character       2
    6  ZIP         Character       5
    7  ACCTNO      Numeric         5
    8  PAIDUP      Logical         1
    9  LASTTRAN    Date            8
   10  CATEGORY    Numeric         2
   11  AREACODE    Character       3
```

```
12   TEL          Character      8
13   SLNAME       Character     15
14   SFNAME       Character     15
15   ORDER        Numeric        3
** Total **                    151
```

The disk directory, when viewed with the sector editor, now appears as shown below. Note that the file size is the only directory information ZAP changes (other than the date and time, of course, which are unimportant here).

```
Directory Editing Mode                                    DiskMinder
[Esc] Displays Main Menu

Filename.Ext     Size     Date       Time    Attr Clu  Reserved
HARRISON.LTR    39391   10/11/88   14:03:21   20  0002  00000000000000000000
ZSAMPLE .DBF     1024   10/28/88   14:39:06   20  0029  00000000000000000000
σOOL    .QTE    20252   10/17/88   16:40:27   20  00D3  00000000000000000000
σISH    .DBF    43801   10/11/88   12:33:09   20  0037  00000000000000000000
        .           0   00/00/80   00:00:00   00  0000  00000000000000000000
        .           0   00/00/80   00:00:00   00  0000  00000000000000000000
```

If we examine the file itself (in the data area of the disk) with the sector editor, we see the following. Pay particular attention to the bytes in boldface. The four starting at the fifth byte of the file are all zero, indicating a zero record count. The byte immediately following the header is the end-of-file marker (1A hex). These changes are made by the ZAP operation and are **the only ones it makes to the file**.

```
File Editing Mode                                         DiskMinder
[Esc] Displays Main Menu

      +0 +1 +2 +3 +4 +5 +6 +7 +8 +9 +A +B +C +D +E +F   0   4   8   C
0000  03 58 0A 1C 00 00 00 00 01 02 97 00 00 00 00 00   ♥X....ù.....
0010  00 00 00 00 00 00 00 00 00 00 00 00 00 00 00 00   ..............
0020  53 55 52 4E 41 4D 45 00 00 00 00 43 03 00 68 68   SURNAME....C.hh
0030  0F 00 00 00 01 00 00 00 00 00 00 00 00 00 00 00   ..............
0040  46 4E 41 4D 45 00 00 00 00 00 00 43 12 00 68 68   FNAME......C.hh
0050  0F 00 00 00 01 00 00 00 00 00 00 00 00 00 00 00   ..............
0060  53 54 52 45 45 54 00 00 00 00 00 43 21 00 68 68   STREET.....C!.hh
0070  23 00 00 00 01 00 00 00 00 00 00 00 00 00 00 00   #.............
0080  43 49 54 59 00 00 00 00 00 00 00 43 44 00 68 68   CITY.......CD.hh
0090  12 00 00 00 01 00 00 00 00 00 00 00 00 00 00 00   ..............
00A0  53 54 41 54 45 00 00 00 00 00 00 43 56 00 68 68   STATE......CV.hh
00B0  02 00 00 00 01 00 00 00 00 00 00 00 00 00 00 00   ..............
  .     .    .    .    .    .    .    .     .    .    .
  .            ( more header information in this area )
  .     .    .    .    .    .    .    .     .    .    .
01C0  53 46 4E 41 4D 45 00 00 00 00 00 43 87 00 68 68   SFNAME.....Cç.hh
01D0  0F 00 00 00 01 00 00 00 00 00 00 00 00 00 00 00   ..............
01E0  4F 52 44 45 52 00 00 00 00 00 00 4E 96 00 68 68   ORDER......Nû.hh
01F0  03 00 00 00 01 00 00 00 00 00 00 00 00 00 00 00   ..............
0000  0D 1A 5A 75 63 6B 65 72 6D 61 6E 20 20 20 20 20   ..Zuckerman
0010  20 41 64 64 69 73 6F 6E 20 42 2E 20 20 20 20 20    Addison B.
0020  34 31 36 20 47 61 72 66 69 65 6C 64 20 41 76 65   416 Garfield Ave
0030  6E 75 65 20 20 20 20 20 20 20 20 20 20 20 20 20   nue
0040  20 20 20 42 6F 73 74 6F 6E 20 20 20 20 20 20 20      Boston
0050  20 20 20 20 20 4D 41 30 32 31 33 30 20 20 38 35        MA02130   85
```

If we now examine the file allocation chain for ZSAMPLE.DBF, we see that it consists of just FAT cell 29 (shown in boldface below) as expected. All other links in the original allocation chain have been cleared and are indistinguishable from the cleared links of the erased files.

```
Fat Editing Mode                                             DiskMinder
[Esc] Displays Main Menu

Clu    +0  +1  +2  +3    +4  +5  +6  +7    +8  +9  +A  +B    +C  +D  +E  +F
0000   FFD FFF 003 004   005 006 007 008   009 00A 00B 00C   00D 00E 00F 010
0010   011 012 013 014   015 016 017 018   019 01A 01B 01C   01D 01E 01F 020
0020   021 022 023 024   025 026 027 028   FFF FFF 000 000   000 000 000 000
0030   000 000 000 000   000 000 000 000   000 000 000 000   000 000 000 000
```

To recover the ZAP'd file using dSALVAGE, we must select it in the Setup and File Selection Menu:

```
───────────────────── Setup and File Selection Menu ─────────────────────
 F1   Help                        F5   Change Directory
 F2   Select Input File           F6   Change Selection Filter
 F3   Type in Name of Input File  F7   Delete File
 F4   Type in Name of Output File F10  Hide/Show Menu
──────────────────────── Press ESC to Continue ────────────────────────

    ZSAMPLE.DBF    1024  10-28-88  14:39:12




──────────────── to position,CR to select ────────────────
```

Now we return to the main menu and press the F5 key to un-ZAP the file. It's easier than falling off a log and far less painful.

```
     Version 1.43              * dSALVAGE *

            (C) Copyright 1987 Comtech Publishing Ltd.

                       M A I N   M E N U

            F2   File Operations
                  ♦  Select Input/Output Files
                  ♦  Change defaults

            F3   Diagnosis and Repair
                  ♦  Internal damage
                  ♦  External (DOS level) damage

            F4   Invoke Editor
                  ♦  Header Editor
                  ♦  Record Editor
                  ♦  Byte Stream Editor

            F5   Unzap Selected File

      F1 = Help                          Press ESC to Quit

Your Choice[ ]
```

Within moments, dSALVAGE displays the following message in a window:

```
┌─────────────────────────────────────────────────────┐
│              853 records recovered                   │
│                                                      │
│ ─────────── Press any Key to Continue ─────────────  │
└─────────────────────────────────────────────────────┘
```

The un-ZAP'er has done its job, recovering all 853 records.

The disk directory now appears as follows:

```
C:\DIR A:

 Volume in drive A has no label
 Directory of  A:\

HARRISON LTR    39391  10-11-88   2:03p
ZSAMPLE  DBF   129317  10-28-88   2:39p
        2 File(s)    192513 bytes free
```

And a display of the FAT verifies the complete rebuilding of the ZAP'd file's allocation chain.

```
Fat Editing Mode                                                DiskMinder
[Esc] Displays Main Menu

┌──────────────────────────────────────────────────────────────────────────┐
│ Clu   +0  +1  +2  +3    +4  +5  +6  +7    +8  +9  +A  +B    +C  +D  +E  +F  │
│ 0000  FFD FFF 003 004   005 006 007 008   009 00A 00B 00C   00D 00E 00F 010 │
│ 0010  011 012 013 014   015 016 017 018   019 01A 01B 01C   01D 01E 01F 020 │
│ 0020  021 022 023 024   025 026 027 028   FFF 02A 02B 02C   02D 02E 02F 030 │
│ 0030  031 032 033 034   035 036 062 000   000 000 000 000   000 000 000 000 │
│ 0040  000 000 000 000   000 000 000 000   000 000 000 000   000 000 000 000 │
│ 0050  000 000 000 000   000 000 000 000   000 000 000 000   000 000 000 000 │
│ 0060  000 000 063 064   065 066 067 068   069 06A 06B 06C   06D 06E 06F 070 │
│ 0070  071 072 073 074   075 076 077 078   079 07A 07B 07C   07D 07E 07F 080 │
│ 0080  081 082 083 084   085 086 087 088   089 08A 08B 08C   08D 08E 08F 090 │
│ 0090  091 092 093 094   095 096 097 098   099 09A 09B 09C   09D 09E 09F 0A0 │
│ 00A0  0A1 0A2 0A3 0A4   0A5 0A6 0A7 0A8   0A9 0AA 0AB 0AC   0AD 0AE 0AF 0B0 │
│ 00B0  0B1 0B2 0B3 0B4   0B5 0B6 0B7 0B8   0B9 0BA 0BB 0BC   0BD 0BE 0BF 0C0 │
│ 00C0  0C1 0C2 0C3 0C4   0C5 0C6 0C7 0C8   0C9 0CA 0CB 0CC   0CD 0CE 0CF 0D0 │
│ 00D0  0D1 0D2 FFF 000   000 000 000 000   000 000 000 000   000 000 000 000 │
│ 00E0  000 000 000 000   000 000 000 000   000 000 000 000   000 000 000 000 │
│ 00F0  000 000 000 000   000 000 000 000   000 000 000 000   000 000 000 000 │
├──────────────────────────────────────────────────────────────────────────┤
│ Editing FAT entry for cluster    029H            FAT1 Sector        1       │
│                        sector      90            FAT2 Sector        3       │
└──────────────────────────────────────────────────────────────────────────┘

        DiskMinder — Copyright 1988 Westlake Data Corporation
```

The case we have just examined is a difficult one for an automatic un-ZAP'er since it involves a fragmented datafile having erased files in its interstitial spaces (clusters 37 through 61 in this case).

Partially Overwritten ZAP'd File

An even more difficult case is that of the ZAP'd file whose data has been partially overwritten. Although overwritten data cannot be recovered, we can recover the non-overwritten part using the manually assisted un-ZAP capability in dSALVAGE Professional.

We will use ZFILE.DBF on drive A to illustrate the process. A directory listing shows:

```
C:\DIR A:

 Volume in drive A has no label
 Directory of  A:\

 ZFILE    DBF    13106  10-19-88  12:28p
        1 File(s)    349184 bytes free
```

When viewed with the DiskMinder sector editor, the directory appears as follows. Note that ZFILE.DBF (shown in boldface) starts in cluster 2:

```
Directory Editing Mode                                      DiskMinder
[Esc] Displays Main Menu

 Filename.Ext    Size    Date     Time    Attr Clu  Reserved
 ZFILE   .DBF    13106  10/19/88  12:28:18  20  0002  00000000000000000000
         .           0  00/00/80  00:00:00  00  0000  00000000000000000000
         .           0  00/00/80  00:00:00  00  0000  00000000000000000000
```

The FAT shows that ZFILE occupies clusters 2 through E (shown in boldface):

```
Fat Editing Mode                                           DiskMinder
[Esc] Displays Main Menu

 Clu    +0  +1  +2  +3    +4  +5  +6  +7    +8  +9  +A  +B    +C  +D  +E  +F
 0000  FFD FFF 003 004   005 006 007 008   009 00A 00B 00C   00D 00E FFF 000
 0010  000 000 000 000   000 000 000 000   000 000 000 000   000 000 000 000
 0020  000 000 000 000   000 000 000 000   000 000 000 000   000 000 000 000
```

We now ZAP the file, after which the directory appears as follows. Note that ZFILE now occupies only a single 1024-byte cluster.

```
C:\DIR A:

 Volume in drive A has no label
 Directory of  A:\

 ZFILE    DBF     1024   3-24-89  10:27p
        1 File(s)    361472 bytes free
```

The FAT shows that the ZAP'd file (indicated in boldface) occupies only cluster 2. Cells 3 through E have been cleared.

```
Fat Editing Mode                                              DiskMinder
[Esc] Displays Main Menu

Clu    +0  +1  +2  +3    +4  +5  +6  +7    +8  +9  +A  +B    +C  +D  +E  +F
0000   FFD FFF FFF 000   000 000 000 000   000 000 000 000   000 000 000 000
0010   000 000 000 000   000 000 000 000   000 000 000 000   000 000 000 000
0020   000 000 000 000   000 000 000 000   000 000 000 000   000 000 000 000
```

We now write another file (START.TXT) to the disk. A directory listing shows:

```
C:\DIR A:

    Volume in drive A has no label
    Directory of  A:\

    ZFILE     DBF     1024    3-24-89  10:27p
    START     TXT     2855    3-12-89  11:44p
              2 File(s)     358400 bytes free
```

On examining the directory with DiskMinder, we see that START.TXT starts in cluster 3.

```
Directory Editing Mode                                        DiskMinder
[Esc] Displays Main Menu

Filename.Ext    Size     Date      Time    Attr Clu  Reserved
ZFILE   .DBF    1024   03/24/89  22:27:27   20  0002  00000000000000000000
START   .TXT    2855   03/12/89  23:44:02   20  0003  00000000000000000000
        .          0   00/00/80  00:00:00   00  0000  00000000000000000000
```

The FAT shows that START.TXT occupies clusters 3 through 5 (shown in boldface), all of which were formerly occupied by ZFILE. Hence, the part of ZFILE that occupied these clusters has been overwritten.

```
Fat Editing Mode                                              DiskMinder
[Esc] Displays Main Menu

Clu    +0  +1  +2  +3    +4  +5  +6  +7    +8  +9  +A  +B    +C  +D  +E  +F
0000   FFD FFF FFF 004   005 FFF 000 000   000 000 000 000   000 000 000 000
0010   000 000 000 000   000 000 000 000   000 000 000 000   000 000 000 000
0020   000 000 000 000   000 000 000 000   000 000 000 000   000 000 000 000
```

Since the automatic un-ZAP'er of dSALVAGE would not find a data match between the end of cluster 2 and any other cluster on the disk, it would not recover any data. Instead, we use the manually-assisted un-ZAP feature of dSALVAGE Professional, starting from its main menu.

```
Version 2.10              * dSALVAGE PROFESSIONAL *

               (C) Copyright 1989 Comtech Publishing Ltd.

                          M A I N   M E N U

            F2   File Operations
                    ◆ Select Input/Output Files
                    ◆ Change defaults
            F3   Diagnosis and Repair
                    ◆ Internal damage
                    ◆ External (DOS level) damage
            F4   Invoke Editor
                    ◆ Header Editor
                    ◆ Record Editor
                    ◆ Byte Stream Editor
                    ◆ Hex Editor
            F5   Unzap Selected File
                    ◆ Automatic Unzap
                    ◆ Manually Assisted Unzap


     F1 = Help                              Press ESC to Quit
```

After we select ZFILE.DBF and press F5, the following screen appears:

```
INPUT FILE........ ZFILE.DBF      dBASE VERSION..... DBASE-III+ / IV
HEADER SIZE....... 545            LAST UPDATED...... 3-24-89
FIELDS PER RECORD. 16             TOTAL RECORDS..... 0
FILE SIZE......... 1024           RECORD SIZE....... 157
                                  CLUSTER SIZE...... 1024
CURRENT DIRECTORY. A:\
OUTPUT WRITTEN TO. A:\ZFILE.DBF
DIRECTORY FILTER.. *.DBF          RECOMMENDED REPAIR: none


┌──────────────────────── Unzap Menu ────────────────────────┐
│                                                             │
│   F1  Help            F2  Unzap        F3  Manually-assisted Unzap
│                                                             │
│                                                             │
└──────────────── Press ESC to return to Main Menu ──────────┘
```

At the above menu, we press F3 to invoke manually-assisted un-ZAP. The screen appears as follows:

```
─────────────────────── Manual Unzap Commands ───────────────────
  F1 Help                   F4 Align Over Damage
  F2 Finish and Exit        F5 Continue Unzap From Here    F7 Try Previous
  F3 Accept Free Cluster    F6 Try Next Free Cluster          Free Cluster
──────────────────── Press ESC to Return to Unzap Menu────────────
                                          ────────── Cluster Counter──────────
  DELETEFLAG :                            Current cluster: 0002 Free cluster: 0006
     SURNAME : Werner   0.0019            Records recovered so far: 3
       FNAME : 86061532617827-
      STREET : 6419Worden          John T.
        CITY : 23 Jankowski
       STATE : Pa
         ZIP : ul D.
      ACCTNO :
      PAIDUP :
     BALANCE :    196
    LASTTRAN : Kenwood
    CATEGORY :
    AREACODE :
         TEL :
      SLNAME :             Bosto
      SFNAME : n               MA
```
No Match at Cluster Boundary

The above display depicts data from two clusters. The non-highlighted area displays data at the end of cluster 2. The highlighted area (highlighting not shown) displays data at the beginning of cluster 6 (the first free cluster beyond the end of START.TXT). Although the data does not match at the boundary, all the data on the screen appears to belong to ZFILE. Therefore, we press F4 to align this part of the file. The result appears in the following screen.

```
─────────────────────── Manual Unzap Commands ───────────────────
  F1 Help                   F4 Align Over Damage
  F2 Finish and Exit        F5 Continue Unzap From Here    F7 Try Previous
  F3 Accept Free Cluster    F6 Try Next Free Cluster          Free Cluster
──────────────────── Press ESC to Return to Unzap Menu────────────
                                          ────────── Cluster Counter──────────
  DELETEFLAG :                            Current cluster: 0002 Free cluster: 0006
     SURNAME : Jankowski                  Records recovered so far: 3
       FNAME : Paul D.
      STREET : 196 Kenwood
        CITY : Boston
       STATE : MA
         ZIP : 02130
      ACCTNO :    299
      PAIDUP : T
     BALANCE :    0.00
    LASTTRAN : 19860629
    CATEGORY : 29
    AREACODE : 617
         TEL : 832-8347
      SLNAME : Wopperer
      SFNAME : Robert T.
```
arrow keys to slide, CR to end

Cluster 6 clearly contains data from ZFILE, so we accept it by pressing F3. Afterward, the following screen appears, showing data at the beginning of cluster 7. We accept it also by pressing F3.

```
 ──────────────── Manual Unzap Commands ────────────────
  F1 Help                   F4 Align Over Damage
  F2 Finish and Exit        F5 Continue Unzap From Here    F7 Try Previous
  F3 Accept Free Cluster    F6 Try Next Free Cluster           Free Cluster

 ──────────────── Press ESC to Return to Unzap Menu ────────────────
                                       ──────── Cluster Counter ────────
  DELETEFLAG :                         Current cluster: 0006 Free cluster: 0007
    SURNAME : Finein                   Records recovered so far: 9
     FNAME : Robert L.
     STREET : 2 Cherokee Circle
       CITY : Boston
      STATE : MA
        ZIP : 02130
     ACCTNO :    161
     PAIDUP : T
    BALANCE :    0.00
   LASTTRAN : 19860701
   CATEGORY : 16
   AREACODE : 617
        TEL : 919-3519
     SLNAME : Wirth
     SFNAME : Gerald R.
```

We continue in this way from cluster to cluster until we find the end of the file. Alternatively, we could press the F5 key at any time to let un-ZAP proceed automatically. Finally, we press F2 to terminate the process. dSALVAGE Professional tells us how many records have been recovered, rebuilds the file's allocation chain, and updates the file size information in the disk's directory.

 Summary

You can recover all the data from a ZAP'd file with dSALVAGE if none of it has been overwritten. If the data has been partially overwritten, you can recover the non-overwritten part with dSALVAGE Professional.

21

Recovery of Cross-Linked Datafiles

In Chapter 7, we discussed cross-linking, the most common form of which is linking between the allocation chains of two files. Figure 21-1 shows a typical example.

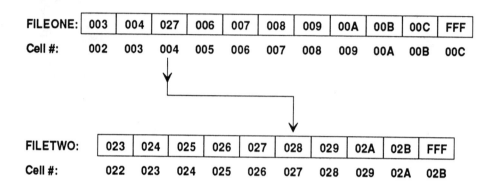

Figure 21-1. Typical Cross-Linking Condition

A link (cell 4) in FILEONE's allocation chain has been corrupted to point to a link (cell 27) in FILETWO's chain. When you examine FILETWO, it appears perfectly normal. When you examine FILEONE, however, it appears normal initially (that is, through the data in cluster 4), but then it seems to contain data from FILETWO (clusters 27 through 2B). The data in clusters 5 through C never appears since DOS no longer regards them as part of FILEONE. If FILEONE were a DBF file, you would see something like the following in BROWSE:

```
SURNAME--------  FNAME----------  STREET----------------------------
Schaeffer       Evan J.          10 Vinton Rd.
Roof            Frederick E.     12 River St.
Reilly          Gerard J.        6841 County Rd. 32
Porravecchio    Harvey D.        4062 Standord
Peek            Jack             337 Avery Street
Orcutt          James G.         1612 Hennessey Rd.
Mench           John J.          5839 Chile Ave.
Mayberry        o ther file, repa ir of the header by means of a spec
 healthy header (from another  file) and the records portion of th
 header.  If th e user does ele ct this option, that file's header
ies.  When view ed from within  dBASE, one cannot determine if an e
f external dama ge), due to cro ss-linking (another type of externa
If the fil e is a copy, data ha ve already been irretrievably lost.
different cause s that are fund amentally different in both nature
ta record.  dBA SE will not ope n a file having this type of damage
f the header.   If the header i s found to be damaged, recovery inv
is merged with  the existing da ta, an offset may be detected by pr
```

| BROWSE | \|<A:>\|FILEONE | \|Rec: 35/65 |

View and edit fields.

In our example, FILEONE is a DBF datafile and FILETWO is an ASCII text file. If you examine FILETWO with a word processor, text editor, or DOS' TYPE, it appears normal. We call it the *affected file.* **You can always determine the direction of the linking. It is very important to know this before starting recovery. The file that appears distorted is the one with the corrupted allocation chain.** In our example, FILEONE appears distorted, as you have seen. We call it the *corrupted file.*

Recovery should begin with the copying of the affected file (FILETWO in this case) to another disk or directory. The copy will be fine since there is nothing wrong with FILETWO's allocation chain.

We consider the following three types of cross-linking:

Category A: The corrupted file is a DBF datafile, but the affected file is not.

Category B: The affected file is a DBF datafile, but the corrupted file is not.

Category C: Both are DBF datafiles.

The recovery steps are slightly different for each category, as we now illustrate.

Category A:
The corrupted file is a DBF datafile, but the affected file is not.

The procedure is:

1. Copy the affected file to another disk.

2. Run CHKDSK without the /F option to spell out the cross-linking situation.

3. Run CHKDSK with the /F option and have it deallocate the lost clusters. Respond negatively to the question about converting lost chains to files.

4. Invoke dBASE, open the corrupted file, and ZAP it to break the cross-link.

5. Un-ZAP the corrupted file.

Category B:
The affected file is a DBF datafile, but the corrupted file is not.

The procedure is:

1. Copy the affected DBF file to another disk.

2. Run CHKDSK without the /F option to spell out the cross-linking situation.

3. Find the size of the corrupted file from a directory listing.

4. Run CHKDSK with the /F option and have it deallocate the lost clusters. Respond negatively to the question about converting lost chains to files. This changes the file size in the directory.

5. Erase the corrupted file to break the cross-link.

6. Use a sector editor (such as DiskMinder) to restore the original size of the corrupted file in the directory.

7. Un-erase the corrupted file using the Norton Utilities or another un-erase program.

This form of cross-linking is insidious in that it is undetectable from within dBASE and is therefore easy to overlook. The DBF datafile appears perfectly normal. However, as you will see shortly, erasing or modifying the corrupted file affects the datafile. For example, if you erase the corrupted file, part of the datafile will disappear also.

Category C:
Both files are DBF datafiles.

The procedure is:

1. Copy the affected file to another disk.

2. Run CHKDSK without the /F option to spell out the cross-linking situation.

3. Run CHKDSK with the /F option and allow it to deallocate the lost clusters. Respond negatively to the question about converting lost chains to files.

4. Invoke dBASE, open the corrupted file, and ZAP it to break the cross-link.

5. Un-ZAP the corrupted file.

In each process, we recommend running CHKDSK without the /F option first, then with it. The reason is that CHKDSK may reveal more complex cross-linking than we have considered. For example, FILE_ONE may be cross-linked to FILE_TWO which, in turn, is cross-linked back into FILE_ONE or to some other file. The problem is that CHKDSK does not report cross-linking until you have committed yourself to a response when it asks about converting lost chains to files.

If you respond affirmatively to this question, CHKDSK creates CHK files in the disk's root directory and assigns the lost clusters to them. If you respond negatively, it deallocates the lost clusters by clearing their FAT cells. When you invoke it with the /F option, you cannot simply tell CHKDSK to do nothing. It will always do one thing or the other. But there are cases in which you may want to do nothing until you explore the FAT in detail. Hence, always run CHKDSK initially without the /F option to get the "lay of the land" before committing yourself.

Our current example falls in category A. We now illustrate the recovery in detail.

A directory listing of our sample disk appears as follows:

```
C:\DIR A:

 Volume in drive A has no label
 Directory of  A:\

 FILEONE   DBF     10751  10-18-88   11:41a
 SAMPLE    DOC     21504   9-12-88   11:21a
 FILETWO   DOC      9646  10-08-88   11:26a
          3 File(s)     319488 bytes free
```

Before proceeding with recovery, we use the DiskMinder sector editor to clarify the problem. This step is not essential, but it is informative. DM shows the directory in the following form. Note that FILEONE starts in cluster 2.

```
Directory Editing Mode                                      DiskMinder
[Esc] Displays Main Menu

 Filename.Ext     Size    Date       Time    Attr Clu  Reserved
 FILEONE .DBF    10751  10/18/88   11:41:02   20  0002  0000000000000000000
 SAMPLE  .DOC    21504  09/12/88   11:21:26   20  000D  0000000000000000000
 FILETWO .DOC     9646  10/08/88   11:26:14   20  0022  0000000000000000000
         .           0  00/00/80   00:00:00   00  0000  0000000000000000000
```

We also examine FILEONE's allocation chain (shown in boldface below) using DiskMinder:

```
Fat Editing Mode                                            DiskMinder
[Esc] Displays Main Menu

 Clu    +0  +1  +2  +3   +4  +5  +6  +7    +8  +9  +A  +B    +C  +D  +E  +F
 0000   FFD FFF 003 004  027 006 007 008   009 00A 00B 00C   FFF 00E 00F 010
 0010   011 012 013 014  015 016 017 018   019 01A 01B 01C   01D 01E 01F 020
 0020   021 FFF 023 024  025 026 027 028   029 02A 02B FFF   000 000 000 000
 0030   000 000 000 000  000 000 000 000   000 000 000 000   000 000 000 000
```

Since the disk contains only three small files, we can easily spot two allocation chain links pointing to cell 27 (namely, cells 4 and 26). This is what we call cross-linking. On a large hard disk containing many files, cross-linking is not so readily apparent.

A great danger in cross-linking is that erasing the "corrupted" file may destroy part of the "affected" file as well. In the screen shown above, for example, FILEONE appears to occupy clusters 2 through 4 and 27 through 2B. As far as DOS is concerned, they contain FILEONE. But you and I know that clusters 27 through 2B are actually part of FILETWO. DOS will, however, deallocate all eight clusters if you erase FILEONE. It would leave clusters 5 through C dangling, not recognized as part of any file. CHKDSK would report them as "lost."

Now for the first step in recovery (after copying FILETWO to a separate disk, of course): namely, running CHKDSK without the /F option. It produces the following report:

```
C:\CHKDSK A:

Errors found, F parameter not specified.
Corrections will not be written to disk.

A:\FILEONE.DBF
    Allocation error, size adjusted.

8 lost clusters found in 1 chains.
Convert lost chains to files  (Y/N)?
```

At this point, it does not matter what you answer since CHKDSK will not do anything anyway. It is warning us, however, that FILEONE's size in the directory would change if the /F option were used. After we answer the question, CHKDSK provides the rest of its report as follows:

```
        8192 bytes disk space
            would be freed.

A:\FILEONE.DBF
    Is cross linked on cluster 39
A:\FILETWO.DOC
    Is cross linked on cluster 39
```

CHKDSK confirms the presence of a cross-link at cluster 39 (or 27 hex), as we already knew from our earlier examination of the FAT.

It is now time to run CHKDSK with the /F option.

```
C:\CHKDSK A:/F
A:\FILEONE.DBF
    Allocation error, size adjusted.

8 lost clusters found in 1 chains.
Convert lost chains to files  (Y/N)?
```

We will respond negatively to the question, thus allowing CHKDSK to adjust the size of FILEONE and deallocate clusters 5 through C. Alternatively, we could respond affirmatively and erase the CHK file produced by CHKDSK. The final outcome is the same.

```
Convert lost chains to files  (Y/N)? N
    8192 bytes disk space freed.

A:\FILEONE.DBF
    Is cross linked on cluster 39
A:\FILETWO.DOC
    Is cross linked on cluster 39
```

A directory listing of the disk now shows:

```
C:\DIR A:

 Volume in drive A has no label
 Directory of  A:\

FILEONE  DBF     8192  10-18-88  11:41a
SAMPLE   DOC    21504   9-12-88  11:21a
FILETWO  DOC     9646  10-08-88  11:26a
         3 File(s)    327680 bytes free
```

Note that FILEONE is now 8192 bytes, whereas it was 10751 bytes before.

Although unnecessary for file recovery, it is instructive to reexamine the FAT now. The eight deallocated clusters appear in boldface:

```
Fat Editing Mode                                        DiskMinder
[Esc] Displays Main Menu
```

Clu	+0	+1	+2	+3	+4	+5	+6	+7	+8	+9	+A	+B	+C	+D	+E	+F
0000	FFD	FFF	003	004	027	**000**	**000**	**000**	**000**	**000**	**000**	**000**	**000**	00E	00F	010
0010	011	012	013	014	015	016	017	018	019	01A	01B	01C	01D	01E	01F	020
0020	021	FFF	023	024	025	026	027	028	029	02A	02B	FFF	000	000	000	000
0030	000	000	000	000	000	000	000	000	000	000	000	000	000	000	000	000
0040	000	000	000	000	000	000	000	000	000	000	000	000	000	000	000	000
0050	000	000	000	000	000	000	000	000	000	000	000	000	000	000	000	000

Note that the offending cross-link pointer is still in cell 4.

Now for the critical step, disposing of the offending pointer. We dispose of it by opening the datafile in dBASE and ZAPping it. After QUITting dBASE, we can once more examine the directory. We see:

```
C:\DIR A:

Volume in drive A has no label
 Directory of  A:\

FILEONE   DBF      1024  10-18-88  12:05p
SAMPLE    DOC     21504   9-12-88  11:21a
FILETWO   DOC      9646  10-08-88  11:26a
          3 File(s)     334848 bytes free
```

Note that FILEONE's size is now 1024 bytes, the size of a single cluster. This cluster contains the file header.

Although unnecessary for the recovery process, it is instructive to look at the FAT once again. As you can see below in boldface, DOS now recognizes only cluster 2 as containing FILEONE. ZAP deallocated clusters 3 and 4 (as well as 27 through 2B, of course, since they were associated with FILEONE). The key point is that the offending cross-link pointer in cell 4 is gone.

At the risk of sounding repetitive, we caution you again very strongly not to write anything to a disk or change anything on one containing a ZAP'd datafile until after you have recovered the file. The deallocated clusters containing the ZAP'd file's data are extremely vulnerable and may be overwritten by the next file written to disk.

```
Fat Editing Mode                                          DiskMinder
[Esc] Displays Main Menu

Clu   +0  +1  +2  +3    +4  +5  +6  +7    +8  +9  +A  +B    +C  +D  +E  +F
0000  FFD FFF FFF 000   000 000 000 000   000 000 000 000   000 00E 00F 010
0010  011 012 013 014   015 016 017 018   019 01A 01B 01C   01D 01E 01F 020
0020  021 FFF 023 024   025 026 027 000   000 000 000 000   000 000 000 000
0030  000 000 000 000   000 000 000 000   000 000 000 000   000 000 000 000
0040  000 000 000 000   000 000 000 000   000 000 000 000   000 000 000 000
0050  000 000 000 000   000 000 000 000   000 000 000 000   000 000 000 000
```

All that we must do now is un-ZAP the datafile, a simple operation in dSALVAGE. Since dSALVAGE reconstructs the file from deallocated clusters in the data area of the disk without using pointer information in the FAT, it will recover the ZAP'd file correctly.

After invoking dSALVAGE and selecting the File Operations option from the main menu, we see the following screen:

```
──────────────── Setup and File Selection Menu ────────────────
F1   Help                        F5    Change Directory
F2   Select Input File           F6    Change Selection Filter
F3   Type in Name of Input File  F7    Delete File
F4   Type in Name of Output File F10   Hide/Show Menu
──────────────── Press ESC to Continue ────────────────

    FILEONE.DBF     1024   10-18-88   12:05:14




Your Choice[ ]
```

After pressing the F2 key to select an input file, Enter to select FILEONE.DBF, and Esc to return to the main menu, we see the following screen:

```
  Version 1.43                * dSALVAGE *

              (C) Copyright 1987 Comtech Publishing Ltd.

                       M A I N   M E N U

              F2   File Operations
                    ♦ Select Input/Output Files
                    ♦ Change defaults

              F3   Diagnosis and Repair
                    ♦ Internal damage
                    ♦ External (DOS level) damage

              F4   Invoke Editor
                    ♦ Header Editor
                    ♦ Record Editor
                    ♦ Byte Stream Editor

              F5   Unzap Selected File

      F1 = Help                          Press ESC to Quit

Your Choice[ ]
```

All we must do is press the F5 key to un-ZAP the file. After a few moments, the following message appears near the center of the screen:

```
                          65 records recovered

                     Press any Key to Continue
```

dSALVAGE confirms the recovery of all 65 records. The job is done. The cross-link has been broken and the datafile has been restored completely.

Although it is not essential, we can examine the disk directory and FAT once again to see the results. The directory confirms the restoration of FILEONE's original size.

```
C:\DIR A:

 Volume in drive A has no label
 Directory of  A:\

FILEONE   DBF    10751  10-18-88  11:41a
SAMPLE    DOC    21504   9-12-88  11:21a
FILETWO   DOC     9646  10-08-88  11:26a
        3 File(s)    319488 bytes free
```

A display of FILEONE's allocation chain (shown in boldface below) shows complete reconstruction.

```
Fat Editing Mode                                          DiskMinder
[Esc] Displays Main Menu

Clu   +0  +1  +2  +3    +4  +5  +6  +7    +8  +9  +A  +B    +C  +D  +E  +F
0000  FFD FFF 003 004   005 006 007 008   009 00A 00B 00C   FFF 00E 00F 010
0010  011 012 013 014   015 016 017 018   019 01A 01B 01C   01D 01E 01F 020
0020  021 FFF 023 024   025 026 027 000   000 000 000 000   000 000 000 000
0030  000 000 000 000   000 000 000 000   000 000 000 000   000 000 000 000
0040  000 000 000 000   000 000 000 000   000 000 000 000   000 000 000 000
0050  000 000 000 000   000 000 000 000   000 000 000 000   000 000 000 000
```

If you need still more confirmation of successful recovery, examine the recovered file in the BROWSE mode of dBASE:

```
       SURNAME-------- FNAME---------- STREET------------------------
       Schaeffer       Evan J.         10 Vinton Rd.
       Roof            Frederick E.    12 River St.
       Reilly          Gerard J.       6841 County Rd. 32
       Porravecchio    Harvey D.       4062 Standord
```

```
Peek         Jack           337 Avery Street
Orcutt       James G.       1612 Hennessey Rd.
Mench        John J.        5839 Chile Ave.
Mayberry     John P.        126 Fulton
Mancini      Joseph A.      19 Greenmoor Way
Liva         Kerney         104 Weld Street
Learmouth    Louis D.       377 Maple Street
Blessington  Michael        53 Cameron Street
Koehler      Michael A.     77 Woodsmeadow
Kennett      Mohan S.       21 Barons St.
Jankowski    Paul D.        196 Kenwood
Holmes       Philip O.      157 Barberry Terrace
Hatch        Richard A.     257 Clay Ave.
```

BROWSE	|<A:>|FILEONE	|Rec: 35/65

View and edit fields.

Now that recovery is complete, we can re-copy FILETWO (which we saved earlier) back onto the disk.

As mentioned above, you may encounter more complex forms of cross-linking than our example. They will require the use of a sector editor. Recovery will, however, still involve the basic procedures just discussed. Armed with the understanding you have gained in this book, a good sector editor such as DiskMinder, and the dSALVAGE file recovery product, you will have an excellent chance to recover cross-linked files of any form.

 ## Summary

Cross-linking makes it appear that one file (the corrupted one) contains part of another (the affected one). It is a FAT problem rather than a file problem.

Cross-linking is like a time bomb since it may exist for a long time without you being aware of it. If you copy the corrupted file, the copy will contain parts of the two files involved. If you erase or modify the corrupted file, the other will be affected adversely.

You should run CHKDSK frequently to determine whether cross-linking is present. Recovery involves removing the cross-link from the FAT and reconstructing the corrupted file's allocation chain. dSALVAGE's unique un-ZAP capability can repair a DBF datafile corrupted by cross-linking.

22

Editing Datafiles with the dSALVAGE Editors

When one thinks about editing dBASE datafiles, one usually thinks in terms of dBASE commands. But the dBASE editors, such as EDIT and BROWSE for records and MODIFY STRUCTURE for the header, have limitations that are sometimes inconvenient or even unacceptable. For example, neither EDIT nor BROWSE allows you to edit the delete status byte found at the beginning of each record. Nor does either let you edit the pointers in memo fields or remove nulls from a file. Thus you cannot use them to correct several common forms of damage.

The MODIFY STRUCTURE command lets you alter field definitions, but not other contents of file headers. It also forces you to recopy your entire file even if you just change a field name.

In addition, although dBASE has data search capabilities through the LOCATE, FIND, and SEEK commands, there is no convenient way to search for data that crosses field or record boundaries or for memo field pointers.

Finally, although dBASE lets you write a datafile in delimited or SDF format, it automatically adds a carriage return/line feed pair at the end of every record. You may not want this addition. For example, you may want to transfer a DBF data stream to a mainframe computer without headers or record delimiters.

dSALVAGE has editors without such limitations. The standard version has three editors: Header Editor, Record Editor, and Byte Stream Editor. dSALVAGE Professional has a fourth, the Hex Editor. This chapter examines their capabilities.

A word of caution is necessary here. Powerful editors, such as dSALVAGE's or the sector editors discussed earlier, have enormous capabilities. They also can do considerable harm if used improperly. A sector editor, for example, can let you write all kinds of garbage into the File Allocation Table or into the boot sector of your hard disk, making your files inaccessible or your disk completely unusable. With dSALVAGE's Header Editor, you could alter the file header in ways that might lock up your computer.

We invoke dSALVAGE Professional's editors from the Editor Menu which is accessed from the Main Menu. The Editor Menu appears in Figure 22-1. You can change editors without losing your place in the file.

```
─────────────────── Editor Menu ───────────────────

   F1   Help              F3    Record Editor        F5   Hex Editor
   F2   Header Editor     F4    Byte-Stream Editor

───────────────── Press ESC to return to Main Menu ─────────────────
```

Figure 22-1. dSALVAGE Professional's Editor Menu

 ## Header Editor

dSALVAGE's Header Editor lets you repair a DBF datafile header to make it consistent with the data in the file. It is not suitable for creating a new header from scratch (although that capability exists in the Class 3 and Class 5 recovery modes of dSALVAGE Professional). It is intended to supplement dBASE's MODIFY STRUCTURE command, not to replace it.

Upon pressing the F1 function key from the Editor Menu, you see the following screen (shown here for the case in which file T1.DBF was selected):

```
INPUT FILE........ T1.DBF        dBASE VERSION..... DBASE-III+
HEADER SIZE....... 1409          LAST UPDATED...... 8-5-87
FIELDS PER RECORD. 43            TOTAL RECORDS..... 35
FILE SIZE......... 21500         RECORD SIZE....... 574
                                 CLUSTER SIZE...... 2048
                  ─────── Edit Header Commands ───────

F1 Help                                    F6  Change Version Number
F2 Select/Count Fields  F4 Change Record Count  F7  Copy Header to New File
F3 Change Record Size   F5 Change Field Count   F10 Hide/Show Menu

                  ─────── Press ESC to Return to Editor Menu ───────

FIELD NAME:DELETEFLAG TYPE:C WIDTH:001 PLACES:000
FIELD NAME:SURNAME    TYPE:C WIDTH:020 PLACES:000
FIELD NAME:FNAME      TYPE:C WIDTH:015 PLACES:000
FIELD NAME:COMPANY    TYPE:C WIDTH:040 PLACES:000
FIELD NAME:STREET     TYPE:C WIDTH:040 PLACES:000
FIELD NAME:CITY       TYPE:C WIDTH:015 PLACES:000
FIELD NAME:STATE      TYPE:C WIDTH:002 PLACES:000
FIELD NAME:ZIP        TYPE:C WIDTH:010 PLACES:000
FIELD NAME:COUNTRY    TYPE:C WIDTH:022 PLACES:000
FIELD NAME:TEL        TYPE:C WIDTH:012 PLACES:000
```

The Record Size, Record Count, Header Size (determined by Field Count), and Version Number all represent data in the first twelve header bytes for dBASE III/III PLUS/IV files. You can change any of them by simply pressing the appropriate function key and entering a new value when asked.

Field name, type, width, and decimal place changes require that you first press the F2 function key and select a field using a point-and-shoot method. Suppose that you select the FNAME field. Upon pressing F2, the following edit screen appears:

```
INPUT FILE........ T1.DBF        dBASE VERSION..... DBASE-III+
HEADER SIZE....... 1409          LAST UPDATED...... 8-5-87
FIELDS PER RECORD. 43            TOTAL RECORDS..... 35
FILE SIZE......... 21500         RECORD SIZE....... 574
                                 CLUSTER SIZE...... 2048
                  ─────── Edit Field Commands ───────

F1 Help              F3 Change Field Type   F5  Change Field Decimals
F2 Change Field Name F4 Change Field Width  F10 Hide/Show Menu


                  ─────── Press ESC to Return to Header Editor Menu ───────

FIELD NAME:DELETEFLAG TYPE:C WIDTH:001 PLACES:000
FIELD NAME:SURNAME    TYPE:C WIDTH:020 PLACES:000
FIELD NAME:FNAME      TYPE:C WIDTH:015 PLACES:000
FIELD NAME:COMPANY    TYPE:C WIDTH:040 PLACES:000
FIELD NAME:STREET     TYPE:C WIDTH:040 PLACES:000
FIELD NAME:CITY       TYPE:C WIDTH:015 PLACES:000
FIELD NAME:STATE      TYPE:C WIDTH:002 PLACES:000
FIELD NAME:ZIP        TYPE:C WIDTH:010 PLACES:000
FIELD NAME:COUNTRY    TYPE:C WIDTH:022 PLACES:000
FIELD NAME:TEL        TYPE:C WIDTH:012 PLACES:000
```

If you press a function key (F2 through F5), you can make the indicated header changes by providing new values when asked. Unlike the situation with dBASE's MODIFY STRUCTURE command, a field name change (or any change enabled here) does not require rewriting of the file.

 **Record Editor**

Pressing F3 in the Editor Menu calls up the Record Editor. It resembles the EDIT mode of dBASE. A typical Record Editor screen appears in Figure 22-2.

```
┌────────────────────── Record Editor Commands ──────────────────┐
│ F1 Help                    ALT-G Goto Record    HOME  First Record    │
│ F2 Count Good Records      ALT-T Show Errors    END   Last Record     │
│ F3 Query By Example        PgUp  Prev Record    ^HOME Beginning of Field │
│ ALT-S/ALT-A Search/Repeat  PgDn  Next Record    ^END  End of Field     │
│ └─────────── F10 Hide/Show Menu  Press ESC to Return to Editor Menu ──┘
│ DELETEFLAG : *
│    SURNAME : EMERSON
│      FNAME : WALTER
│    COMPANY : EMERSON & WILCOX, INC.
│     STREET : 78 ROSEDALE ROAD
│       CITY : ALLENTOWN
│      STATE : PA
│        ZIP : 77541
│      NOTES :        124
│        TEL : (215) 555-1212
│      ODATE : 19871219
│   SSURNAME : HUMPERDINCK
│     SFNAME : CAROLINE
│   SCOMPANY : EMERSON & WILCOX, INC.
│    SSTREET : 78 ROSEDALE ROAD
│      SCITY : ALLENTOWN
└───────────────────────────────────────────────────────────────┘
              Record 27        file position 16334
```

Figure 22-2. Typical dSALVAGE Record Editor Screen

There are major differences between the Record Editor and dBASE's EDIT mode, specifically:

- The delete status byte is displayed and can be edited. In the example, the asterisk in the DELETEFLAG indicates that the record has been marked for deletion. To recall it, merely type a space over the asterisk.

- Memo field pointers can be edited. (See the NOTES field in the example above).

- Dates appear as they are stored in the data file. (See the ODATE field which contains 12/19/87).

- Fields that are wider than the available screen space are not wrapped, but can be scrolled horizontally.

- Individual records can be checked for damage by pressing Alt-T.

- A simple form of Query-by-Example allows you to find records matching any data pattern.

Figures 22-3 and 22-4 illustrate the Query-by-Example feature.

```
──────────────────── Record Editor Commands ────────────
  F1 Help                    ALT-G Goto Record    HOME  First Record
  F2 Count Good Records      ALT-T Show Errors    END   Last Record
  F3 Query By Example        PgUp  Prev Record    ^HOME Beginning of Field
  ALT-S/ALT-A Search/Repeat  PgDn  Next Record    ^END  End of Field
  ──────── F10 Hide/Show Menu  Press ESC to Return to Editor Menu ──────

  DELETEFLAG : ?
     SURNAME : ??????????????????
       FNAME : ??????????????
     COMPANY : ????????????????????????????????????????????
      STREET : ??????????????????????????????????????????
        CITY : ??????????????????
       STATE : ??
         ZIP : ?????????
     COUNTRY : ?????????????????????????
         TEL : ?????????????????
     TEL_EXT : ???????????????
    SSURNAME : ?????????????????????
      SFNAME : ??????????????????
    SCOMPANY : ???????????????????????????????????????????
     SSTREET : ???????????????????????????????????????????
       SCITY : ??????????????????

  fill in template, press Enter        Record 27       file position 16344
```

Figure 22-3.   *dSALVAGE Record Editor's Query-by-Example Feature*

If you fill in the template as shown in Figure 22-4, dSALVAGE will find every record having "B" as the first character of the SURNAME field, "NY" in the STATE field, and "381" as the telephone exchange.

```
┌──────────────────────── Record Editor Commands ────────────────────────┐
│ F1 Help                      ALT-G Goto Record      HOME   First Record │
│ F2 Count Good Records        ALT-T Show Errors      END    Last Record  │
│ F3 Query By Example          PgUp  Prev Record      ^HOME Beginning of Field │
│ ALT-S/ALT-A Search/Repeat    PgDn  Next Record      ^END   End of Field │
│ └──────────── F10 Hide/Show Menu  Press ESC to Return to Editor Menu ─┘ │
├────────────────────────────────────────────────────────────────────────┤
│ DELETEFLAG : ?                                                          │
│    SURNAME : B?????????????????                                         │
│      FNAME : ?????????????????                                          │
│    COMPANY : ?????????????????????????????????????????                  │
│     STREET : ?????????????????????????????????????????                  │
│       CITY : ?????????????????                                          │
│      STATE : NY                                                         │
│        ZIP : ??????????                                                 │
│    COUNTRY : ?????????????????????                                      │
│        TEL : ??????381??????                                            │
│    TEL_EXT : ????????????                                               │
│   SSURNAME : ?????????????????????                                      │
│     SFNAME : ?????????????????                                          │
│   SCOMPANY : ??????????????????????????????????????????                 │
│    SSTREET : ??????????????????????????????????????????                 │
│      SCITY : ?????????????????                                          │
├────────────────────────────────────────────────────────────────────────┤
│ fill in template, press Enter          Record 27       file position 16344 │
└────────────────────────────────────────────────────────────────────────┘
```

Figure 22-4.   Sample Query in dSALVAGE Record Editor

 **Byte Stream Editor**

The Byte Stream Editor (Figure 22-5) lets you view and edit file data as a continuous character stream in a format exactly as it is stored (i.e., without carriage returns, line feeds, or any other field or record delimiters). It also lets you search for character sequences; mark, move, copy, and delete blocks of data; write a marked block of data to an external file; and perform cut-and-paste operations (paste is available in dSALVAGE Professional only).

The status line at the bottom of the screen always indicates the cursor position by both record number and file position (byte number).

```
┌──────────────── Byte Stream Editor Commands ──────────────┐
│ F1    Help         │ALT-B Mark Block │ALT-W Write Block│ALT-F Write File│
│ F10   Hide/Show Menu│ALT-M Move Block │ALT-G Goto Byte  │PgUp/PgDn       │
│ ALT-S Search       │ALT-C Copy Block │ALT-U Undelete   │HOME Top of File│
│ ALT-A Repeat Search │ALT-D Delete Block│ALT-P Paste File │END  End of File│
└──────────────── Press ESC to Return to Editor Menu ───────┘

┌─────────────────────────────────────────────────────────────────┐
│  CONNERS            PHILLIP        ST. VITUS DANCE SCHOOL         │
│            4325 SUMMIT AVENUE                 ST PAUL             │
│     MN55101                                                      │
│                                                                  │
│                                                                  │
│                            PCWEEK   1987030219870302MAIL         │
│ 119.950.00    22.4519870302CC-240407        /  11600             │
│                                ZS6622-01                         │
│    CASH              N 2.50F 0.00 0.00T    22.45     0.00         │
│                          COMPUTERS UG                            │
│           22 WESTERN ROAD                   BIRMINGHAM           │
│     8184599   ENGLAND                                            │
│                                                                  │
│                                                                  │
│                     FLYER    1987030219870302AIR     1           │
│ 0.000.00    6.0019870321M            /  11601BRITISH US          │
└─────────────────────────────────────────────────────────────────┘
Your Choice[ ]                  Record 1        file position 1410
```

Figure 22-5. *dSALVAGE Byte Stream Editor*

 **Hex Editor**

Pressing F5 from the Editor Menu calls up the Hex Editor (dSALVAGE Professional only). It allows you to edit any character in any region of a file, including the header. When you invoke this editor after selecting a DBF file, the cursor starts at the first byte of the first record. You can move it to the beginning of the file (that is, to the first byte of the header) by pressing the Home key.

An initial screen might appear as shown in Figure 22-6. The initial position of the cursor is in boldface. The Tab key switches the cursor from the hex display at the left to the ASCII one at the right. You can edit either display.

```
──────────────────── Hex Editor Commands───────────────
 F1     Help          PgUp  Prev Screen        HOME  Beginning of File
 F10    Hide/Show Menu PgDn  Next Screen        END   End of File
 ALT-S  Search              Arrow keys to move cursor  TAB   Hex  ASCII Display
 ALT-A  Repeat Search
──────────────── Press ESC to Return to Editor Menu──────────
```

```
43 4F 44 00 00 00 00 00 00 00 00 4E 2C 02 B1 61  COD        N,a
05 02 00 00 01 00 00 00 00 00 00 00 00 00 00 00
4C 41 42 45 4C 4D 41 44 45 00 00 4C 31 02 B1 61  LABELMADE  L1a
01 00 00 01 00 00 00 00 00 00 00 00 00 00 00 00
41 4D 54 50 41 49 44 00 00 00 00 4E 32 02 B1 61  AMTPAID    N2a
08 02 00 00 01 00 00 00 00 00 00 00 00 00 00 00
42 41 4C 41 4E 43 45 44 55 45 00 4E 3A 02 B1 61  BALANCEDUE N:a
08 02 00 00 01 00 00 00 00 00 00 00 00 00 00 00
0D 20 43 4F 4E 4E 45 52 53 20 20 20 20 20 20 20     CONNERS
20 20 20 20 20 20 50 48 49 4C 4C 49 50 20 20 20        PHILLIP
20 20 20 20 20 53 54 2E 20 56 49 54 55 53 20 44     ST. VITUS D
41 4E 43 45 20 53 43 48 4F 4F 4C 20 20 20 20 20  ANCE SCHOOL
20 20 20 20 20 20 20 20 20 20 20 20 20 34 33 32                432
35 20 53 55 4D 4D 49 54 20 41 56 45 4E 55 45 20  5 SUMMIT AVENUE
20 20 20 20 20 20 20 20 20 20 20 20 20 20 20 20
20 20 20 20 20 53 54 20 50 41 55 4C 20 20 20 20     ST PAUL
```

Record 1   file position 1410

Figure 22-6. dSALVAGE Professional Hex Editor

Pressing the Home key moves the cursor to the first byte of the file (shown in boldface below).

```
─────────────────── Hex Editor Commands ───────────────
  F1     Help            PgUp  Prev Screen         HOME  Beginning of File
  F10    Hide/Show Menu  PgDn  Next Screen         END   End of File
  ALT-S  Search          Arrow keys to move cursor TAB   Hex  ASCII Display
  ALT-A  Repeat Search
  ──────────────── Press ESC to Return to Editor Menu ───────────
```

```
 03 57 08 05 23 00 00 00 81 05 3E 02 00 00 00 00  ♥W#     ü
 00 00 00 00 00 00 00 00 00 00 00 00 00 00 00 00
 53 55 52 4E 41 4D 45 00 00 00 00 43 05 00 B1 61  SURNAME    C♣ a
 14 00 00 00 01 00 00 00 00 00 00 00 00 00 00 00  ¶
 46 4E 41 4D 45 00 00 00 00 00 00 43 19 00 B1 61  FNAME      C↓ a
 0F 00 00 00 01 00 00 00 00 00 00 00 00 00 00 00
 43 4F 4D 50 41 4E 59 00 00 00 00 43 28 00 B1 61  COMPANY    C( a
 28 00 00 00 01 00 00 00 00 00 00 00 00 00 00 00  (
 53 54 52 45 45 54 00 00 00 00 00 43 50 00 B1 61  STREET     CP a
 28 00 00 00 01 00 00 00 00 00 00 00 00 00 00 00  (      ˙
 43 49 54 59 00 00 00 00 00 00 00 43 78 00 B1 61  CITY       Cx a
 0F 00 00 00 01 00 00 00 00 00 00 00 00 00 00 00
 53 54 41 54 45 00 00 00 00 00 00 43 87 00 B1 61  STATE      Cç a
 02 00 00 00 01 00 00 00 00 00 00 00 00 00 00 00
 5A 49 50 00 00 00 00 00 00 00 00 43 89 00 B1 61  ZIP        Cë a
 0A 00 00 00 01 00 00 00 00 00 00 00 00 00 00 00
```

Header position 1

You should have an intimate understanding of header information before using the editor to alter it.

The Hex Editor is not restricted to dBASE files. It can be used to examine and edit files of any type. Since you can edit in hex mode, you can write anything, including control characters and graphics characters, into a file.

 **Summary**

The basic purpose of the dSALVAGE editors is to let you examine a file during repair, and change header information for consistency with the file's data. Their great power, however, makes them useful for many other file exploration and modification activities.

The Byte Stream and Hex Editors, for example, can be used with files of any type. A novel application came from a dSALVAGE user who applied them to the task of converting non-DBF file formats to dBASE-compatible format.

An unusual application of the Byte Stream Editor involved the recovery of a dBASE II file containing almost 80,000 records, thereby exceeding the 65,535 record limit. dBASE would not access more than about 15,000 of them since the header's record counter (like an automobile odometer) had wrapped. By marking the entire record area as a block, writing it to an external file, and merging it with a new dBASE III PLUS header in dSALVAGE, all the records were recovered.

The dSALVAGE editors provide great power that you should use intelligently and cautiously. Their usefulness is limited only by your skill and ingenuity. As Winston Churchill said, "Give us the tools and we will finish the job."

Appendix A

dBASE Datafile Reference

The header bytes and field types for versions of dBASE appear below. The first byte of the header is byte 1.

dBASE IV File Header

Byte(s)	Meaning
1	8B if memo fields present, 03 if not. 63 if SQL control file.
2-4	Date of last update
5-8	Record count
9-10	Header size in bytes
11-12	Record length
13-14	Reserved
15	Incomplete transaction flag
16	Encryption flag
17-28	Reserved for local area network use
29	Indicates presence of production MDX file
30-32	Reserved
33 to end minus one	Field definitions in groups of 32 bytes. Within each group, the meanings are as follows:
1-10	Field name padded with nulls
11	Zero
12	Field type (see Table A-1)
13-16	Reserved
17	Field width
18	Number of decimal places for numeric fields
19-20	Reserved
21	Work area identifier
22-31	Reserved
32	MDX key flag
last byte	0D

Table A-1. dBASE IV Field Types		
Designation		**Type**
ASCII	**Hex**	
C	43	Character
D	44	Date
F	46	Floating Point
L	4C	Logical
M	4D	Memo
N	4E	Numeric

dBASE III PLUS File Header

Byte(s)	Meaning
1	83 if memo fields present, 03 if not
2-4	Date of last update
5-8	Record count
9-10	Header size in bytes
11-12	Record length
13-32	Reserved
33 to end of header minus one	Field definitions in groups of 32 bytes. Within each group, the meanings are as follows:

Byte	Meaning
1-10	Field name padded with nulls
11	Zero
12	Field type (see Table A-2)
13-16	Reserved
17	Field width
18	Number of decimal places for numeric fields
19-32	Reserved
last byte	0D

Table A-2. dBASE III PLUS Field Types		
Designation		**Type**
ASCII	**Hex**	
C	43	Character
D	44	Date
L	4C	Logical
M	4D	Memo
N	4E	Numeric

dBASE III File Header

Byte(s)	Meaning
1	83 if memo fields present, 03 if not
2-4	Date of last update
5-8	Record count
9-10	Header size in bytes
11-12	Record length
13-32	Reserved
33 to end of header minus two	Field definitions in groups of 32 bytes. Within each group, the meanings are as follows:

	1-10	Field name padded with nulls
	11	Zero
	12	Field type (see Table A-3)
	13-16	Reserved
	17	Field width
	18	Number of decimal places for numeric fields
	19-32	Reserved
	next to last byte	0D
	last byte	Reserved

Table A-3. dBASE III Field Types

Designation ASCII	Hex	Type
C	43	Character
D	44	Date
L	4C	Logical
M	4D	Memo
N	4E	Numeric

dBASE II File Header

Byte(s)	Meaning
1	02
2-3	Record count
4-6	Date of last update
7-8	Record length
9-521	Field definitions in groups of 16 bytes. Within each group, the meanings are as follows:

1-10   Field name padded with nulls

11   Zero

12   Field type (see Table A-4)

13   Field width

14-15   Reserved

16   Number of decimal places for numeric fields

Table A-4. dBASE II Field Types		
Designation		**Type**
ASCII	**Hex**	
C	43	Character
L	4C	Logical
N	4E	Numeric

Appendix B

DEBUG Commands

You can invoke DEBUG with or without a filespec. Enter DEBUG at the DOS prompt to invoke it without a filespec. To invoke it with the file TEST.DBF in the DATA directory of drive E, enter DEBUG E:\DATA\TEST.DBF.

DEBUG's major commands are listed alphabetically below. All commands may be either uppercase (as shown) or lowercase.

COMMAND	FUNCTION
D	Display next 128 memory locations starting at the current address
D <addr>	Display next 128 memory locations starting at a specified address
	Example: D 20A displays next 128 memory locations starting at address 020A.
D <addr1>,<addr2> or **D <addr1> <addr2>**	Display memory between two addresses **Example:** D 603 A1F displays all memory locations from address 0603 through address 0A1F.
E <addr> [list]	Change memory
	Examples: E 24D 47 replaces the value at address 024D with 47 hex.
	E 302 47 54 57 63 49 replaces the five values starting at address 0302 with the five hex values entered.
	E 7B8 "Accounts" replaces the eight values starting at address 07B8 with the hex values of the characters in the word Accounts.

273

COMMAND	FUNCTION
F <addr1> <addr2> <value> or **F <addr1> <addr2> <"char">**	Fill memory with a specified value or character **Examples:** F 42B 5B7 20 replaces all addresses from 042B through 05B7 with hex 20. F 42B 5B7 "z" replaces all addresses from 042B through 05B7 with the character z.
H <value1>,<value2> or **H <value1> <value2>**	Do hexadecimal addition and subtraction **Examples:** H 6B31 42C8 yields ADF9 (the sum) and 2869 (the difference). H 42C8 6B31 yields ADF9 (the sum) and D797 (the difference). In this case, the difference is negative, but DEBUG does not mark it.
L [<addr>]	Load a file from disk while DEBUG is active. If the load address is not specified, the file is loaded at offset 0100. **Example:** L 42D loads a copy of the file specified by the N command so that its first byte lies at address 042D.
M <addr1>,<addr2>,<addr3> or **M addr1 addr2 addr3**	Move a block of memory to a new location. The block extends from addr1 to addr2. The new location starts at addr3. **Example:** M 46D2 8BA9 3A7B moves the block of memory extending from address 46D2 through address 8BA9 forward to address 3A7B, thereby overwriting memory starting at 3A7B. The first two addresses specified must lie within a contiguous 64K region. See Appendix E for more details.

COMMAND	FUNCTION

N <filespec>

Identify a file to be loaded from or written to disk while DEBUG is active.

Example: N TEST.DBF sets up file control blocks for the L and W commands. Following this command, the L command would load the file TEST.DBF into memory. The N command is unnecessary if DEBUG was invoked with a filespec.

Q

Exit (to DOS)

R

Display CPU registers

Example: The R command produces a display like the following:

AX=0000 BX=0001 CX=C000 DX=0000
SP=FFEE BP=0000 S I = 0000 DI =0000

DS=26D4 ES=26D4 SS=26D4 CS=26D4
IP=0100 NV UP DI PL NZ NA PO NC

For file recovery, the only important numbers here are the BX and CX registers (the file size), and the DS (data segment) and CS (code segment) registers that define the current segment number. The BX and CX values here (0001 and C000) indicate that the file is 1C000 hex (114688 decimal) bytes long. See Appendix E for further discussion of CPU registers.

S <addr1>,<addr2>,<value>
or
S <addr1> <addr2> <value>

Search an area of memory for a value. The area extends from addr1 to addr2.

Examples: S 34B EF78 1A searches memory from address 034B through address EF78 for the hex value 1A.

S 100 9AB7 "Harry" searches memory from address 0100 through 9AB7 for the character string "Harry".

COMMAND	FUNCTION
W	Write file to disk

Example: W writes the file (loaded when DEBUG was invoked or specified by the N command) to disk.

Appendix C

ASCII Table

Character	Binary	Decimal	Hex	Character	Binary	Decimal	Hex
NUL or ^@	00000000	0	00	space	00100000	32	20
SOH or ^A	00000001	1	01	!	00100001	33	21
STX or ^B	00000010	2	02	"	00100010	34	22
ETX or ^C	00000011	3	03	#	00100011	35	23
EOT or ^D	00000100	4	04	$	00100100	36	24
ENQ or ^E	00000101	5	05	%	00100101	37	25
ACK or ^F	00000110	6	06	&	00100110	38	26
BEL or ^G	00000111	7	07	'	00100111	39	27
BS or ^H	00001000	8	08	(	00101000	40	28
HT or ^I	00001001	9	09	)	00101001	41	29
LF or ^J	00001010	10	0A	*	00101010	42	2A
VT or ^K	00001011	11	0B	+	00101011	43	2B
FF or ^L	00001100	12	0C	,	00101100	44	2C
CR or ^M	00001101	13	0D	-	00101101	45	2D
SO or ^N	00001110	14	0E	.	00101110	46	2E
SI or ^O	00001111	15	0F	/	00101111	47	2F
DLE or ^P	00010000	16	10	0	00110000	48	30
DC1 or ^Q	00010001	17	11	1	00110001	49	31
DC2 or ^R	00010010	18	12	2	00110010	50	32
DC3 or ^S	00010011	19	13	3	00110011	51	33
DC4 or ^T	00010100	20	14	4	00110100	52	34
NAK or ^U	00010101	21	15	5	00110101	53	35
SYN or ^V	00010110	22	16	6	00110110	54	36
ETB or ^W	00010111	23	17	7	00110111	55	37
CAN or ^X	00011000	24	18	8	00111000	56	38
EM or ^Y	00011001	25	19	9	00111001	57	39
SUB or ^Z	00011010	26	1A	:	00111010	58	3A
ESC or ^[	00011011	27	1B	;	00111011	59	3B
FS. or ^\	00011100	28	1C	<	00111100	60	3C
GS or ^]	00011101	29	1D	=	00111101	61	3D
RS or ^^	00011110	30	1E	=	00111101	61	3D
US or ^_	00011111	31	1F	>	00111110	62	3E

Character	Binary	Decimal	Hex	Character	Binary	Decimal	Hex
?	00111111	63	3F	'	01100000	96	60
@	01000000	64	40	a	01100001	97	61
A	01000001	65	41	b	01100010	98	62
B	01000010	66	42	c	01100011	99	63
C	01000011	67	43	d	01100100	100	64
D	01000100	68	44	e	01100101	101	65
E	01000101	69	45	f	01100110	102	66
F	01000110	70	46	g	01100111	103	67
G	01000111	71	47	h	01101000	104	68
H	01001000	72	48	i	01101001	105	69
I	01001001	73	49	j	01101010	106	6A
J	01001010	74	4A	k	01101011	107	6B
K	01001011	75	4B	l	01101100	108	6C
L	01001100	76	4C	m	01101101	109	6D
M	01001101	77	4D	n	01101110	110	6E
N	01001110	78	4E	o	01101111	111	6F
O	01001111	79	4F	p	01110000	112	70
P	01010000	80	50	q	01110001	113	71
Q	01010001	81	51	r	01110010	114	72
R	01010010	82	52	s	01110011	115	73
S	01010011	83	53	t	01110100	116	74
T	01010100	84	54	u	01110101	117	75
U	01010101	85	55	v	01110110	118	76
V	01010110	86	56	w	01110111	119	77
W	01010111	87	57	x	01111000	120	78
X	01011000	88	58	y	01111001	121	79
Y	01011001	89	59	z	01111010	122	7A
Z	01011010	90	5A	{	01111011	123	7B
[	01011011	91	5B	I	01111100	124	7C
\	01011100	92	5C	}	01111101	125	7D
]	01011101	93	5D	~	01111110	126	7E
^	01011110	94	5E	DEL	01111111	127	7F
_	01011111	95	5F				

Appendix D

Understanding Hexadecimal

Decimal Numbers

Since long before recorded history, people have had 10 fingers. It is not surprising, therefore, that they developed a number system based on 10. Today we call it the *decimal system* and the numbers it uses *decimal numbers*.

Ten symbols can represent any quantity as a decimal number. The symbols are the everyday 0,1,2,3,4,5,6,7,8, and 9. We need only one to represent a quantity less than 10, but we must group them to represent larger quantities.

When we group them, their positions are important. For example, the numbers 4362 and 6243 differ in value although they consist of the same symbols.

We define the positions as follows. The rightmost position is the *units* position. The succeeding positions to the left are the *tens* position, *hundreds* position, and so forth. In other words, each position represents a power of 10. The rightmost position is 10 to the zeroth power (or 1), the next position to the left is 10 to the first power (or 10), the next one is 10 to the second power (or 10 times 10 or 100), and so on.

We can express a decimal number as a sum of the products of digit values and position values. For example, we can express 4362 as:

4 times 1000	or	4 times 10 raised to the third power	or	4000
+ 3 times 100	or	3 times 10 raised to the second power	or	300
+ 6 times 10	or	6 times 10 raised to the first power	or	60
+ 2 times 1	or	2 times 10 raised to the zero power	or	2
			sum:	4362

Binary Numbers

Although the decimal system is convenient for 10-fingered people, it is inconvenient for 2-fingered computers. We call computers "2-fingered" because their basic counting devices have only two states: ON and OFF. If we represent OFF by 0 and ON by 1, we can develop a number system based on powers of 2 rather than on powers of 10. We call it the *binary system*. In it, we use only two symbols (**0** and **1**), called *binary digits* or *bits*, to represent any quantity.

279

Just as with decimal numbers, we can group binary digits to represent large quantities. Any quantity larger than 1, in fact, requires more than one bit. The concepts discussed above about groups of decimal digits are also true about groups of bits, although the specific values differ.

As with decimal numbers, position is important with groups of bits. For example, 1010 and 1100 differ in value although they consist of the same symbols.

In the binary system, each position represents a power of 2. The rightmost position is 2 to the zeroth power (or 1), the next position to the left is 2 to the first power (or 2), the next position is 2 to the second power (or 2 times 2 or 4), and so on.

We can also express a binary number as a sum of products. For example, we can express 1101 as:

1 times 8	or	1 times 2 raised to the third power	or	8
+ 1 times 4	or	1 times 2 raised to the second power	or	4
+ 0 times 2	or	0 times 2 raised to the first power	or	0
+ 1 times 1	or	1 times 2 raised to the zero power	or	1
			sum:	13

Hence, 1101 binary equals 13 decimal.

Hexadecimal Numbers

Let's consider one more number system. It is called the *hexadecimal system*, and it is closely related to the binary system. It is based on powers of 16 and would probably be our standard if we had 8 fingers on each hand.

Just as a system based on powers of 10 requires 10 symbols to represent any quantity, and one based on powers of 2 requires 2 symbols, a system based on powers of 16 requires 16 symbols to represent any quantity. This is a problem since no one ever bothered to invent 6 more symbols to represent the 6 extra digits required in hexadecimal. The common practice is to use the first six letters of the alphabet (A, B, C, D, E, and F—either capital or lowercase).

Hence the complete set of sixteen symbols in the hexadecimal number system is: 0,1,2,3,4,5,6,7,8,9,A,B,C,D,E and F. While using letters is convenient and well-suited to keyboard entry, it does produce strange-looking numbers such as 9A and FC.

Just as with decimal and binary digits, hexadecimal (or simply **hex**) digits can be grouped to represent large quantities. Any quantity larger than 15 requires more than one hex digit.

In the hex system, each position represents a power of 16, with the rightmost position being 16 to the zeroth power (or 1). The next position to the left is 16 to the first power (or 16), the next is 16 to the second power (or 16 times 16 which is 256), and so on.

For example, we can express the hex number 3AE7 as:

3 times 4096	or	3 times 16 raised to the third power	or 12288
+ A times 256	or	10 times 16 raised to the second power	or 2560
+ E times 16	or	14 times 16 raised to the first power	or 224
+ 7 times 1	or	7 times 16 raised to the zero power	or 7
			sum: 15079

Hence 3AE7 hex equals 15079 decimal.

Converting Among Number Systems

Now that you have been exposed to the three number systems of interest when working with computers, let's combine this information as shown in Table B-1. It illustrates counting in the three systems.

Table D-1. Counting in Binary, Decimal, and Hex

Decimal	Binary	Hex	Decimal	Binary	Hex
0	0	0	17	10001	11
1	1	1	18	10010	12
2	10	2	19	10011	13
3	11	3	20	10100	14
4	100	4	21	10101	15
5	101	5	22	10110	16
6	110	6	23	10111	17
7	111	7	24	11000	18
8	1000	8	25	11001	19
9	1001	9	26	11010	1A
10	1010	A	27	11011	1B
11	1011	B	28	11100	1C
12	1100	C	29	11101	1D
13	1101	D	30	11110	1E
14	1110	E	31	11111	1F
15	1111	F	32	100000	20
16	10000	10	33	100001	21

One thing that should be obvious from Table D-1 is that you must be careful to indicate which number system you are using. In some cases it is clear, but in others it is not. For example, the number 10 represents different quantities, depending on whether it is decimal, binary, or hex. If someone offered you 1000 dollars, you would probably be disappointed if the number were binary. Didn't read the fine print, did you? On the other hand, you would be over four times wealthier than you expected if 1000 were a hex number. Do you see why?

Just as you can do arithmetic in the familiar decimal system, you can also do it in binary, hex, or any number system. Perhaps more important than doing arithmetic, however, is the ability to convert between number systems. We particularly stress converting between decimal and hex since it is a frequent problem when working with computers.

You have seen an example of converting from hex to decimal. Unfortunately, converting from decimal to hex is not as easy. Some inexpensive pocket calculators can do binary, decimal, or hex arithmetic and perform conversions among the systems. If you do a lot of work in hex, we suggest you buy one. There is even software (such as Westlake Data's DiskMinder or Borland's Sidekick) that provides a hex calculator on your computer's screen.

Besides its intrinsic value in tasks such as file repair, hex is also an important status symbol. It is the computer equivalent of being able to write prescriptions in Latin, long equations in strange-looking mathematical symbols, or documents in "legalese" ("whereas the party of the first part"). It is an excellent way to impress the uninitiated with your expertise and make them willing to pay ridiculous consulting fees.

Appendix E

Handling Small Files That Are Larger than 64K Bytes

In this book, we distinguish between small files and large ones. We define a "small" file as one that fits in your computer's low memory together with DEBUG and any "terminate and stay resident" software that might also be there. Any other file is large.

There is actually an intermediate file size, larger than 64K, but still small enough for DEBUG to load. Files in this size range present unique difficulties if you use DEBUG to work with them. In particular, they require deeper understanding of the computer's registers and memory addressing scheme than you would otherwise need.

Memory Addressing

The 'brain' of your computer is the Central Processing Unit (CPU). It can communicate with memory locations, each of which has an *address.* Some addresses are reserved for the computer's own use, but 655,360 (or 640K) of them are available to you as *low memory* for holding programs and data.

Each address has a number that distinguishes it from other addresses, much like your house number differs from others on your street. Unlike house numbers (thank goodness!), computer addresses are most conveniently expressed in hexadecimal. Just imagine where your mail would go if you gave your street address in hex.

In the PC, we refer to addresses in two different ways:

- absolute address

- segment number plus offset

To make matters more confusing, we often refer to offsets as *relative addresses* and to segment numbers as *segment addresses.*

Let's consider *absolute addresses* first. We will assume that your computer has 640K of memory. Five hex digits are necessary to form a number as large as 640K since 655,360 decimal is A0000 hex. If the first address of contiguous memory is 0, the last one is 9FFFF.

283

The leading (most significant) digit of a five digit hex number represents a block of 65536 decimal (or 64K) memory locations. Thus, for example, there are 10000 hex (65536 decimal or 64K) addresses between 40000 hex and 50000 hex.

Although a 64K block can start anywhere, it is often convenient to think of memory as consisting of such blocks, each starting at an address that is a multiple of 10000 hex. In this view, absolute addresses 0, 10000, 20000, 30000, and so forth mark the beginnings of 64K blocks of memory.

For reasons not pertinent to this discussion, we do not usually deal with addresses in absolute form. DEBUG, for example, always shows addresses in the *segment/offset* form, but you must know how to convert from one form to the other.

The segment/offset notation expresses an absolute address as two 4-digit hex numbers separated by a colon. The four hex digits to the left are the *segment number* and indicate a particular 64K block of addresses. The four hex digits to the right form the *offset*; they indicate a particular address within the block.

To convert from segment/offset address to absolute address, append a zero to the segment number and add the result to the offset.

A few examples should clarify this:

1. The segment/offset address is 3000:5000. The segment number is 3000 and the offset is 5000. You can determine the absolute address by appending a zero to the segment number and adding the result to the offset as follows:

    $$\begin{array}{r} 30000 \\ +\ 5000 \\ \hline 35000 \end{array}$$

    Hence, segment/offset address 3000:5000 is the same as absolute address 35000.

2. The segment/offset address is 425D:0100. The segment number is 425D and the offset is 0100. The absolute address is:

    $$\begin{array}{r} 425D0 \\ +\ 0100 \\ \hline 426D0 \end{array}$$

    Hence, segment/offset address 425D:0100 is the same as absolute address 426D0.

When converting segment/offset addresses to absolute addresses, you get a unique result, as we have just seen. But converting the other way does not produce a unique result. For example, we can express the absolute address 426D0 in many different ways such as:

```
426D:0000   since   426D0 + 0000 = 426D0
426C:0010   since   426C0 + 0010 = 426D0
425D:0100   since   425D0 + 0100 = 426D0
416D:1000   since   416D0 + 1000 = 426D0
4000:26D0   since   40000 + 26D0 = 426D0
   etc.
```

Now you might ask why any sane person would create such an addressing scheme. There are actually some good reasons for it, just as there are for tax laws, airline schedules, and sports playoff systems (aren't there?). Regardless of whether it seems reasonable, it is the scheme you must use.

We pointed out earlier that it is often convenient to think of memory as consisting of 64K blocks starting at absolute addresses that are multiples of 10000 hex. Now that you understand the relationship between absolute and segment/offset addresses, you can also think of memory as consisting of 64K blocks whose segment numbers are multiples of 1000 hex. In this view, segment numbers 0, 1000, 2000, 3000, and so forth mark the beginnings of 64K blocks of memory. In other words, if you increase the most significant digit of the segment number by 1 while leaving the other 3 digits unchanged, you are specifying a new memory location exactly 64K higher in memory. For example, if you have the address

```
2000:0100
```

then the address

```
3000:0100
```

is exactly 64K higher in memory.

Now, of course, 64K blocks of memory need not have segment numbers that are multiples of 1000. They can have any values. For example, a 64K block of memory could be segment number 2A6C. In this event, the next higher block would be segment number 3A6C. Any address in the lower block (such as 2AC6:4C04) would have a corresponding address (such as 3AC6:4C04) in the next higher block.

DEBUG and CPU Registers

At some points in this book, we tell you to load a file into memory and examine it with the DEBUG Dump command, sometimes by merely giving the command D and sometimes by giving D followed by an address. In the latter case, we use an offset since the entire file is small enough to fit into a single 64K segment. Thus we need not specify the segment number.

Specifically, to dump the next 128 memory locations starting at offset 21B0, you would give the command

```
D 21B0
```

Since you did not provide a segment number, you might wonder how DEBUG knew which 21B0 to use. The answer is in the contents of special CPU registers. When DEBUG loads a file into memory, it loads certain registers. They include the CS (code segment) and DS (data segment) registers. CS and DS normally contain the same value, but you can change either or both as you will see. When you give a Dump command and specify only the offset, DEBUG uses the segment number in the DS register. Sometimes you need to refer to two different 64K segments. In such cases, you will want different values in these registers.

A more complete form of the Dump command specifies the segment register as follows:

```
D DS:21B0
```

If DS and CS contain the same values, the following command produces the same result:

```
D CS:21B0
```

There are also instances in the book where we tell you to move a block of memory to another location using the DEBUG Move command in the form:

```
M <start address of block> <end address of block>
<destination address>
```

In all cases, the specified addresses are offsets since the file is small enough to fit into a single 64K block and the destination address is also in the same block. Here again, when you specify only offsets, DEBUG uses the segment number in the DS register.

Sometimes you need to know what DS and CS contain and how to change them.

DEBUG lets you examine the CPU registers by simply giving the Register command R. It produces a display like the following (although specific values will, of course, vary).

```
-R
AX=0000  BX=0001  CX=C000  DX=0000  SP=FFEE  BP=0000  SI=0000 DI=0000
DS=26D4  ES=26D4  SS=26D4  CS=26D4  IP=0100   NV UP DI PL NZ NA PO NC
```

Most of this display need not concern you, but pay particular attention to the DS, CS, BX, and CX registers. DS and CS both contain 26D4, indicating the segment into which the file is loaded. BX and CX contain the file size. In this case, BX and CX contain 1C000 hex indicating that the file's size is 114688 bytes (1C000 hex = 114688 decimal). The IP register contains 0100, confirming that the file is loaded at offset 0100.

The R command also lets you change register values. For example, to change the CS register from 26D4 to 36D4, you would give the command

```
R CS
```

DEBUG displays

```
CS 26D4
:_
```

The cursor is on the next line as shown. Now type 36D4 and press the Enter key to load the new value into CS.

Small Files That Exceed 64K

At this point you have enough background to handle a dBASE file that is small but larger than 64K.

Let's consider a file containing 1C000 hex (114688 decimal) bytes. You load it into memory with the command

DEBUG filename

Before proceeding, let's be sure you understand where DEBUG puts the file. Since it is larger than 64K but smaller than 128K, it occupies one full 64K memory segment and part of another. If DEBUG selects 26D4 as the segment into which it loads the file, it puts the first byte at address 26D4:0100. Subsequent bytes go in subsequent memory locations up to 26D4:FFFF. DEBUG puts the next byte at the first memory location of the next 64K segment—that is, at address

36D4:0000. From here it continues filling memory locations through the end of the file which lies at 36D4:C100. (You will see in a moment why this is where the end lies).

The R command shows that registers CS and DS both contain 26D4, the segment number of the memory-resident file. But since the file is larger than 64K, you know that only a part of it is in that segment. We can examine the part with the Dump command

```
D 100 FFFF
```

To examine the part of the file that resides in the next 64K segment, you can, for example, change the CS register to 36D4 using the R CS command. Then give the command

```
D CS:0 FFFF
```

which displays the entire 64K block beginning at address 36D4:0000.

Block moves using DEBUG are more complicated for files larger than 64K. Recall that the Move command is

M <start address of block> <end address of block> <destination address>

M lets you specify a segment number and an offset for the **start address of block** and **destination address**, but requires that the **end address of block** be specified as an **offset** only. In other words, the entire block must lie within a single 64K segment. Hence, if you want to move a block larger than 64K or one that crosses a 64K boundary, you must do it in multiple steps.

Consider our sample file above. Its length is 114688 decimal (1C000 hex) bytes and its first byte is at the segment/offset address 26D4:0100 (or absolute address 26E40). Adding 1C000 hex and 26E40 hex gives 42E40 hex as the absolute address of the end of the file. 42E40 hex is equivalent to segment/offset address 36D4:C100. As you saw earlier, the absolute address 42E40 corresponds to many different segment/offset addresses. We select 36D4 here since it represents the next higher 64K segment above 26D4.

Now suppose that you want to move the block of memory, beginning at 26D4:58F0 and extending to the end of the file, down to address 26D4:0100. You must move it in two steps since the file straddles the 64K block boundary between segments 26D4 and 36D4. The two steps are:

1. Move part 1 of the file (the part residing in segment 26D4, starting at offset 58F0 and extending through offset FFFF) down to offset 0100.

2. Move part 2 of the file (the part residing in segment 36D4) down to the first address following the end of the relocated part 1.

You must do some arithmetic here. Before the move of step 1, the total piece of the file in segment 26D4 extended from offset 0100 through offset FFFF. However, we are only interested in preserving the part extending from offset 58F0 through offset FFFF. We will move it down in memory to offset 0100, thereby overwriting whatever was in memory from 0100 through 58F0. The total number of bytes moved in step 1 is A70F hex (FFFF minus 58F0). Afterward, the byte that was at offset FFFF will be at offset A80F. The very next byte is, of course, at offset A810, the destination address for the move of step 2.

Before giving the move commands, change the CS register to 36D4 with the command

```
R CS
```

DEBUG will display

```
CS 26D4
:_
```

Type 36D4 at the prompt and press the Enter key.

You can confirm the change with the R command:

```
-R
AX=0000  BX=0001  CX=C000  DX=0000  SP=FFEE  BP=0000  SI=0000  DI=0000
DS=26D4  ES=26D4  SS=26D4  CS=36D4  IP=0100    NV UP DI PL NZ NA PO NC
```

You are now ready to perform the two moves with the commands:

```
M 58F0 FFFF 100
M CS:0 C100 A810
```

You must enter them in the order shown. Otherwise, you will overwrite the data in 26D4:58F0 through 26D4:FFFF before you can move it out of the way.

Summary

You can easily handle files smaller than 64K with DEBUG. But using it with small files that are larger than 64K is more difficult. You must understand the computer's memory organization and CPU registers. If you use dSALVAGE to repair file damage, you can ignore the information provided here.

Appendix F

DOS Essentials

Disk Organization

There are four main regions on an MS-DOS disk: boot sector, File Allocation Table, root directory, and data area.

The boot sector contains information used by DOS. It is the one region of the disk that you should not touch. First, you would not understand the information it contains. Second, changing it can make your disk unusable.

The root directory holds a master list of all files and subdirectories stored on the disk. Each subdirectory, in turn, can contain a list of files and subdirectories. Each file or subdirectory entry has a name, extension, size, date and time of last update, attribute, and a number indicating where it starts in the data area. The DIR command displays some of this information.

The File Allocation Table (FAT) is a map showing where the various parts of files are located in the data area. DOS uses the directory to find where a file starts, and uses the FAT to find the rest of it. Each disk has two copies of the FAT; the second is presumably just a backup, as DOS never uses it.

The data area contains the files and subdirectories. Subdirectories are similar to files, but they have a distinguishing attribute value.

Filenames and Filespecs

DOS files have names consisting of two parts. The first part consists of up to 8 characters of your choice. The second part (called the *file extension*) consists of up to 3 characters (not always of your choice). When writing filenames, you must separate the parts with a dot or period. The symbols * and ? can appear in a filename in most commands. "*" represents any continuous sequence of characters, "?" represents any single character. The filename TY*.?XT, therefore, specifies all files having TY as the first two characters in their names, and having three-character extensions with XT being the last two. These symbols (often called *wildcards*) are useful to group files for copying and other operations and to find files when you are unsure of their exact names.

To fully specify a file not in the current directory, you must provide the drive letter and the path as well as the file's name. This combination of information is called a *filespec*.

A *path* defines a location in the hierarchy of directories. For example, \BIN\SALES defines a directory SALES below a directory BIN that is, in turn, below the primary root directory. The filespec for a file SAMPLE.DBF in this directory on the C drive would be

```
C:\BIN\SALES\SAMPLE.DBF
```

Major DOS Commands

Major DOS commands used in this book are:

CD	Change directory
CHKDSK	Check the FAT
COPY	Copy files
DEL or ERASE	Delete file
DIR	Directory
MD	Make directory
TYPE	Display a text file

We may describe them further as follows. Here anything enclosed in square brackets [ ] represents an optional part of a command. Anything enclosed in angle brackets is required. [d:] indicates that you may include a drive letter such as C:.

CD

Syntax: **CD [[d:]path]**

Purpose: Move to a different directory if arguments are given. Display current directory name if no arguments are given. Type "CD .." to move to parent directory.

CHKDSK

Syntax: **CHKDSK [d:][/f]**

Purpose: Analyze, and optionally repair, a FAT.

COPY

Syntax: **COPY [d:][path]<source filename> [d:][path]**
                 <target filename>

Purpose: Copy a file. You need to specify the target filename only if the
                 target file is to have a different name from the source file.

DEL or ERASE

Syntax: **DEL [d:][path]<filename> or ERASE [d:][path]<filename>**

Purpose: Remove file(s) from the directory. Use DEL with care! When
                 files are deleted, they are lost forever (unless you have an
                 un-erase utility).

DIR

Syntax: **DIR [d:][path][filename]**

Purpose: Display filenames, sizes, and dates and times of last update.

MD

Syntax: **MD [d:]<path>**

Purpose: Make (create) a new directory

TYPE

Syntax: **TYPE [d:][path]<filename>**

Purpose: Display the contents of a text file. Not suitable for COM, EXE,
                 or other machine language files. Display will stop as soon as a
                 1A hex is encountered.

Appendix G

Symptom Table

SYMPTOM	PROBABLE CAUSE	SEE CHAPTER
Improper field highlighting in BROWSE	Nulls in file	14
Cannot create a good index file	Nulls or extra EOFs in file	14, 15
Region of non-ASCII trash in datafile	Electrical power problem	14, 22 (Byte Stream Editor)
Fewer records shown in a LISTing than indicated in file STRUCTURE	Extra EOFs	15
STRUCTURE listing appears abnormal	Damaged header	16
dBASE says "not a dBASE database" when you try to open the file	Damaged or missing header	16, 18
Progressive offset from record to record	Header does not match file data	16, 18
Data is offset or displaced from field boundaries in LIST or BROWSE	Lost clusters or copy of file with lost clusters	17,19
File accidentally ZAP'd		20
Datafile appears to contain part of an unrelated file	Cross-linking	21

Glossary

ASCII Acronym for American Standard Code for Information Interchange. Usually refers to the set of 128 characters having numeric values from 0 through 127 decimal (0 through 7F hex or 0 through 1111111 binary).

Binary Number system based on powers of 2.

Bit Binary digit, also the fundamental unit of data storage in a computer.

Byte Group of 8 bits that defines a character.

CHKDSK DOS utility for checking and correcting a disk's File Allocation Table.

Control characters The 32 ASCII characters having numeric values from 0 through 31 decimal (0 through 1F hex).

Cross-linking File Allocation Table problem in which a link in one file's chain points to a link in another's chain or to an earlier link in its own chain.

Data area of a disk Physical part of the disk surface where files are stored.

Decimal Number system based on powers of 10.

Directory The listing of files and subdirectories stored on a disk. Usually called the root directory, it is stored in a specific part of the disk. It contains file names, sizes, attributes, and starting clusters.

End-of-file marker Character with ASCII value 1A hex (26 decimal). Also called Ctrl-Z, it identifies the end of the record area in a DBF datafile.

Extended ASCII The 128 characters having numeric values from 128 through 255 decimal (80 through FF hex). Also called graphics characters.

FAT File Allocation Table. The map used by DOS to find the parts of files stored on disk. The FAT is stored in a specific part of the disk surface.

Fragmentation Condition that exists when consecutive parts of a file do not occupy logically contiguous clusters in the data area of the disk.

Header or **File Header** First part of a DBF datafile. It contains both field definitions and information about the file as a whole.

Hexadecimal (hex) Number system based on powers of 16.

Lost clusters Clusters in the data area of the disk not recognized by DOS as being part of any file because of errors in the File Allocation Table.

Nibble 4 bits or 1 hex digit.

Null Character with ASCII value zero.

PACK dBASE command for physically removing deleted records from a datafile.

Record area of a file Part of a DBF datafile where the records are stored.

Skipped clusters Clusters originally part of a file allocation chain that have become disassociated from the file. Skipped clusters are a special case of lost clusters.

TSR Terminate-and-stay-resident program, an MS-DOS program that loads into memory in such a way as to prevent other programs from overwriting it. It can thus be activated at any time (usually by pressing a special combination of keys) without being loaded from disk.

ZAP dBASE command for removing all records from a datafile.

Index

Notes

"This book is especially important in documenting current dBASE dialects. The multiplicity of divergent implementations has created an obvious need for a comprehensive, cohesive guide. David Kalman's book fulfills this need."—**C. Wayne Ratliff, inventor of dBASE.**

The DATA BASED ADVISOR® Series
Lance A. Leventhal, Ph.D., Series Director

The dBASE® Language Handbook

by David M. Kalman
Editor-In-Chief, Data Based Advisor

The one-stop supermarket for dBASE information including Quicksilver, Clipper, dBASE III, dBASE III PLUS, dBASE IV, dBXL, and FoxBASE+.

Here is the first standardized reference for the popular dBASE language and its dialects. David Kalman, Editor-in-Chief of *Data Based Advisor*, has provided a book all dBASE users and developers will want to have on their shelves. It is the only book that provides an alphabetical listing of all commands from dBASE III PLUS and dBASE IV, as well as the leading compatible systems (Clipper, dBXL, FoxBASE+, and Quicksilver). It also contains many practical examples, drawn from a wide variety of applications. This handbook is an essential reference for dBASE consultants, developers, managers, programmers, teachers, trainers, users, and vendors, as well as OEMs, VARs, and analysts.

Special Features of the Book are:
■ Standardized descriptions for each entry that include syntax, definition, options, limits and warnings, recommended use, variations, and cross-references.

■ Up-to-date coverage of all systems, including windowing, SQL, and networking commands.

■ Clear explanations and practical examples.

■ Discussions of all options and variations, including those in compatible systems.

■ Extensive comparisons of systems, highlighting their differences and ways to simulate missing or enhanced features.

■ Many hints and warnings drawn from actual experience.

$29.95, ISBN 0-915391-30-9, 1024 pages, 7 x 9, trade paperback, illustrations

Available from your favorite book or computer store or use the order form on the next page.

Slawson Communications • 165 Vallecitos de Oro • San Marcos, CA • 92069-1436

"Rick Spence has taken on the formidable challenge of writing the definitive Clipper text."—**Brian Russel, Nantucket Corporation**

The **DATA BASED ADVISOR®** Series
Lance A. Leventhal, Ph.D., Series Director

Clipper® Programming Guide

by Rick Spence

Nantucket's Clipper compiler for dBASE programs is one of the most popular productivity tools in the database world. Rick Spence, co-developer of Clipper and expert columnist in *Data Based Advisor* and *Reference: Clipper* magazines, provides an up-to-date description of how to use Clipper effectively. He includes many examples drawn from actual applications and extensive discussions of arrays, user interfaces, query methods, memo fields, direct file access, networking, and file structures. He also explains the details of how to interface C programs to Clipper and presents complete sample programs for hot key management, mouse interfaces, and serial communications. The book starts where the manual leaves off; it provides new and advanced material, not duplication. As Brian Russell of Nantucket Corporation states in his foreword, "...no other author could explain Clipper so succinctly..."

Special Features of the book are:

- Up-to-date coverage of Clipper
- Extensive description of C programming for Clipper
- Detailed procedures and examples for using Clipper on local area networks
- Description of advanced query techniques involving multiple databases and multiple relations
- Many new functions, tips, hints, and warnings derived from the author's extensive experience as both a developer and user of Clipper
- Uses modern programming techniques throughout—all examples are modular, well-structured, and well documented.
- All Clipper and C code in the book is also available on disk.

$24.95, ISBN 0-915391-31-7, 680 pages, 7 x 9, trade paperback, illustrations.

Available from your favorite book or computer store or use the order form in this book.

Slawson Communications • 165 Vallecitos de Oro • San Marcos, CA • 92069-1436

ORDER FORM

Thank you for purchasing this Microtrend™ book. To order additional copies or this book or any of our other titles, please complete the form below. Or call 1-800-SLAWSON.

Name_____

Address_____

City_____ State_____ Zip _____

Qty	Title	Price Each	Total	

Dept. SDDB

	Subtotal		
U.S. SHIPPING Books are shipped UPS except where a post office box is given as a delivery address.	Sales Tax: CA residents add 7%		
	Shipping charge: $3.00 per book		
	TOTAL		

FORM OF PAYMENT

☐ Visa   ☐ MasterCard   ☐ Check

Card #: | | | | | | | | | | | | | | | |

Expiration date: _____

Signature: _____Date _____

Mail this order form to:

Microtrend™ Books
Slawson Communications, Inc.
165 Vallecitos de Oro
San Marcos, CA 92069-1436

619/744-2299

Reader Comments
Salvaging Damaged dBASE Files

This book has been edited, the edited material reviewed, and the program matter tested and checked for accuracy; but bugs find their way into books as well as software. Please take a few minutes and tell us if you have found any errors, and give us your general comments regarding the quality of this book. Your time and attention will help us improve this and future products.

Did you find any mistakes? _____

_____

_____

Is this book complete? (If not, what should be added?)_____

_____

_____

What do you like about this book? _____

_____

_____

What do you not like about this book? _____

_____

_____

What other books would you like to see developed?_____

_____

_____

Other comments:_____

_____

_____

If you would like to be notified of new editions of this and/or other books that may be of interest to you, please complete the following:

Name_____

Address: _____

City/State/Zip_____

Mail to: **Microtrend™ Books**
                 Slawson Communications, Inc.
                 165 Vallecitos de Oro
                 San Marcos, CA 92069-1436

FOUR-WAY BONUS CARD

FREE ISSUE

Get a free issue of *Data Based Advisor*! Simply enclose payment with your order, and we'll extend your subscription by one additional month!

SAVINGS OF $12.40

Your subscription will save you an entire dollar every single month on your issue of *Data Based Advisor*!

DATA BASED ADVISOR®
Database Management Systems Magazine

❏ **YES,** Send *Data Based Advisor* for one year (12 issues) for just $35, and since I'm enclosing payment now, add a *FREE* issue onto my subscription! *(13 issues for the price of 12)

❏ 1 year - $35

PLUS, along with my subscription, sign me up for the *Data Based Advisor* **Readers Exchange** electronic bulletin board for just $10 more.

❏ Readers Exchange with subscription - $45

Savings based on cover price of $3.95.

Add $10 for Canada and Mexico magazine subscriptions, U.S. funds only. All other countries, add $30, international money orders only.

Name _____

Company _____

Address _____

City _____ State _____ Zip _____

❏ Check (made payable to *Data Based Advisor*)

❏ Visa/MasterCard

Card # _____

Expiration date _____

❏ Bill me (does not include bonus issue)

Call Toll Free 1-800-336-6060

3FCP

MONEY BACK GUARANTEE

If, at any time, for any reason, you no longer want *Data Based Advisor*, we'll give you a complete refund on all unmailed issues.

$25 OFF READERS EXCHANGE

Our new electronic bulletin board - the Readers Exchange - gives you on-line access to database experts, free software, and *Data Based Advisor* program code! Best of all, order your BBS subscription with your magazine subscription and pay only $10 more - a whopping $25 off the regular price!

❏ **YES,** Send *Data Based Advisor* for one year (12 issues) for just $35, and since I'm enclosing payment now, add a *FREE* issue onto my subscription! *(13 issues for the price of 12)

❏ 1 year - $35

PLUS, along with my subscription, sign me up for the *Data Based Advisor* **Readers Exchange** electronic bulletin board for just $10 more.

❏ Readers Exchange with subscription - $45

Savings based on cover price of $3.95.

Add $10 for Canada and Mexico magazine subscriptions, U.S. funds only. All other countries, add $30, international money orders only.

Name _____

Company _____

Address _____

City _____ State _____ Zip _____

❏ Check (made payable to *Data Based Advisor*)

❏ Visa/MasterCard

Card # _____

Expiration date _____

❏ Bill me (does not include bonus issue)

Call Toll Free 1-800-336-6060

3FCP